# BASIC INCOME

## *for*

# CANADIANS

From the **COVID-19 Emergency** to
**Financial Security for All**

EVELYN L. FORGET

James Lorimer & Company Ltd., Publishers
Toronto

James Lorimer & Company Ltd., Publishers acknowledges funding support from the Ontario Arts Council (OAC), an agency of the Government of Ontario. We acknowledge the support of the Canada Council for the Arts, which last year invested $153 million to bring the arts to Canadians throughout the country. This project has been made possible in part by the Government of Canada and with the support of Ontario Creates.

Cover design: Tyler Cleroux
Cover image: Anna Kraynova / Shutterstock.com

Library and Archives Canada Cataloguing in Publication

Title: Basic income for Canadians : from the COVID-19 emergency to financial security for all / Evelyn L. Forget.
Names: Forget, Evelyn L., 1956- author.
Description: New and revised edition. | Includes bibliographical references and index.
Identifiers: Canadiana (print) 20200260537 | Canadiana (ebook) 20200260723 | ISBN 9781459415683 (softcover) | ISBN 9781459415690 (EPUB)
Subjects: LCSH: Income distribution—Canada. | LCSH: Basic income—Canada. | LCSH: Income maintenance programs—Canada. | LCSH: Poverty—Canada. | LCSH: Economic security—Canada. | LCSH: Social security—Canada.
Classification: LCC HC120.I5 F68 2020 | DDC 362.5/820971—dc23

James Lorimer & Company Ltd., Publishers
117 Peter Street, Suite 304
Toronto, ON, Canada
M5V 0M3
www.lorimer.ca

Printed and bound in Canada.

# BASIC INCOME
## *for*
# CANADIANS

*For all the people I met in church basements, libraries, community halls and lecture theatres across Canada who shared their stories and helped me to understand; and,*
*For Naomi and Louis, who already make this world better.*

*Courage, my friends: 'Tis not too late to build a better world.*
                                                    – Tommy Douglas

# Contents

## LIST OF FIGURES

## LIST OF TABLES

# Introduction

Before the end of 2019, reports of a new kind of pneumonia from Wuhan, China, began to circulate. By mid-March 2020, the World Health Organization labelled COVID-19 a pandemic and, one after another, countries around the world repatriated their citizens, closed their borders and shut down restaurants, theatres, bars and most workplaces to contain the virus.

As the pandemic persisted, millions of people lost their jobs or had their work hours cut, exposing the economic insecurity with which Canadian families were already living. Half of Canadians were already struggling from paycheque to paycheque with little left over for savings, and household debt was at a record high. Few had enough set aside to pay the rent or put food on the table for even a short period of time. This situation wasn't caused by COVID-19; it reflected changes that had been ongoing for decades. More than a third of the workforce was working in precarious employment before the pandemic — on contract, in temporary jobs, self-employed or working part-time when they would have preferred full-time work.

In Canada, the economic shutdown had two immediate effects. It revealed the inequality and economic insecurity people were already living with, and it forced us to acknowledge the limitations of our existing social safety net. People displaced from their usual employment turned to Employment Insurance and learned that fewer than 40 per cent of them qualified for any support. Those who did qualify received payments too little even to pay the rent. When the federal government responded by putting in place a much-needed set of emergency support programs, it was discovered that the online system of accounts designed by the Canada Revenue Agency (CRA) to facilitate income tax collection was capable of working far better than we'd had any reason to believe it could. Using these accounts, the government could deliver emergency support to applicants in a matter of days. It could respond to changing circumstances. All that was necessary was a directive to administrators not to approach applicants with suspicion, withholding support until every detail of every application was verified and documented. Eligibility issues could be sorted out after people's lives had stabilized and any overpayments could be recovered through the income tax system. That initial level of trust was soon challenged, but it was clear that it wasn't technology that limited the ability to respond rapidly to changing circumstances.

The emergency supports, particularly the Canada Emergency Response Benefit (CERB), were important and necessary. For the most part, they were well delivered. However, the CERB was not a basic income. Support was conditional; the CERB was limited to people who had worked and earned at least $5,000 in the previous twelve months, and who lost their jobs or had their hours of work reduced by the economic effects of the pandemic or who had child care responsibilities associated with school closures. There were also design and implementation issues associated with the CERB that are very relevant to a discussion of basic income.

When the federal government announced at the end of July 2020 that CERB would end at the end of August and recipients would be transitioned to Employment Insurance in order to facilitate the reopening of the economy, it also acknowledged that Employment Insurance would not be adequate. Another new transitional program would be required to meet the needs of the many people in need who would not qualify. Instead of seizing the opportunity to build a comprehensive program that would address emerging challenges, they chose instead to slap another patch on a creaky and bloated program designed for a bygone era. Yet all of this informal experimentation with income support programs, part of the government's attempts to respond to the pandemic's effects, provided evidence that could be used to design a better, more comprehensive program designed to meet the needs of the future rather than the past.

How might things have been different had a basic income been in place? Over the past few years, proposals for a Canadian basic income have coalesced around a design sometimes called a guaranteed livable income or basic income guarantee. A person with no income, for whatever reason, would receive enough money to live a modest yet still dignified life. Low-waged working people living in poverty would receive a partial benefit — enough to ensure that they can live above the poverty line and that they benefit financially from working. Every dollar earned would reduce the benefit by less than a dollar until, for middle- and higher-income earners, the basic income disappears entirely. Basic income would replace the inconsistent and expensive set of monetary benefits currently offered by the federal and provincial governments — the GST credit, the Canada Workers Benefit, provincial income assistance and provincial income replacement for people with disabilities. It would be supplemented by publicly provided services — public health insurance, public education, child care, special supports for people with disabilities and many others. Basic income doesn't replace public services; it provides discretionary income that people can use however they like to meet their own unique needs.

Someone who had lost a job due to the economic shutdown caused by the coronavirus would be treated in exactly the same way as someone who lost a job for any other reason — because they or a family member were ill, for example, or a private employer faced bankruptcy. They would go to their online government account and enter the details of their income from all sources. Within a matter of days, a payment based only on their other income would be deposited to their bank account. Administrators would check eligibility and verify income, and any overpayment could be recovered through the tax system. There would be no intrusive and stigmatizing home checks, "means tests" or work requirements. Applicants would be approached with trust and treated with dignity. No one would need to determine whether an applicant deserves support; applicants would receive support based on their income alone.

As the pandemic persisted, many people began to ask whether we needed a permanent income replacement benefit — a guaranteed livable income. It was clear that existing income supports were inadequate and, if retained, would have to be fundamentally restructured to include more people, provide greater levels of support, treat people with dignity and to ensure that the program itself didn't discourage people from working. However, questions remained. Did we have the capacity to create and deliver such a benefit? Was it technically feasible and, if so, what exactly should it look like? How high should the basic guarantee be, and how quickly should it be reduced as other income increases?

This book addresses many of the concerns readers might have with such a proposal. Will people still work if they know they will receive enough to live on anyway? Perhaps we should guarantee everyone a job instead. What if someone leaves a job voluntarily; should they still receive a basic income? How will a guaranteed livable income relate to all our other programs and public services? People are very different from one another, and each one of us has unique needs and strengths. Will all Canadians benefit from a basic income or do some people need the assistance of a caseworker to ensure that they still have food and housing when the money is gone? Should some people get more than others, and what will happen to prices and wages? And something no one could ignore as the deficits associated with the pandemic continued to grow, can we afford it?

Designing and implementing a basic income is not simple, but the issues involved are exactly the same as those that accompanied the introduction of the Canada Child Benefit. Who qualifies and who doesn't? How much should recipients get, and how will it be financed? How should the payments be delivered? How can changing needs be accommodated? All these questions and more were addressed, and the resulting Canada Child Benefit lifted thousands of kids out of poverty. Every income-support policy requires income to be defined, and decisions must be made about how to treat wealth. There is no perfect way to answer these questions, but they have been answered in the past and can be again. How should a family be defined, and what exactly is family income? Any decision advantages some kinds of families and disadvantages others. There is no "correct" or "neutral" or "objective" definition, and the decisions should not be left to a team of "experts." These decisions entail value judgments and all Canadians should be part of the conversation. This book identifies the issues and details of the trade-offs involved.

Some people who care deeply about lifting the floor and helping everyone reach their fullest potential argue that "guaranteed services" should be offered instead of basic income. Guaranteed services, they claim, will allocate resources on the basis of need while basic income is just money. No sensible proposal for a basic income imagines that money alone is sufficient. Canadians need public services, and to characterize the discussion as basic income versus public services is a false dichotomy. However, public services work much better for some people than for others. Public services are designed, implemented and evaluated by members of the dominant culture. That is, perhaps, one of the reasons why *The Final Report of the National Inquiry into Missing and Murdered Indigenous Women and Girls* recommended a guaranteed livable income for all Canadians. Basic income has sometimes been dismissed as a "one size fits all" solution, but it is precisely the opposite. As soon as someone has money, that money can be transformed into all manner of services and goods that address their unique needs — needs that they identify, and that they can address in their own way and on their own timetable.

Imagine, for a moment, what health care may look like for a pregnant woman from northern Manitoba. When she is seven or eight months pregnant, she will be flown from her remote community to a large, urban centre for the last several weeks of her pregnancy — alone, without her family and friends to support her. This ensures that she has access to the best technology and appropriate medical skills if something unexpected happens during delivery. But she leaves her kids behind, often staying with grandmothers or aunties or other friends and relatives or left in the care of older brothers and sisters. In Winnipeg or Thompson or Brandon, she will live without family support, but she may have access to support workers and will certainly meet many health care providers. These workers often will not share her family background, and their support and advice will sometimes run counter to the way things are done in her community. The message she gets, unintended but still there, is that there is something wrong with her and she needs education, or there is something backward about her culture and it should change.

How would a basic income help this mother? It won't bring better health care to rural and remote communities. But a basic income would allow her to pay someone to come into her home to care for her kids so she doesn't have to worry so much. It would allow her to share some financial support with her mother or sister who may be caring for her kids while she waits to give birth. It would allow her to buy a plane ticket so her sister or cousin can travel with her to keep her company in the city. It might even allow her to hire a doula from her own cultural background who can help her communicate with well-meaning care providers. Whatever she chooses to do with her basic income, she is the person who will make that decision. She is in a position to decide what her most pressing needs are and how to best meet them. No public service can be everything to everyone, no matter how large the budget or how well meaning the people who deliver it.

Canadians need services, and sometimes we need our services to be better than they are, but we also need money — money that we can depend upon and that we can spend on our own needs, in our own way and on our own timetable.

# Chapter 1

# A Guaranteed Livable Income for Canadians

As COVID-19 swept across the globe in early 2020, the World Health Organization reluctantly labelled the infection a pandemic. Country after country restricted international travel, and then shut down schools, bars, restaurants and workplaces to contain the virus. Many workers were sent home and others had their work hours reduced. The lucky ones, those in the knowledge economy especially, continued to work remotely — many with the added stress and distraction of children home from school. Some, the frontline workers in health care as well as the warehouse workers, supermarket cashiers, delivery drivers and food production technicians, had essential jobs that required them to put their own and their families' health at risk by continuing to work outside their homes.

Workers who lost their jobs or had their hours reduced as a consequence of a government decision to shut down large swaths of the economy turned to existing social programs for help. More than half of the people who lost their jobs found existing programs such as Employment Insurance (EI) inaccessible because they hadn't worked enough hours to qualify for support, or because they left their jobs to care for children home from school. Others did qualify for support but the amount of money they would receive and how long they would receive it depended on their previous work history, and where in the country they lived. Sometimes they discovered that a program into which they had paid would give them too little to meet their rent. As a consequence, there were renewed calls for a basic income to address economic insecurity and the pockets of deep poverty that persist in Canada.

The pandemic did not create the need for a basic income. It revealed and amplified economic trends that had been growing for decades. The labour market was polarized and becoming more so; young people, racialized people, newcomers and women were more likely to be in low-paid precarious work, and this kind of work was growing as a proportion of all jobs. Consumer debt was at an all-time high, and half of Canadian households were living paycheque to paycheque, unable to meet even a small unexpected expense or deal with a single week without pay. People who had been surviving on provincial income assistance or disability, which offered support well below the poverty line in every province, were already relying on food banks and charities. These supports shrivelled as the volunteer labour and donations they relied upon disappeared during the pandemic. Women, who had made great strides in the labour market in the past fifty years, recognized how fragile those gains were when they were still called upon to provide child care after the elementary schools and daycares closed. Unpaid care work was always an important component of the economy, but COVID-19 meant that many more women were called upon to provide many more hours. All of these trends highlighted how poorly our social programs, especially EI and provincial income assistance, addressed the poverty and economic insecurity that already existed in Canada well before the pandemic. COVID-19 offered many more Canadians the opportunity to experience their inadequacy first-hand.

The federal government responded by creating a series of temporary emergency economic supports for workers displaced by the pandemic.

The Canada Emergency Response Benefit (CERB) was created for workers who lost their jobs, as long as they had earned at least $5,000 in the previous year. This was a program designed specifically to support workers temporarily out of work because of factors related to the pandemic; it was not a basic income and some of its features and effects demonstrate why a basic income would be a better response. The CERB paid $2,000 a month and was intended to offer sixteen weeks of support, which was later extended. The program was soon expanded to include workers whose hours had been reduced; as long as they earned no more than $1,000 a month, workers retained the full benefit. If they earned $1,001, they lost the entire benefit. This particular feature of the program would cause difficulty when the economy began to recover and people were called back to work. The CERB also provided support for people unable to work at their regular jobs because of child care responsibilities or quarantine requirements. It was, however, conditional. Workers were eligible only if they were out of work for specific reasons, and only if they had earned at least $5,000 in the previous twelve months. It was also temporary and offered a maximum of sixteen weeks of support, later extended to twenty-four weeks. A second program was introduced for students, with different eligibility requirements and obligations, which paid a lower amount. Students with children under twelve or living with a disability received a supplement. Seniors and children received a one-time tax-free payment through existing programs. Various loans, grants and wage subsidies were created for employers — small and large businesses, the non-profit sector and charities.

These new programs were essential to stabilizing the economy in the initial weeks after the lockdown. People applied for the CERB through an online account with the Canada Revenue Agency and the money was delivered into their bank account within days. This unexpectedly rapid response was due to a directive to administrators to pay the support to applicants and wait to verify eligibility until people's lives had stabilized. There were, however, limitations. Some people, such as adults who relied upon provincial income assistance or disability support, were not eligible. Others, including seniors with relatively high incomes, were either not eligible or had their payments clawed back by the provinces. Income was delivered inconsistently; the CERB and student benefits delivered taxable income, while seniors and children received payments tax-free. Income taxes were not withheld at source, which created potential difficulties for people when they next filed taxes, and it was unclear how money received by people later found to be ineligible would be treated. Some applicants were confused about which program they might fall under and applied to the wrong one. Others who were not eligible applied anyway, even though they would later be required to repay benefits. Despite these difficulties, the program had two particular strengths: it could respond quickly to need, leaving eligibility issues to be sorted out later, and it offered a sense of safety to workers whose lives had been disrupted by closures and layoffs.

The CERB also created particular challenges as workplaces began to reopen. Many Canadians discovered just how little some of their neighbours were paid; the monthly CERB payment of $2,000 was about equal to what a minimum-wage worker in most provinces would earn if they were lucky enough to get full-time hours. As employers struggled to re-open when public health regulations were relaxed, few were in a position to guarantee a minimum number of hours, and restaurant employees who relied on tips were particularly disadvantaged by new work models that relied on takeout. Therefore, workers were put in an almost impossible situation where they bore all the risk of the reopening. If they returned to work and their employer could offer only part-time employment, they might earn more than $1,000 and lose the entire CERB, but less than the $2,000 they would receive if they stayed home. The CERB was inconsistent with reopening the economy and its effects were amplified by the lingering effects of the shutdown. Elementary schools remained closed and child care was not readily available. Many employers could not provide a workplace that kept workers safe from infection. The CERB, for all its innovation, was not a basic income.

By the end of July 2020, the federal government began to imagine what changes to the CERB might be required to support an economy emerging from months of lockdown. They announced that the CERB would end as planned and that recipients would be transitioned to Employment Insurance. However, too many people still without work would not qualify for Employment Insurance, and therefore the federal government announced yet another transitional program to support these people, including parents with childcare responsibilities, gig workers and the self-employed.

Wouldn't it have been simpler, many asked, to introduce a basic income? After all, the two groups of Canadians who already received a form of basic income — families with children younger than eighteen who received the Canada Child Benefit (CCB) and seniors who received Old Age Security (OAS) and the Guaranteed Income Supplement (GIS) — continued to receive their incomes during the pandemic, unlike adults of working age. Had a basic income been in place for adults, it would have automatically provided the necessary extra support for those who lost jobs or had their hours reduced during the pandemic. The time spent creating a somewhat inconsistent set of emergency measures that still left some people vulnerable, would have been unnecessary. A well-designed basic income would have provided additional support to displaced workers as the economy closed down, but it would also have supported the tentative re-opening after the first weeks of infection. As firms started to call workers back, workers would not have a financial incentive to stay home instead. They could take a chance on their employer, knowing that they could still count on a basic income to meet their needs if their employer faltered and they were paid for fewer hours than they'd hoped to work. Neither workers nor employers would have to bear the full risks of re-opening because basic income would act as an insurance policy against the unexpected.

## What is a Basic Income?

Over the past few years, most proposals for basic income in Canada have taken a particular form sometimes called a guaranteed livable income or basic income guarantee. There are other forms of basic income, most notably one that sends everyone the same amount of money whether they need it or not. Unlike a guaranteed livable income, this other form has never found much traction in Canada for reasons that will become clear when costs are discussed in Chapter 9. By contrast, a guaranteed livable income has been supported by advocates as distinct from one another as the Senate Finance Committee, the commissioners behind *The Final Report of the National Inquiry into Missing and Murdered Indigenous Women and Girls*, the bishops of the Anglican Church of Canada, the Canadian Association of Social Workers, the Canadian Alliance to End Homelessness, a coalition of 270 organizations and individuals in the arts community representing tens of thousands of workers and a wide range of civil society organizations. Basic income was first advanced in Canada by the Special Senate Committee on Poverty headed by David Croll in 1971, then called for again a decade later by the Royal Commission on Economic Union, and then again by the 2009 report of the Senate Standing Committee on Social Affairs entitled *In From the Margins: A Call to Action on Poverty, Housing and Homelessness*.[1] COVID-19 lent a new urgency to calls for reform.

A guaranteed livable income ensures that anyone with no other source of income would receive an amount sufficient to live a modest but dignified life. Anyone who works but still lives in poverty would receive a partial benefit. For every dollar earned, the benefit would be reduced by less than a dollar until it disappeared entirely for middle- and high-income earners. The amount received would depend only on income; there would be no "means tests" and no obligation to report to a caseworker or to demonstrate efforts to find work. Basic income would replace other monetary benefits for low-income individuals, such as the GST credit and the Canada Workers Benefit (CWB) but it would not replace the full range of public services necessary in a high-income country such as Canada.

Basic income would become part of the social safety net rather than a replacement for it. Public health care, education and other social supports would still be necessary. Parents who work outside the home would still need access to daycare at a reasonable cost. People living on reserve would still need safe water and basic infrastructure. People with disabilities would still require access to supportive devices and programs designed to address their specific needs, even if they also receive a basic income. People who use substances would still require access to safe injection sites and treatment programs. Some people would continue to need social housing, particularly in high-rent jurisdictions, or specific programs designed to deal with local issues such as the very high cost of food in northern Canada. People living in rural and remote areas would still need public transportation and digital access. Youth aging out of the foster care system would continue to require more than just financial support. A basic income is not designed to replace these necessary programs. Rather, it sets a financial floor beneath which no one in a high-income country like Canada should be required to live.

Basic income could be delivered through Canada Revenue Agency accounts, in much the same way that the CERB was delivered, or it could use a similar but unrelated set of online accounts. The delivery of the CERB showed that the technical capacity to deliver a responsive basic income exists. An individual would log in each month, enter the details of their income and the appropriate amount of support would be deposited directly into their bank account. The few people without online access could be accommodated through simple paper applications, and payments could be delivered in other ways to people without bank accounts. Benefits could vary each month, as family structure and earned income might vary. Eligibility, of course, would be determined and income validated, but these details can wait. People would have access to the support they needed as soon as they needed it. The system would be based on trust — then validated.

This seems an almost revolutionary way of treating adults who seek financial assistance. Instead of designing systems to catch the small minority of people who intentionally misrepresent their situation, programs could be designed to address the needs of the vast majority of people who are honest. Applicants who received support in error could pay it back later. The few who cheat, and there are always some no matter how well designed a system might be, would pay back benefits fraudulently received along with additional penalties. This is precisely what happens with high-income individuals when they pay their income taxes, and with private sector firms who collect and remit the GST to the federal government. If trust can be extended to people earning hundreds of thousands of dollars a year, and firms with millions of dollars in annual revenue, both of whom have far more capacity and incentive to cheat than low-income individuals, surely the same trust can be extended to those living on much less.

Extending trust and delivering support without intrusive means-testing and verification upfront is not only more respectful, it leads to better outcomes. In the Trust Experiments conducted in the Netherlands, researchers wanted to know if, for people receiving support for the long-term unemployed, they removed the obligation to satisfy a caseworker that they were actively seeking work. Researchers found that people without such obligations were more likely to find full-time jobs and work towards independence than were those who were required to meet regularly with caseworkers, develop job search plans and demonstrate compliance. Similar results characterized the Basic Income Experiment in Finland.[2] The follow-up survey of participants in the short-lived Ontario Basic Income Guarantee Experiment also showed that people receiving a basic income were more likely to find a regular, full-time job than those who did not receive a basic income.[3] Trusting people seems to work, and there is little evidence that it encourages dishonesty.

## How Does a Basic Income Differ From Existing Benefits?

The federal government did not have a functioning basic income in place when the virus began to circulate and the decision was made to shut down the economy. What would have happened if they had relied on the existing system to support workers? There is a complex set of supports for working-age adults offered by all levels of government, but there are two key programs designed to provide income for working age adults: Employment Insurance (EI) and income assistance, sometimes called welfare, offered by the provinces and territories.

### Employment Insurance

The first benefit that any Canadian would seek if they lost their job would be Employment Insurance. Unemployment Insurance was first introduced in Canada in 1940 as a response to the Great Depression and was financed from the beginning by contributions from employees, employers and the federal government. Since then, it has undergone many transformations. It has never been without controversy. Some critics have always argued that the system was far too generous and encouraged people who could and should work to remain idle instead. Others have always pointed to its limitations, arguing that too few people were actually able to obtain support when they needed it because of the strict eligibility requirements, and those who were supported received too little.

Unemployment Insurance was created primarily to address issues of cyclical unemployment — to support workers who lost their jobs because the economy had fallen into a recession. This was clearly a temporary situation and workers required, more than anything, temporary support to meet their immediate needs while they waited to be called back to work as the economy recovered. The original plan covered only about 42 per cent of the workforce, and explicitly excluded seasonal workers, teachers, government employees, hospital employees and many others. Workers could be disqualified if they had ever participated in a strike and were penalized if they left their job voluntarily or refused work. Workers who were unable to work because of illness, pregnancy or injury were not covered.

Unemployment Insurance was first expanded to about 75 per cent of the labour force in 1955 when seasonal workers were integrated into the program. The 1960s saw a number of revisions and, in 1971, the program was reoriented to include a number of active services for jobseekers, including retraining. Since then, the program has undergone a number of transformations and revisions. In 1990, the federal government eliminated its financial obligations under the plan, making it entirely self-financed through contributions from employers and employees. In 1993, workers who voluntarily left their jobs or refused work were entirely disqualified and benefits were again lowered. In 1996, when the program was renamed Employment Insurance, benefits were lowered once again and workers who applied repeatedly were penalized.

Throughout it all, the amount of support a worker could expect depended on how many hours they had worked in the previous year and how much they had earned, up to a maximum. Beginning in 2009, workers could only claim benefits if they worked a certain number of insured hours in the previous twelve months, which varied across the country depending on regional levels of unemployment. In areas with lower unemployment rates, applicants had to work more hours before they qualified.

As EI underwent transformation, so too did the economy in which it operated. Some parts of the country still had a resource-based economy with large numbers of seasonal workers, while other areas that had relied on the steady work associated with manufacturing began to see many jobs offshored or replaced by technology. There were always new jobs created to replace those that were lost, but the new jobs in the expanding service sector were increasingly precarious. Many had no guaranteed hours, paid very low wages and very few had union support or the kind of workplace benefits that had characterized manufacturing jobs. Young people just entering the labour force knew they would be retraining, probably more than once, for jobs that they could not yet imagine. Long before the pandemic shut down the economy in 2020, the economy was already characterized by far fewer lifetime jobs with benefits, decent wages and union protection and many more contingent jobs — short-term contracts, self-employment and permanent part-time work. Young workers, women and racialized people were the most vulnerable, but they were not alone. Older workers displaced from jobs in the resource or manufacturing sectors found that their skills were not enough for them to find employment that paid as well as the jobs they left behind. As factories and mines closed, big box stores opened. New opportunities paid lower wages and offered fewer benefits. Many costs that used to be associated with employing labour, such as the provision of a pension and benefits such as health care, were shifted to taxpayers. The number of contingent workers in Canada grew from 4.8 million in 1997 to 6.1 million in 2015. Almost one-third of Canadian jobs were for contingent workers, yet temporary positions paid 30 per cent less on average than permanent positions, and only 24 per cent of Canadian workers were covered by private sector pension plans.[4]

Over time, these changes in the labour market made EI less and less adequate. When workers lost their jobs in the 2008 recession, many discovered that they did not qualify for EI because they had not met the prior work requirement. Others were self-employed and did not receive support. Still others worked part-time because they had a disability, often invisible, that made full-time work impossible. Meeting the work requirement was especially hard for people with disabilities. The economy recovered after that recession, but the issues with EI remained. When COVID-19 led to public health measures that shut down a number of workplaces, it was apparent that EI could not handle the expected volume of applications and, even if it could, it would not protect workers from financial devastation. The only applicants who could receive support were those who worked close to full-time and did not leave their jobs voluntarily. There was no support for people who stopped working to care for their kids when elementary schools closed. People who were immune-compromised and feared for their health if they returned to work were not covered. The self-employed were inadequately covered. Fewer than 40 per cent could expect to receive any support from EI in normal times, and the amount they received and the length of time they would be supported would be limited by their prior work history.

Applicants were confronted with another problem. Employment Insurance is based on a philosophy of profound mistrust. Each application required independent verification of work history and cause for termination before benefits would be extended. There was no database in place that was continually updated with information about earnings and employment history. Therefore, the verification required took time and applicants in need could expect to wait several weeks to receive support, even if they ultimately received retroactive payments. Many faced significant hardship while they waited for back payments. The system was simply not capable of dealing with a massive influx of applications, each of which needed independent verification of every detail. It would be overwhelmed.

The pandemic made it clear that EI could not meet the needs of contemporary workers. It was not flexible enough to deal with a changing economy, nor was it generous enough. Its philosophy of mistrust was inconsistent with what is known about human motivation. Most of all, it was just not possible to distinguish between those who "deserved" support and those who were "undeserving" of support. Did the woman who faced relentless harassment from her colleagues leave her job voluntarily? Should it be up to her employer to make that call? Or should judging applicants be the prerogative of a government bureaucrat? Should the young man who has trouble keeping a job because his social skills are affected by his mental health be punished for his invisible disability? There are appeal panels, but how long should one wait to receive support?

For all its limitations, however, there was one group of workers for whom EI worked relatively well — adults in regular, full-time jobs. For those who earned at or above the median wage, EI paid a maximum benefit of $2,484 a month in 2020, which exceeded the CERB and most basic income proposals. A recipient was permitted to work while on claim, and their benefit would be reduced by fifty cents for every dollar earned up to 90 per cent of previous earnings. Additional earnings reduced the benefit on a dollar for dollar basis. Recipients could receive support for somewhere between fourteen and forty-five weeks depending on their prior work history and the job market in the region where they lived. Employment Insurance also provided some sick leave and parental leave to those who qualified. For those who qualified, this program worked well enough. However, EI was an insurance program entirely paid for by contributions from workers and employers. It required those in precarious jobs, who were disproportionately young, female and racialized, to pay into a system that benefitted primarily those in regular, relatively well-paid jobs. The self-employed, along with those who left jobs because of health or child care responsibilities, didn't qualify. Employment Insurance, on its own, could never meet the needs of all working-age Canadians.

The inadequacies that had been growing for decades became abundantly clear when the government proposed to end the CERB and transition everyone on to EI. If they did not create a new transitional benefit for the self-employed, parents with care responsibilities and those with too little work experience to qualify for EI, the end of the CERB would have left many with no choice but to apply for provincial income assistance. These programs, administered by the provinces, are variously known as social assistance, income assistance or, more commonly, welfare depending on the province — programs of last resort.

## Provincial Income Assistance

Adults under age sixty-five with no other means of support and an insufficient work history to qualify for EI could apply for provincial income assistance. The amount offered varied by province as did the precise regulations, but every province provided a level of support well below the poverty line and imposed a complex and inconsistent set of regulations designed to ensure that applicants exhaust all other avenues of support first, and meet a set of obligations designed to demonstrate that they are actively seeking work while receiving benefits. In each case, the province would try to encourage recipients to find paid employment or someone else to support them by imposing strict eligibility requirements and employing caseworkers whose job is to identify and disqualify recipients who do not meet the eligibility rules.

To apply for income assistance, an applicant was required to provide documentation that included their social insurance number, provincial health card and birth certificate. They were required to document their income, assets and debt by providing bank statements and income tax forms. Age, education, immigration status, past employment, housing costs and the number of people in the family were verified. A caseworker had the authority to arrive at any time during normal business hours, without notice, and ask to inspect an applicant's home. They were entitled to verify the information provided by contacting the bank and the Canada Revenue Agency. In most provinces, a recipient could have no more than $10,000 in assets.[5]

The amount of support provided varied by family size and province. In 2020, for example, a single adult in Ontario was eligible for a maximum shelter allowance of $390 and a basic needs allowance of $343, for a total of $733 per month. Recipients also received extended health benefits that paid for dental, vision, drugs, hearing and other related costs. Some might also have been eligible for some federal and provincial refundable tax credits, if they had applied. Tax credits were not automatic and they varied by province. The total of these benefits was still considerably less than the minimum monthly income of $1,529.91 that a single adult could receive, without condition, from Old Age Security and the Guaranteed Income Supplement the moment they turned sixty-five.

To continue receiving provincial income assistance, recipients had a number of obligations. Everyone was required to meet with their caseworker every three months and take part in approved activities designed to help them find a job. However, a recipient was not permitted to register in an educational program without the explicit consent of their caseworker. Recipients were required to report any income they received and keep receipts and statements to document income, assets and expenses. Recipients were required to report any changes in circumstances, such as a new job, opening or closing a bank account, having a baby, moving or having a partner move in. Any gift, including even a gift of groceries from a family member, was listed as income and reduced the benefit. Recipients were required to obtain any other income or support they were entitled to, including child support from previous partners. Recipients were required to provide any document or information requested by their worker. If they did not comply, they could be disqualified or have their benefits reduced. If they did not meet the deadline for submitting requested documents, their next payment might have been delayed, reduced or denied.

The amount of money an applicant was entitled to receive from provincial income assistance was not easily determined. With over 800 rules, 240 benefit rates, 50 children's benefit rates and 30 plus specialized benefits in Ontario's social assistance programs, which is very similar to other programs across the country, applicants faced a good deal of uncertainty. Some recipients received different amounts of money each month, as gifts, needs, income and special benefits came into play.[6]

If a recipient worked while on income assistance in Ontario, they were allowed to earn $200 per month with no penalty. When earnings exceeded this, benefits were reduced by fifty cents for every dollar earned. This was one of the most generous treatments of employment income in Canada, and it was intended to encourage people to become independent of income assistance. Most provinces continued to reduce benefits on a dollar-for-dollar basis after a small allowance.

However, many people who relied on income assistance in Ontario still found it difficult to leave the program because they relied upon extended health benefits that were tied to income assistance. Most low-income workers could not receive income assistance because of the rigid eligibility requirements. Some had assets greater than $10,000 or owned a vehicle worth more than $15,000, or (especially in rural areas) a boat or snowmobile, while others were not prepared to pursue a former partner for child support.

Provincial income assistance across Canada paid too little to allow recipients to live adequately. It relied on caseworkers to interpret a complex system of regulations, which meant that recipients could never know with certainty how much they were entitled to receive, or when they would receive it. Moreover, it could not deal seamlessly with low-wage working people. Provincial income assistance was based on regulation and surveillance; it was intrusive and stigmatizing. It worked by taking away from recipients the ability to decide for themselves how to live their lives and how to spend their money.

The additional benefits tied to income assistance in many provinces, such as extended health benefits, could and should be made available to everyone based on level of income rather than source of income. Manitoba and Saskatchewan offered pharmacare to low-income working people as well as to those receiving income assistance; support for prescription drugs in these two provinces was based on the level of family income, rather than its source. Access to dental, mobility, vision and hearing care and appliances, along with other similar supports, could also be based on income rather than restricting such support to people who receive income assistance or disability support. This would extend support to those who work for low wages and eliminate the risk that discourages people who receive income assistance or disability support from trying to work.

The biggest difference between a basic income and provincial income assistance is that basic income would not rely on the discretion, intervention or interpretation of a caseworker. The amount received would be based solely on income. Some critics have argued that poverty is complex and people living with low incomes would still need the guidance of a caseworker to make good decisions and to overcome the challenges that keep them in poverty, as well as to navigate special programs and to deal with unanticipated events.

This honourable intention — the attempt to meet the unique needs of different people through discretion — has a dark side. A complex array of programs designed to meet the needs of different people at different life stages with different challenges could make it almost impossible for someone dealing with a complex family situation and perhaps inter-generational trauma to figure out how much they would be entitled to receive. People often have not received their benefits because they didn't understand how to apply or even know what might have been available. The caseworkers who were supposed to help them were simultaneously required to act as gatekeeper, ensuring that no one received benefits to which they were not entitled. In some provinces, they have been instructed not to tell clients about special programs unless the client asks. Few clients would think to ask about a program they didn't know about. It could be difficult to both help and police your client at the same time, or to build trust while checking with landlords, banks and employers to make sure a client was telling the truth.

Many antipoverty programs have tried to help people succeed — to get and keep a job, for example, by encouraging them to adopt the behaviour and make the kinds of decisions valued by mainstream culture. Indigenous people, immigrants, people of different genders or abilities have rarely been the ones who decide which programs should be available to, or mandated for, those who need support. Navigating a complex system that takes the form of particular services delivered in particular ways has been part of a historical legacy at the root of much poverty and dysfunction.

## Poverty in Canada

The economic shutdown devastated many families who were just making ends meet in normal times. However, well before the pandemic, there were many people in Canada who were already living well below the poverty line and trying to access support through the existing, inadequate social programs. In 2018, 8.7 per cent of Canadians had incomes below the official poverty line; of these, 6.6 per cent were adults of working age and 1.6 per cent were children under eighteen living with poor parents. Only 0.6 per cent of Canadians were sixty-five or older and living in poverty.

FIGURE 1.1 Persons Living Below the Poverty Line (market basket measure), 2018

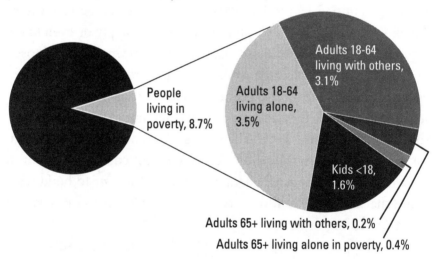

Source: Statistics Canada. Table 11-10-0135-01 (formerly CANSIM 206-0041).

People without enough money to meet basic needs require a guaranteed, adequate and predictable income. Those who are economically insecure need an insurance policy to protect them against the risk of poverty and loss. A basic income is designed to meet both needs.

FIGURE 1.2 Poverty Rates by Age (market basket measure), 2018

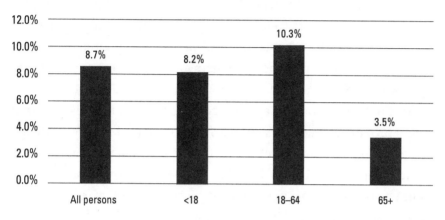

Poverty Rates in Canada by Age Group

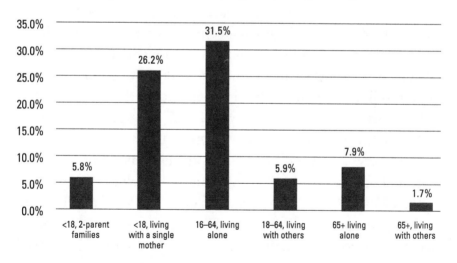

Poverty Rates in Canada by Age and Living Arrangement

Source: Statistics Canada. Table 11-10-0135-01 (formerly CANSIM 206-0041).

Families with children younger than eighteen have access to the Canada Child Benefit, a type of basic income, and people sixty-five and over have access to Old Age Security and the Guaranteed Income Supplement. These two sets of programs have ensured that the poverty rate of children and seniors has been lower than it has been for adults of working age. Among people aged sixty-five and older, 3.5 per cent have been living in poverty as have 8.2 per cent of children eighteen and younger, compared with 10.3 per cent of working-age adults. There is still much work to be done. In 2018, seniors living alone faced a poverty rate of 7.9 per cent while 26.2 per cent of children living with single mothers were poor because their mothers were poor. Working-age adults who lived alone faced a poverty rate of 31.5 per cent.

The poverty of working-age adults was entirely due to the fact that EI and provincial income assistance had not evolved to accommodate the changing labour market. By 2016, 8.2 per cent of workers were already employed in gig work — that is, as self-employed independent contractors hired for particular projects. While many of these workers were highly skilled and commanded high hourly wages, the episodic nature of their employment could be associated with income insecurity.[7] Not all workers had equal access to high-quality jobs. In 2016, employees with a high school diploma or less were more likely to hold jobs with inflexible schedules, low autonomy, few benefits and less opportunity for training. Younger workers were more likely to hold jobs with involuntary and irregular work schedules.[8] In 2019, only 76 per cent of employees were in full-time permanent work, with younger and female employees more likely to be represented in temporary, casual and part-time work.[9] Episodic work, part-time work and self-employment have all made it difficult to qualify for EI.

These changes have become a permanent feature of the changing economy and were well established long before COVID-19 forced many more people to deal with economic insecurity. Our social programs were already failing; the pandemic brought these failures to our attention in a very dramatic way. As early as June 2020, a Statistics Canada report by René Morissette suggested that "One plausible hypothesis is that the COVID-19 pandemic might accelerate the automation of certain tasks. Likewise, the COVID-19 pandemic might lead to a permanent increase in rates of telework and, more generally, to changes in work arrangements (e.g. shiftwork, configuration of office spaces) that facilitate physical distancing."[10]

## A Basic Income Is More than an Antipoverty Program

A basic income does more than meet the needs of those living in poverty; it also provides insurance for everyone. Even someone who holds a good, solid, middle-class job can no longer assume that they will do so for the rest of their working lives. Everyone has always been vulnerable to poor health and accidents that force some people to stop working before they are old enough to receive pensions. But the changing economy, alongside such unexpected events as global pandemics, has introduced new kinds of job insecurity.

A basic income can address the problems associated with the growth of precarious employment. It used to be easier to distinguish between workers, retirees, people facing short-term unemployment, people not in the workforce, students and people with disabilities. Consequently, Employment Insurance was created for the short-term unemployed, Disability Support for people with disabilities, special programs for students, Old Age Security, the Guaranteed Income Supplement and the Canada Pension Plan for the retired and income assistance for people not in the workforce. All of these programs were, and continue to be, associated with strictly enforced eligibility criteria to make sure that individuals access the correct program for their needs. The growth of precarious employment, however, has made these distinctions almost meaningless. Workers may have tried to support families with part-time jobs when they would have preferred full-time work that was not available to them, or they may have been subsisting between short-term contracts. People who wanted to work might have found themselves effectively "retired" many years before they would have liked to be. Some people with disabilities, especially mental health and other invisible disabilities, were rejected when they applied to programs for people with disabilities yet were still unable to find and keep jobs in standard workplaces unwilling or unable to accommodate their needs. Students may have had child care and senior care responsibilities along with job responsibilities. People on income assistance would often like to work but feared the loss of drug or extended health benefits that they or their family members relied on and received as part of their income assistance.

A basic income would supplement the incomes of those who retire too early because their jobs end, and fill gaps between jobs for those who make do with short-term contracts. It would support those unable to work because of the illness or disability of a family member or because of their own health challenges. It would supplement the incomes of low-wage workers, especially young people struggling to find permanent work in a changing economy, and subsidize individuals who choose to engage in job training or other education.

A basic income that effectively addresses the issues of poverty and economic insecurity would have many other consequences for Canadian society. Income affects our sense of self and the opportunities we have to consume, to invest, to save and to give, and each of these affects our health, our social well-being, our ability to parent, our education and our ability to withstand adversity.

### Health and Well-Being

Our health care system has been doing a reasonable job of addressing illness, but it has done little to keep people well. Many of the people treated at inner-city clinics and busy hospital emergency departments are there because of the lives they have lived. Our health is affected by our income, the social support we can rely on, our social status, our education, the social and physical conditions in which we work and live, our personal health practices and coping skills and the opportunities we had as children. These social determinants of health are all interrelated, but income is fundamental. It affects the kind of housing and neighbourhoods we live in and our ability to access education and to offer opportunities to our children.

Income also affects our ability to access health care not provided by the province or federal government. While hospital services and visits to family doctors have been routinely available to all Canadians, dental work and prescription medications have not. Some provinces have provided means-tested pharmaceutical coverage for all adults, but others have not. People who have depended on provincial income assistance have had access to extended health care, and those who work at good jobs have had access to these services through their benefits packages at work, but people who have worked part-time and on short-term contracts have often had no coverage for such fundamental needs. The implications have gone beyond the suffering associated with unmet health needs. Dental health, for example, is one of the informal markers of social status in our society. People with bad teeth present poorly in job interviews and are often not hired into higher-level positions that require interaction with the public. This makes it harder to escape from poverty and to become self-supporting. People with inadequate pharmaceutical coverage miss time at work and are sometimes hospitalized because they cannot adequately control their health conditions.

## Education and Training

In a rapidly evolving labour market, continuing education is fundamental. Basic income would support education throughout our lives. Young children, growing up in households with adequate incomes, could go to school secure and well fed. Educational outcomes improve when families who can afford to pay the rent move less often, and children can continue in the same school. As adolescents, children in families with adequate incomes and less parental stress may be less vulnerable to neighbourhood risk factors associated with leaving school early, such as early pregnancies. They may feel less pressure to leave school before graduation and become independent if their parents have the resources to support them. For adults, a basic income could provide the resources necessary to take time out of the labour market to access further training.

The ability to use a basic income to fund retraining could make it possible to get a better job. Instead of a lifetime of working at minimum wage or near-minimum wage jobs, an individual with a basic income could retrain to meet the changing demands of the labour market. This would make it possible to compete for better-paid permanent jobs with benefits instead of dealing with the income insecurity associated with low-wage, part-time work. Basic income would provide a structure that could support individuals as they worked to better their conditions; it would not simply be a source of short-term support for people mired in inadequate work.

### Financial Resilience

A basic income would do more than allow people to meet their day-to-day needs for survival. People could count on receiving their basic income without worrying about how a caseworker would choose to interpret and apply a set of confusing and inconsistent regulations. They would know how much they would receive and when it would appear in their bank accounts. While these may seem like small matters, it is almost impossible to plan and to save without an adequate, dependable, predictable income. When breaking a regulation you didn't know about might result in financial penalties, as is the case with income assistance, it seems reasonable to spend money as soon as it appears in case it is snatched back. When regulations associated with provincial income assistance reduce benefits for those with assets, it makes little sense to save for the future. Why save for unexpected (or even expected) needs when there might be funding available through the discretion of a caseworker if need can be demonstrated? Provincial income assistance has been a system predicated on crisis and dependence. It was established to respond to crisis, and it perpetuates a situation where a recipient is always on the edge of crisis.

By contrast, a predictable basic income would allow individuals to make decisions about how to allocate their money and how to save for future purchases or unexpected events. Having an adequate, predictable income would allow people to take control of their own lives. It would allow people to make choices about how they live, and with the ability to choose comes autonomy and self-respect.

### Healthy Labour Market Attachment and Creativity

At the heart of much of the controversy associated with basic income is the fear that a basic income will free workers to work less or not at all. But there are many people who do important work outside the traditional labour market. Artists and actors have rarely earned enough to pay the rent without a side job in a café or elsewhere. Many entrepreneurs have faced a long period before their new enterprise generates enough income to pay a salary. Other people do not work for pay but spend much of their time working for their families and communities. All of these activities contribute to the richness of the society in which we live.

If people do choose to spend less time in paid work, at least some of them will contribute to our social well-being. Even those who choose to spend less time working and more time in traditional leisure activities might ultimately be more productive in the labour market as a result of the time away from work. Basic income encourages us, among other things, to have a broader conversation about the meaning of work in our lives.

### Responsible Citizenship

The most important consequence of basic income is that it would allow all Canadians to decide for themselves how to live their lives without the coercion of grinding poverty, the stress of income insecurity or the humiliation associated with income assistance. It would allow each Canadian the basic resources we need to participate in our society. We could register our child in theatre or hockey. We could enjoy the small pleasures of going to a coffee shop or a neighbourhood pub without worrying about the few dollars involved. We may find time to volunteer in our communities or to help our neighbours and family members who require additional support. All of us would have the same opportunities to make our own decisions and to live with the consequences of those decisions.

## Economic Insecurity, Persistent Poverty and Basic Income

As the first wave of COVID-19 began to wane, governments at every level began to face two issues simultaneously. The pandemic made it clear that our existing safety net not only allowed poverty to persist among those who had always struggled on inadequate provincial assistance, but also was unable to address the needs of the growing ranks of workers in precarious employment. The temporary benefits that these governments offered, however, came with their own very significant costs. By June 2020, as the first provinces began to cautiously lift their public health restrictions, 8.1 million Canadians had applied for support through the CERB. The official unemployment rate rose to 13.7 per cent in May, but that number would be more than 23 per cent if we adjusted it for the reduced hours of those who continued to work and the displaced workers who were not actively seeking employment. By the end of April, the Parliamentary Budget Officer was already projecting a federal deficit of more than $252 billion for 2020, against the expected $21 billion before the pandemic, and expected the debt to exceed $1 trillion in a year when the economy was expected to shrink by 12 per cent. By July, the projected deficit had reached $343 billion, and the debt was expected to reach $1.2 trillion. Vast sums of money were being spent in a context of profound uncertainty.

Epidemiologists told us that we could expect successive waves of the virus over the next few years until a vaccine was developed. Some of the firms that closed during the pandemic would never re-open and, while a good deal of entrepreneurial spirit was evident in the attempts business people made to stay afloat, this was hardly an ideal time to seek financial support to start a new business. Many of those firms that did survive would use the opportunity of the pandemic and government support to adopt new technologies, some of which would displace the human labour that they had previously relied upon. Machines are, after all, not vulnerable to viruses. As it became clear that the economy would not recover quickly, we also began to recognize that the pandemic was reinforcing economic changes that had been underway for a long time, such as the decline of oil and gas as a driver of the economy, technological change and the growing precarity of work.

Social and income inequality, too, became very apparent; it's much easier to self-isolate in a 1,500-square-foot house with a backyard and a regular income than in a one-bedroom apartment with two kids. We were also forced to recognize that women and racialized people were among the first to lose their jobs during the shutdown, and they were also prominent among the frontline workers who continued to work the cash registers, stock the grocery store shelves and provide care to vulnerable seniors in nursing homes. As workplaces started to reopen, women were less able to take advantage of opportunities because the schools were still closed and children still needed care. The need for better protection against economic insecurity was clear, but we struggled with the need to provide better and more cost-effective income supports at the same time that our capacity to pay for additional programs was strained.

# Chapter 2

# Canadian Experiments with Basic Income

Our experience with COVID-19 was unprecedented, and the need for our various levels of government to provide support to Canadians while the economy shut down to contain the infection was, for most of us, something we could never have imagined. There was nothing unique, however, about the suggestion that some form of a basic income might be a useful response. There has been a policy interest in a targeted basic income — a guaranteed income — in Canada for decades. As the Canada Pension Plan was introduced, medicare was rolled out in the early 1970s and what was then called Unemployment Insurance was made more generous, Canadian policymakers were looking for a way to deliver income support that would eliminate some of the obvious flaws of "welfare" — its inadequacy, its gaps, the stigma associated with its use and, especially, the design features that made it difficult to escape a life of poverty and dependence and discouraged people from working.

Americans were experimenting with what they called a Negative Income Tax — a system identical to a targeted basic income. In the US, interest in the Negative Income Tax came about because of the civil rights movement of the 1960s. Young, idealistic students travelled from New York and Boston and New Haven to southern states to register voters and were shocked to see Americans living in conditions they associated with low-income countries. The media brought the discovery into living rooms across the nation. There was growing popular support for antipoverty interventions in the US and, eventually, one response was the creation of four experiments as part of President Johnson's War on Poverty. These were conducted in various parts of the US, for varying lengths of time and with different designs. The purpose of all of these experiments was to answer a simple question: If you give people income support in the form of a targeted basic income, will they work less? More importantly, is it possible to design the basic income in a way that doesn't discourage work?[1]

Canadian policymakers watched these US experiments with interest and, in 1974, the federal government decided to conduct a Canadian experiment called Mincome. They sought a research site and Manitoba, under its first ever NDP provincial government, leaped at the chance to partner. Between 1975 and 1978, many families in Winnipeg, Dauphin and several rural communities received a targeted basic income.

## Rediscovering Mincome

In 1974, I was a first-year student at Glendon College in Toronto intending to major in psychology. I found myself registered in an economics class, almost by accident, and vowed to make the best of what I expected to be a rather boring term. I was interested in people — not interest rates and tax expenditures! It was a time of optimism and social change, and, like many of my classmates, I wanted to help make the world a little more just and the lives of ordinary people a little bit easier. I didn't expect economics to have much to say about the world I'd grown up in.

During the course of that year, and under the mentorship of an extraordinary professor named Ian McDonald, I came to understand my own relationship to money. I was the oldest of three children, and my father died when I was twelve. My mother had few job skills; like many women of her generation, she never expected to have to support a family on her own. She raised us, first on Mother's Allowance and later through a series of low-skilled and not particularly well-paid jobs. I learned very quickly how important money is, and how vulnerable anyone becomes when they have no money of their own. People with money have choices and opportunities that others don't have. I knew that my widowed mother struggled financially to support three young children. However, I had the opportunity to complete high school because my mother chose to allow me to live at home even when I was old enough to work. I could make the choice to go to college, unlike many of my friends, because I was fortunate enough to receive a scholarship. The availability of money then, and for many years of schooling to come, gave me a life that my parents couldn't have imagined, and that most of my friends didn't share.

The year 1974 was important on many levels. Professor McDonald told a story about an experiment that was just being set up in Western Canada called Mincome that would, he was convinced, transform the way we delivered social programs in Canada. With charts and graphs, he showed us how the current system of income assistance created walls that prevented people from becoming independent; if they earned a little money, they lost not only their welfare cheque but also all the benefits, such as drug and dental care, that accompanied income assistance. He explained that working was no guarantee against poverty; low-wage workers struggled to provide for themselves and their families. He used the tools of economics to show us how families were always worse off when they received support directly in the form of goods, such as food, than they would be if they received the equivalent amount of money. People who have money, he reminded us, have the opportunity to spend that money however they think best, and people always know better than bureaucrats or charities what their families need most. It seemed to me that the greatest gift of income security is the ability to take risks and to imagine different outcomes. If Mincome was successful, it would create income security for many more families, and allow young people in particular to imagine different kinds of lives than their parents lived.

I decided to change my major to economics.

## The Basic Income Experiments

Mincome was constructed in the same atmosphere of possibility and expansion that led us to introduce the Canada Pension Plan in 1966 and nationwide universal health insurance by 1972, and to make Unemployment Insurance and disability support payments more generous. The world was being remade and, in Canada, what was then called guaranteed annual income was perceived to be one pillar of a just society — just like medicare.[2]

Mincome took place in three sites in Manitoba — Winnipeg, Dauphin and a set of smaller rural communities. The small town of Dauphin, an agriculturally dependent town in central Manitoba with about ten thousand residents, was unique because it was the only site in any of these experiments that was designated a saturation site: every family (rather than a selected few) that lived in the town was invited to participate. They would receive cash payments only if their family income was low enough to qualify. The amount of money they received would depend on the size of their family and the amount of income they received from other sources. The payments were modest: for a family of four with no other income, the basic income would be $3,800 (just over $22,000 in today's dollars). As income from other sources increased, the value of the basic income would decline by fifty cents for every dollar earned. A family of four earning $7,600 or more would receive nothing.

For people who had previously been receiving income assistance, these rates were only very slightly more generous. Their material circumstances would not be greatly affected. They would, however, have the freedom to spend their time and their money as they saw fit. If they wanted to attend school, they did not need the permission of a caseworker. If they wanted to open a business, they could do so. As long as their income was low enough to qualify, they received support. Perhaps because they were not treated with suspicion by caseworkers, families did not perceive their Mincome stipend as welfare and reported that they felt no stigma.[3] The people for whom Mincome made a profound financial difference were working people. As in many small towns, Dauphin had a number of seasonal, low-paid jobs, and many people were self-employed. They suffered a great deal of income insecurity because of the nature of agricultural work, and their earned incomes were often low enough that they qualified for partial stipends from Mincome even when they worked. The standard of living and economic security of the working poor in Dauphin improved dramatically during Mincome.

## The Death and Rediscovery of Mincome

The money flowed into Dauphin for only three years between 1975 and 1978, as planned. I completed my degree in economics and went on to graduate school, where economics had more to do with mathematics than with the living conditions of the poor. I lost track of Mincome. In fact, I was not alone. The 1970s were a turbulent time, both politically and economically. Oil prices increased as oil-producing countries in the Middle East recognized their newfound power. In Canada, high unemployment and inflation were running hand in hand, which seemed to contradict the way economists expected the world to work. Inflation exceeded 10 per cent a year, and many seniors suffered as the value of their savings evaporated. Young people buying houses faced interest rates of 18 per cent. Governments borrowed and spent money to stimulate the economy and create jobs, facing opposition over growing deficits and government debt. Workers went on strike, demanding cost-of-living increases. The 1970s began in idealism, and there was a clear focus on reducing poverty; by 1978, battered governments were trying to shore up the economy on many fronts. Poverty took a back seat. In the United States, the same economic challenges were compounded by political challenges as the experiments lost support in the House of Representatives and in the Senate.

Governments in Canada paid a price for economic upheaval. The social-democratic NDP government in Manitoba fell in 1976 and was replaced by a Progressive Conservative government. Few governments are keen to invest in the special projects of their predecessors. They continued the experiment, but with little enthusiasm. The Liberals in office federally were a minority government with most of their attention focused on survival. Mincome was cost-shared, with the federal government paying 75 per cent of the costs, and the province paying 25 per cent. As Mincome payments drew to an end, the researchers conducting the experiment petitioned the funders for more money to complete the analysis. They were refused and ordered to "archive the data for future analysis." The experiment ended with data in 1,800 cardboard boxes in a rented office suite in downtown Winnipeg, and at least two levels of government bickering about who should pay the rent.

The stated purpose of all the basic income experiments was to determine the impact on the labour market: would people work less if they were offered a basic income? Several years after the project ended, Derek Hum (the second research director of Mincome) and Wayne Simpson (a labour economist at the University of Manitoba) attempted to answer that question. They examined the Winnipeg sample and discovered that for adult men and single women, there was little effect. Two groups of people, however, reduced their work effort significantly. New mothers, who were entitled to only four unpaid weeks of maternity leave at the time, chose to use the Mincome stipend to buy themselves longer maternity leaves. And "young, unattached males" — that is, men aged fifteen through twenty-four without families to support — reduced their work effort substantially.[4]

But policy attention had shifted, and the results of Mincome were not at the top of anyone's mind. These young, unattached males, however, held an important clue I would later investigate.

In the meantime, I finished my PhD and was hired as a professor of economics at the University of Manitoba. By 2000, I was working in the medical school, and every project I was involved with highlighted the intimate relationship between income and health outcomes. The disparities are profound: lower incomes are associated with shorter life expectancies, higher rates of self-harm and higher rates of chronic conditions. Having become ill, low-income individuals are more likely to suffer complications from their conditions. Even universal health care did not guarantee equal health outcomes for everyone. These statistical findings became real when I walked through the Health Sciences Centre in Winnipeg that treated many low-income residents of the surrounding neighbourhood as well as people flown in from northern communities for treatment. I talked to patients in the cafeteria, the hallways and the garden and soon came to understand a little better how the many different aspects of deprivation build on one another to undermine health. I saw a thirty-five-year-old who lost a leg to diabetes, and teenagers diagnosed with tuberculosis. It was clear enough that poverty was associated with poor health outcomes, but I wondered whether reducing the poverty in which people lived would actually improve their health. Then I remembered Mincome.

I went in search of the Mincome data. The data tape that Derek Hum and Wayne Simpson had used for their labour market analysis had become obsolete and, in any case, focused only on the Winnipeg sample. However, I knew the boxes were somewhere. I tracked them down to a regional office of Library and Archives Canada, where I confronted the full visual impact of 1,800 cubic feet of data.

Overwhelming as the data was, my graduate students and I began combing through the boxes and contemplating different ways of uncovering the impact of Mincome on health. The boxes contained not only the regular labour-market surveys that had informed Derek Hum and Wayne Simpson's work on labour markets, but all kinds of short surveys, letters from participants, information booklets, newspaper articles and the kind of ephemera that gives historians a sense of the period. We began to work through the boxes, and news of our work spread. Former participants phoned and emailed to tell me stories about the impact Mincome had had on their lives. Some of the participants who reflected on their experiences after three decades reported that the extra money had made life just a little bit easier. Mincome had allowed families living close to the edge to indulge in the small, everyday luxuries that made life tolerable. It reduced the stress of unexpected expenses. People reported that accepting the money did not make them feel bad because "everyone was the same." Others told stories of being able to make decisions with long-term consequences. One single mother with two young daughters reported that she had left welfare to join Mincome because she would have the freedom to take some job training, which her otherwise supportive welfare caseworker couldn't see the point of. Forty years later, she reflected on the pride she felt in having modelled independence for her daughters. A farm family that sold vegetables at a local market had faced hardship when their farm truck had broken down; Mincome had allowed them to buy a new truck and stay in business. Another woman told the story of how she and her husband, both in their early twenties at the time, had opened a small record shop, relying on Mincome to pay their living expenses during the challenging early years of the business.

All the stories, whether they were about the small businesses that participants had started or been able to keep alive, or about children going off to college, or even adults able to take job training and make better decisions for their families, confirmed what I had been taught in my first year of university: families know better than any bureaucrat what they need. And what poor people undeniably need is money. Money gives people choices and opportunities.

## Education and Mincome

My project, however, was focused on health and well-being. The Mincome money had flowed for only three years, and I was confronted with a limited budget and 1,800 boxes. Would the experiment have lasted long enough to affect people's lives? And would I be able to show the impact? I knew that I would require funding to complete the research, and that granting agencies would be skeptical that such old material could yield anything of interest. I thought again about the "young, unattached males" that reduced the number of hours they worked when Mincome was introduced. Translating social science into English, I knew that we were talking about adolescent boys — young men the same age I was in 1973, when I decided to complete grade thirteen in Toronto rather than quit school to take a job as a bank teller or telephone operator.

When I quizzed some of the Mincome participants about their lives, several people from Dauphin explained that before Mincome was available, their older brothers and cousins had been under a significant amount of family pressure to become self-supporting as soon as possible, so that families could concentrate their financial resources on younger children. No one quite saw the point of staying in school when you could work and earn decent money. When Mincome came along, many of these families decided that they could support their adolescent sons a bit longer. Whether these boys went back to school because they aspired to a larger lifetime income, or just because they wanted to play football for another year, it would have a significant impact on their future lives. But how could we find these results in the data?

I called the provincial Department of Education and asked for enrollment data for all Manitoba high schools. I wondered whether the impact of Mincome would be large enough to show up in such aggregate data. I divided the data into Dauphin high schools, Winnipeg high schools and high schools in the rest of Manitoba. To get a crude measurement of high school completion rates, I divided grade twelve enrollments by the previous year's grade eleven enrollments:

Figure 2.1 Grade 12 Enrollment as Per cent of Previous Year Grade 11 Enrollment

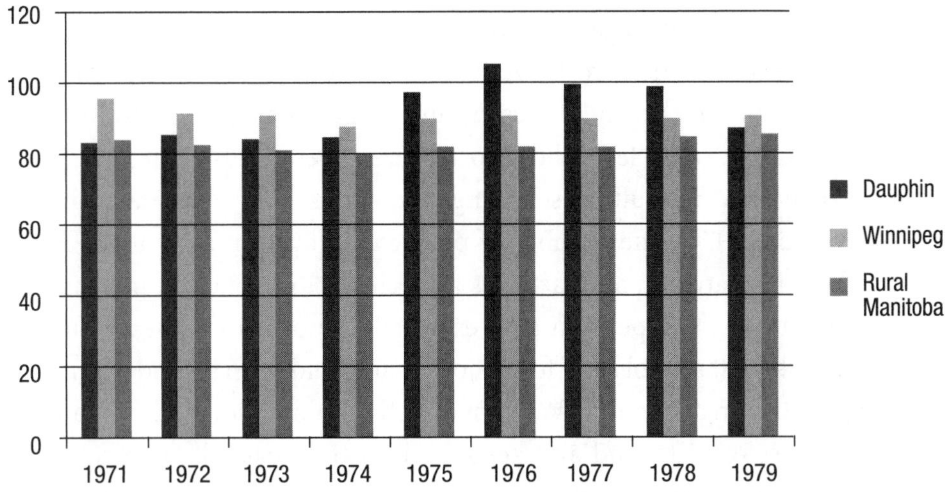

Source: Evelyn L. Forget, "The Town With No Poverty," *Canadian Public Policy* 37, no. 3 (2011).

If everyone in grade eleven continues to grade twelve, and there is no change in the underlying population, the bar in Figure 2.1 will reach 100. The larger the dropout rates between grade eleven and grade twelve, when most children are old enough to leave school legally, the lower the bar. Before 1975, there is little difference between Dauphin and the rest of rural Manitoba. As we might expect, adolescents living in Winnipeg were more likely to go on to grade twelve. When Mincome was introduced, the continuation rate in Dauphin increased above even the Winnipeg rate. In 1976, the bar exceeded 100 per cent; students who had left school were returning to complete grade twelve. In 1977 and 1978, the Dauphin continuation rate hovered near 100 per cent. When Mincome ended in 1979, Dauphin continuation rates fell back to the level of the rest of rural Manitoba. Mincome allowed a lucky cohort of "young, unattached males" to aspire to a much better life than they might have expected had they left school to work like their older brothers and cousins. The decline in hours worked documented by Derek Hum and Wayne Simpson, which on the surface seems to support the fear that basic income will encourage laziness, is actually a good news story.

Imagine the next forty years for someone who did not finish high school in the mid-1970s. Young men had access to good jobs. In Dauphin, they left school to take relatively well-paying jobs in agriculture, agriculture-servicing industries and manufacturing. Since the 1970s, the number of people employed in agriculture has fallen dramatically, and factories have closed in the face of increased international competition and, especially, automation. These young men who left school early found jobs that would soon be undermined by a changing economy. Without a high school diploma, they would have struggled to find and keep work as time passed. High school graduates are much less likely to experience periods of unemployment than those without a diploma, and when they are laid off they are more likely to be re-employed at wages comparable to those of the jobs they left behind. Their lifetime earnings are higher and the opportunities they can offer their children greater.

## Mincome and Health Outcomes

My project, though, was especially concerned with health outcomes. Did reducing poverty make people healthier? Mincome was not designed to gather health data; its purpose was to address the fear that families who were offered a basic income would reduce the number of hours they worked for wages. I was able to find the health outcomes only because of a set of lucky accidents. By 1972, all provinces in Canada had introduced universal health insurance. One of the features of Canadian medicare is that it routinely collects a great deal of data as we use the health care system. Every time an individual interacts with hospitals or physicians, a record of that interaction is created. Hospitalizations are recorded in a database along with records of the patient including, most significantly, how long they were hospitalized, what happened to them in the hospital, and why they were hospitalized in the first place. Every time someone goes to a family doctor, the doctor completes a billing claim for the province. The billing claim identifies the patient, the date and the reason for the consultation.[5] As you might imagine, this is highly confidential data, and great care is taken to protect the privacy of Canadians.

Over time, these data in Manitoba have been de-identified — that is, patient names and identifying characteristics have been removed — and made available to qualified researchers under very restricted conditions. Consequently, the database contains everyone who lived in Dauphin during the Mincome experiment. It was also possible to find people of the same age and sex who lived in similar kinds of families and similar towns. Therefore, we could create a set of matched controls — three other people of the same age, sex, family type and living arrangements — for every person who lived in Dauphin. By examining how these controls fared and comparing their results to the Dauphin residents, we found that:

- Hospitalizations for Dauphin residents fell 8.5 per cent relative to the controls;
- "Accidents and injuries" and "mental health" accounted for most of the decline;
- Visits to family doctors by Dauphin residents fell relative to the controls;
- "Mental health" issues accounted for most of the decline in visits to family doctors.

"Accidents and injuries" is a very big category that includes such things as car and workplace accidents, self-harm and accidental poisoning, assaults and family violence and so on. Low income and "accident and injury" hospitalizations are often linked, partly because low-income people tend to work at more dangerous jobs and live in more dangerous housing and neighbourhoods. The link between mental health and low income also seems reasonable; the constant stress of money worries can lead to anxiety and depression. Health did seem to improve for Dauphin residents, relative to the controls, during Mincome. Mental health improvements were especially important.

## How Did Mincome Make People Healthier?

The statistical analysis of Mincome participants showed undeniably that people used fewer health services when they had a basic income available to them. They were hospitalized less frequently and visited family doctors less often. We also know that improved mental health seemed to play a key role. Statistical analysis, however, cannot explain how or why something happened. What was the mechanism through which health improved? For that, we need the memories of participants.

Without question, Mincome reduced material deprivation. Mincome rates in Dauphin were set at a level just slightly more generous than income assistance. The monetary benefit for income assistance recipients who switched to Mincome was minimal. However, Mincome also offered stipends to low-income working people who had previously not had access to such benefits. These working people, who outnumbered income assistance recipients, did see their income increase.

Eric Richardson, who was about twelve when his family participated in Mincome, has a vivid memory of going to the dentist for the first time: "They didn't take you to the dentist unless you were in pain. No one had extra money for that. I remember being lined up with my brother and sister and marched off to the dentist about then. I ended up with a mouthful of fillings. So — thanks, Mincome!"

Mincome meant money was available for non-emergency care that could lead to better health, even if the benefits eluded a twelve-year-old. There is, however, reason to believe more was going on.

More important than the money received by Mincome recipients was the insurance aspect of basic income. Everyone in Dauphin received the promise that they could receive income support if their income fell below the program threshold. This had the effect of dramatically reducing income insecurity in a town in which much employment and employment income was dependent on agriculture, either directly or indirectly. A bad year for canola reduced the income of the farmer, but it also reduced the incomes of farm labourers, truck drivers, used car salespeople, hairdressers, restaurant owners, small shopkeepers and almost everyone else in town. If this was the nature of small-town employment forty years ago, it is increasingly coming to characterize much larger segments of the labour market today. Precarious employment is growing as a proportion of all employment in Canada and is strongly associated with worse employee health.[6]

Even people who never actually collected a stipend from Mincome knew that the program existed and benefited from it as a form of insurance, particularly those near to the qualifying threshold. Many people didn't know in advance whether they would qualify for Mincome support; it would depend on the weather and other unpredictable events. One question asked of Mincome recipients by the research team was "Why did you choose to participate in Mincome?" The most frequently cited response was "because it would be there if I needed it."[7] Just as in the case of fire or car insurance, a basic income benefits even those who do not need to collect. Anxiety is reduced simply because the insurance exists.

Mincome was also associated with a strong feeling of community in Dauphin. The program did not materially affect the degree of income inequality, largely because even the highest incomes in Dauphin — those of physicians or high school principals — were not nearly as far removed from the incomes of ordinary workers as those of high-income earners in large urban centres are today. The poorest residents were a little less deprived under the program. However, the way that Mincome affected life in this small town reflected the kind of social cohesion often associated with better community health.

I remember those years as really good years. There was just
a little bit of money around. We started a small shop — we
sold record players and records — and people were always out
on the streets. Everyone had enough extra money to go out
for a beer after work. People socialized a lot. The shop never
actually paid us a salary. It paid its way, but Mincome helped
us a lot. When Mincome ended, things just got hard again. We
closed a year or so after Mincome — 1980, I think. — Lois

The marked increase in high school completion rates reflects these
social effects as well. Imagine how a seventeen-year-old decides whether
to go back to school to complete grade twelve or to leave and take a job.
He and his parents will consider the income available to the family, and
whether they can afford to support another year of school. If the family
expects to receive support from Mincome should they need it, parents
might encourage children to stay in school. The young man in question
will consider how the money he might earn would affect his life, but
he will also consider the attractions of continuing his education. One
of those attractions will be what his friends decide to do. If more of
his friends go back to school, he is more likely to consider the option.
It matters whether his friends are in families that might also benefit
from a basic income. The more families that participate, the more
likely it will be that boys continue to grade twelve. Even young men in
families who do not receive support from Mincome will be influenced
by the decisions that their friends make. That is, the social attitudes that
govern community life will be influenced by a basic income.

This sense of community solidarity was also reflected in many of
the comments made by participants with whom I spoke:

"We were all in it together."

"Everyone was the same, so there was no shame."

"We all helped each other out. When we got the truck, we were
always hauling for people. Dad had the best truck, so if someone had
some lambs to ship, they used our truck."

It is possible that Mincome was associated with social solidarity because the town itself worked that way whether or not people received support through Mincome. None of the other experiments in North America during the 1970s had a saturation site where everyone in town had a similar offer. Normally, these experiments are conducted as randomized controlled trials, as was the case in the Winnipeg site. A randomized controlled trial means that the researchers came to town and selected a fairly small proportion of the total population to participate. These participants were then put into either the treatment group that received support through Mincome, or a control group that did not. The idea was that if you compared the results of the two groups, any differences would be due to the existence of Mincome. The participants in the experiment in a randomized controlled trial would know each other only by accident. Therefore, you would not see the kind of social effects that people remember so fondly from the Dauphin site.

## The Ontario BIG Experiment

One of the legacies of Mincome was the attempt to conduct a similar basic income experiment several years later. In the summer of 2017, researchers in Ontario began to approach some people living in Hamilton to participate in a three-year experiment designed to test the feasibility and impact of a basic income guarantee. Over the next several months, participants in Hamilton, Thunder Bay and Lindsay slowly came forward and agreed to open their lives to researchers — to provide data on everything from their health, their work habits, their decision-making skills and the way they participate in society. As the first participants began to receive a basic income, some told their stories to journalists, sharing the satisfaction of buying their first new winter coat in years, or the pride associated with deciding to register in community college, or the simple satisfaction of providing a bedroom for their children.

This project was introduced in the last year of the mandate of an unpopular Liberal government. In June 2018, a provincial election brought the Progressive Conservative Party to power and, despite a campaign promise to complete the experiment, the minister of Social Services announced the cancellation of the project in July 2018. It was, she claimed, "failing." There was no data to support that claim; participants had only completed one survey when they began the program and had not yet been asked how their lives had changed when they began to receive a basic income. The experiment was cancelled before any data collection took place. In August 2018, the provincial government announced that recipients would receive their promised payments until March 2019, when they would be transitioned off the program, but that there would be no evaluation of the experiment.

However, a determined research team from McMaster University in Hamilton captured as much of its impact as possible. They used an online survey and interviewed some of the participants in the Hamilton-Brantford site.[8] The results they reported must be used carefully because their study evaluated outcomes only for the small subset of subjects who volunteered to participate, the results were self-reported and the participants had already been informed that the experiment would be cancelled. This might have affected how they responded. Nevertheless, 217 participants responded and the results are intriguing.

All respondents claimed they had benefited in some way from the basic income guarantee. The vast majority (79.4 per cent) reported better physical and mental health and use of health services declined since many participants reported visiting health practitioners and hospital emergency rooms less often. Mental health was affected even more than physical health, with most reporting reduced anxiety and depression and improvements in family and social relationships. Housing stability and financial status improved, participants found it easier to pay their debts, and use of food banks declined.

Most of those who were working when the pilot began continued to work during the experiment (76.1 per cent). More than a third of those who were working when the pilot began reported that the basic income helped them find higher-paying jobs with better working conditions. Only 3 per cent found themselves working in worse conditions or for less pay. Almost all of those who worked less were working in precarious jobs with low pay and few benefits before the experiment started, and some took the opportunity to go back to school or to spend more time with children or other relatives.

Almost all participants reported that basic income improved their lives, but the results were greatest for those who had been working before the experiment began. That is, the benefits of a basic income were particularly important for the working poor, improving their mental health, reducing stress and opening greater opportunities in the labour market. The people in the most precarious working conditions at the outset had the greatest opportunities to transform the nature of their lives, either by moving into self-employment, changing their jobs or reducing their involvement in the labour market in order to spend more time in caregiving activities.

Some of the participants interviewed were not working for pay before the experiment began, or were working very little, often because of disabilities or other health issues. Few of these participants increased their labour market participation during the experiment, but almost all reported improvements in their physical and mental health and the quality of their relationships.

Overall, several themes were noted from the interviews. Many of the participants reported that receiving a basic income had transformed their lives in significant ways, offering them the opportunity to go back to school or engage in job training. They reported greater confidence and well-being and better social and family relationships.

## Do We Need More Experiments?

After the 2008 financial crash, several high-income countries began to experiment with the concept of basic income, although each meant something different by basic income. During the Democratic primaries before the 2020 US election, and even before the 2020 pandemic, basic income was much discussed. A number of pilots, many including only small numbers of participants, were underway in various US cities. Barcelona introduced a large pilot, and other jurisdictions introduced experiments or announced feasibility studies.

The purpose of an experiment is to answer a research question, and the experiment is designed to answer that question as well as possible. Therefore, a basic income experiment will not necessarily look like a basic income that might be introduced as a regular policy. For example, the purpose of the original Mincome experiment was to determine whether people worked more or less when the financial incentives for working varied. As a consequence, they tested several versions that allowed recipients to keep different portions of their earned income. If a basic income were to be introduced as a permanent policy, however, only one version would be offered. Many of the more recent experiments focused on other aspects of basic income. For many European nations, income assistance is already quite generous. They were not especially interested in whether an increase in income would improve mental and physical health; they already knew it would. However, their income assistance programs are rule-heavy and very bureaucratic. Therefore, they were particularly interested in the "unconditionality" of basic income. What if we stop requiring recipients to prove they are looking for work and just leave them alone? Is it possible that they will actually work more hours or find better jobs?

Several cities in the Netherlands experimented with basic income, and Finland conducted a large two-year experiment that offered previously unemployed individuals — those receiving long-term support for the unemployed — a stipend they called a basic income. This was offered without the usual requirements to engage in job-training and work-search activities or to report regularly to caseworkers, but the amount of money they received and the financial incentives to work were the same as for other unemployed individuals who acted as a comparison group. They hoped that by eliminating some of the bureaucratic oversight, unemployed individuals would have greater time and incentive to look for work. Interim results were scathingly dismissed in the international media as a "failure" because, as was the case in Hamilton, the long-term unemployed were not more likely to work when they received a basic income, although they were also not any less likely to work than those who received traditional benefits for the unemployed. Participants also reported improved mental and physical health and, most importantly, social trust improved dramatically.[9]

The final report on the Finnish experiment received much less international attention, but the results of this very large and well-conducted experiment were similar, in many ways, to the preliminary outcomes of the Ontario experiment while its large size allowed researchers to collect more information about particular groups of people. Researchers reported that employment in the final year of the experiment increased for those who received their benefit without having to demonstrate that they were seeking work more than it did for those who were required to report to a caseworker. (The effect was heightened because policy changes actually increased bureaucracy for the control group during the experiment.) Less bureaucracy and greater individual autonomy encouraged work, especially for newcomers to Finland and for families with children. Moreover, this group reported higher levels of social trust, less anxiety, less depression, less financial stress and better cognitive functioning. Social participation increased for people who received their benefits unconditionally.[10]

The final report of the Utrecht experiment in the Netherlands is similarly intriguing, and its results mirror the findings from Finland and Ontario. Again, this is a large and very well-conducted experiment that looked at the impact of different aspects of basic income on three test groups of people receiving benefits for the long-term unemployed. The first group no longer had to report regularly to a caseworker to demonstrate that they were seeking work, although they were free to choose to be counselled if they wanted to be. This is similar to the Finnish experiment. The second group received additional supports from their caseworker. They would be assigned to a permanent caseworker who had greater discretion to help clients access the supports they required, and who would offer positive feedback and assistance that was largely client-led. The third group was offered financial incentives to work; they were allowed to keep a greater proportion of their benefits as their income increased. All three test groups were compared to people who continued to receive regular income assistance.

The differences between the three test groups are very interesting because they help us to understand a little more about how a basic income affects the way people work. There was little effect on any of the groups in the first months of the study. The first group that was left alone and received unconditional support were most likely to find permanent, full-time work. This effect took time to appear, which suggests that the absence of work requirements gave them the freedom to seek a better job rather than taking any job offer. Towards the end of the two-year study, it appeared that these people were more likely to become financially independent and to no longer need income supports. The second and third groups — those who received positive support and those who received financial incentives to work — were more likely to work than the autonomous group, but the jobs they took tended to be part-time, temporary, precarious work. There was no indication that they were becoming financially independent. This suggests that unconditionality may be a more important aspect of a basic income than financial incentives, if the goal is to encourage independence and permanent jobs.

Different people benefit from different treatments. One unexpected outcome is that the least educated seemed to benefit the most when they are left alone. The researchers theorized that if less educated workers are given additional supports, their confidence that they had the ability to get and keep a job without extra help might be reduced. For the long-term unemployed with significant barriers to work, only intensive services from a caseworker seemed to be effective, and the success was limited to the attainment of "small" jobs — precarious, part-time, temporary work.[11]

There have been many other experiments, mostly in low- and middle-income countries such as Kenya and India, in which entire villages were treated (as was the case with Dauphin). In almost all cases, researchers documented similar kinds of social outcomes. Mental and physical health improved, investment in education increased, the lives of women and girls improved and, most importantly, social solidarity was enhanced. In Malawi, families that received a basic income were more likely to send their daughters to school than families that received no support. Girls in families that received support were less likely to marry early and give birth at very young ages. It was even found that HIV incidence was lower in villages where families received a basic income, a result that researchers attributed to fewer young women engaging in transactional sex work.[12] In India, social transformation was at the heart of findings.[13] Similar kinds of findings emerged in almost all cash transfer experiments. When people were offered a basic income, whether the stipend depends on income or is received by everyone, social attitudes were transformed. In low-income countries, development goals such as female education were met; in middle-income countries, children were less likely to work at menial tasks while women were empowered to make independent decisions about their lives and work.[14, 15]

In every experiment undertaken, whether these were conducted in low-, middle- or high-income countries, the results are astoundingly similar. Basic income improves lives. Physical and mental health improves. The lives of women and girls, in particular, are enhanced. People who were working when the experiment began continued, for the most part, to work during the experiment. Those who were in toxic job situations when a basic income was introduced were empowered to change their lives. Families invested in education, both for adults and children. Financial resilience improved. Housing conditions improved. Social trust was enhanced.

Nevertheless, these experiments have not yet led any jurisdiction to introduce a basic income. The Canadian experience is particularly telling. In both of our basic income experiments, Mincome and the Ontario BIG, changes in government led to a loss of interest in the outcomes of the experiment. There are plenty of reasons for critics to dismiss the results of basic income experiments.

Experiments, by their very nature, are "unrealistic." Only some members of society receive support, so participants are very often isolated from one another. By definition, experiments are temporary, and people might behave differently when they know the basic income they receive will end one day than they would if they believed the basic income to be a permanent policy. Experiments are also incomplete; we can examine how lives are changed by receiving a basic income, but we cannot capture the effects of higher taxes that might be required to pay for the basic income.

Advocates sometimes believe and argue that the outcome of an experiment will be so overwhelmingly positive that policy will change as a consequence. However, the one result we can all agree on is that scientific results do not necessarily lead to political change. Basic income experiments take a very long time to implement and evaluate and they cost a lot of money because of their size and complexity. Not only do we need to give participants a basic income, we need to pay for data access and analysis. Canada's history with basic income experiments doesn't give us a lot of hope that they will bring about change.

By contrast, policy change is much more likely to occur when there is popular recognition that the policies we have in place are inadequate for their purposes. In the wake of COVID-19, Spain was the first to announce a permanent basic income which looks remarkably like the targeted basic income tested in the Canadian experiments. Economic disruption encourages experimentation — not in the formal sense of randomized controlled trials, but in the everyday sense of trying to come up with better solutions to obvious challenges.

# Chapter 3

# Basic Income and Population Health

When the city of Toronto released data showing the concentration of COVID-19 cases by neighbourhood, areas of the city with high rises and large numbers of low-income people fared the worst. Viruses may seem democratic, infecting rich and poor alike, but as with every infectious disease before it, COVID-19 was more common among people with low incomes and, among those who became infected, low-income people were more likely to die. This is the way infectious diseases usually spread. During the 1918 "Spanish flu," an identical pattern repeated itself in cities across Canada. In Winnipeg, the first person to be diagnosed was a woman living in a high-income neighbourhood who brought the infection back from a visit to her daughter in Montreal. Her housekeeper soon became infected and took the virus home with her — north of the railroad tracks that marked the boundary to the north end of the city that was home to the low-income immigrant population. The flu spread rapidly in the over-crowded housing of the north end and, without alternatives, people continued to go to work when they were infected, spreading the infection further. Many who became ill were already weakened by poor nutrition and chronic illness and were much more likely than those living in wealthier parts of the city to succumb.[1]

One of the reasons that COVID-19 took so many of us by surprise is because infectious diseases have become much less common in high-income countries due to routine childhood immunization and antibiotics. Influenza has always been lethal, but usually its victims are elderly people already weakened by other health conditions. Only rarely does a disease attack people of working age with such ferocity. As infectious diseases grew less common and required fewer health care resources, chronic conditions became more prevalent. At least in the prosperous south of Canada, we were living long enough to experience cardiovascular disease, diabetes, rheumatoid arthritis, cancer and other chronic conditions. However, like infectious diseases before them, these new killers were far from democratic.

As Canadians, we often take pride in our universal health care system, and we think it means everyone has access to medically necessary care, notwithstanding perennial concerns about wait times that do not seem to be much worse for low-income than for high-income Canadians. With a bit more thought, we realize that many health services are not paid for by the government but require individual insurance or out-of-pocket payments: dental care and prescription medications are most pressing. However, almost all income assistance programs offer recipients extended health benefits that include dental care and prescriptions. In some provinces, all children and seniors receive these services. If access to health services were the primary determinant of how healthy we are, then our health would not depend as much as it does on our incomes.

And yet our hospitals are full of people who are there not because they have bad luck or faulty genes, but because they have spent years living in deteriorating housing, working badly paid and physically demanding jobs, eating inadequate diets and living with economic insecurity and the stigma associated with poverty. Their bodies are not injured as much as worn out; chronic conditions such as diabetes, hypertension, arthritis and cardiovascular disease have replaced infectious diseases as the primary causes of hospitalization and death, and chronic conditions even more than infectious diseases are strongly influenced by the broader circumstances of our lives.[2] Stress associated with economic insecurity encourages behaviours such as smoking and alcohol and drug consumption, which worsen health conditions. In the poorest neighbourhoods in Canada, men die on average a full four years before their counterparts who live in the wealthiest neighbourhoods. For women, the difference is two years.[3] In Winnipeg, the numbers are even more startling: in East St. Paul, the neighbourhood with the highest median income, women lived on average to 87.5 years in 2011, and men lived until 82.3, but in the income-challenged North End, women only lived to be 70.9 years old, and men died on average at 66.7. That means a woman in the wealthiest neighbourhood of Winnipeg outlived her counterpart in the poorest neighbourhood by 16.6 years, while a man living in the wealthiest neighbourhood lived 15.6 years longer than a man in the poorest neighbourhood. And that gap is growing. Five years earlier, the life-expectancy gap for men was 13.4 years.[4] Stroke and heart attack rates show similar patterns, and rates of dementia are almost twice as high for the poorest as for the richest, even when we adjust for age and sex.

At every stage of our lives, our health is affected by our biological and genetic inheritance, our physical environment, our behaviour, our access to health services and the social and economic factors that surround us. Children from poor families are more likely to be born too early and too small, which affects their health and education throughout childhood. Mothers who suffer stress during pregnancy bear children with a higher risk of developing diabetes. Young mothers who are depressed have children with higher rates of educational difficulties and poorer health outcomes. Children raised in poverty are less likely to live in safe neighbourhoods and safe housing and more likely to suffer accidents and injuries. Rates of asthma are higher for poor children, and educational attainment is lower. They are more likely to be behind in school and to score poorly on standardized tests. Children from the poorest families change schools more often and come to the attention of Child and Family Services more frequently.[5] As they get older, they are more likely to give birth as adolescents (early births are associated with poorer outcomes for children and parents) and to be diagnosed with sexually transmitted infections. Children raised in poverty are, as adults, more likely to experience addictions, mental health difficulties, physical disabilities and premature death (defined as any death before age seventy-five). They are also less likely to graduate from high school on time, and more likely to live in poverty as adults. Poor adults are diagnosed with chronic diseases at younger ages and suffer more complications. They have more accidents throughout their lives and are more likely to suffer dementia before their too-early deaths.[6] Even people who eventually escape from poverty must deal with the consequences of the health conditions they acquired earlier in life.

In work conducted for the World Health Organization, Sir Michael Marmot identifies the social determinants of health as "the conditions in which people are born, grow, live, work and age. The conditions are shaped by the distribution of money, power and resources at local, national and global levels — sometimes termed structural determinants of health inequalities."[7] While health services and biology are important, they are not as important as the social and physical surroundings in which we live. The Public Health Agency of Canada lists twelve key determinants of health:[8]

1.  Income and Social Status

2.  Social Support Networks

3.  Education and Literacy

4.  Employment/Working Conditions

5.  Social Environments

6.  Physical Environments

7.  Personal Health Practices and Coping Skills

8.  Healthy Child Development

9.  Biology and Genetic Endowment

10. Health Services

11. Gender

12. Culture

This list is not definitive. Dennis Raphael lists fourteen closely related determinants of the health of Canadians: aboriginal status, disability status, gender, early life, income and income distribution, education, race, employment and working conditions, social exclusion, food insecurity, housing, social safety net, health services, unemployment and job security.[9] However we define them, the social and physical conditions in which we live have a strong impact on how healthy we are at every stage of our lives.

These factors interact with one another in complex ways. For example, education influences the kind of job people have and the level of income they earn. It affects how likely they are to be unemployed. Income determines the kind of housing they have and the neighbourhood they live in. The level of education they attain can affect their coping skills, but their coping skills also influence the level of education they are likely to achieve. Gender, race and culture influence income and job prospects. Health is determined by individual lifestyle factors, social and community networks and the general socioeconomic, cultural and environmental conditions in which individuals and families live.[10]

Over the past five decades, the evidence linking our social and physical environments to our health has become overwhelming.

Most of the statistical evidence we have collected shows a correlation between income and health for a wide variety of health outcomes: premature death, rates of chronic and infectious diseases, rates of disability, complication rates after surgery, and various health indices. This association holds not only for the poorest among us; at every income level, people with higher incomes are healthier than people with slightly less income. This has led to a set of theories attempting to explain how health and income are linked.

How do we know for sure that poor health is caused by low incomes and not the other way around? Perhaps low incomes and poor health are correlated because sick people are less likely to work, more likely to take more time off work when they are employed and they are likely unable to work at peak efficiency even when they do work. It certainly is the case that people with health conditions and disabilities suffer challenges in the job market and usually earn less than healthy people and people without disabilities. However, income is strongly related to birth outcomes and child health outcomes, and children are not normally expected to be working. Other studies look at when income changes and when health changes; they note that income is more likely to decline before health declines and not the other way around. The evidence that low income causes poor health is overwhelming. The fundamental role played by income is so profound that income is sometimes referred to as the determinant of determinants. There are several pathways through which low income is believed to cause poor health; some pathways affect the individual and some influence outcomes through their impact on the organization of society.

## Material Deprivation

The most direct effect of low income is through material deprivation. Families with low incomes cannot easily afford to buy nutritious food or to live in decent housing in safe neighbourhoods. One indicator of material deprivation identifies those families who struggle to put food on the table. Scholars such as Valerie Tarasuk use food insecurity as a measure of extreme deprivation. Tarasuk has shown that low income is the best predictor of food insecurity. Lynn McIntyre has shown that food insecurity declines markedly as soon as a low-income individual turns sixty-five, largely because their income from Old Age Security and the Guaranteed Income Supplement is much greater than it was under provincial income assistance. Low-income families have difficulty accessing health care that is not provided without charge. Low-wage workers without a drug plan at work may scrimp on prescription drugs. Their oral health will suffer if they cannot pay a dentist through workplace benefits. They might not visit clinics for routine or follow-up visits if public transport is not readily available. All these health-related decisions and many others will be compromised by inadequate incomes.[11]

However, if material deprivation alone were the cause of poor health outcomes, we would expect to see the health disparities related to income disappear once incomes reach a fairly moderate level. Middle-income Canadians can afford dental care, most prescription drugs, decent diets, adequate housing and reasonable transportation. Why would the disparity persist as incomes increase even more? One suggestion is that income affects health through the experience of chronic stress.

Chronic stress has been linked to a variety of hormonal and neurological changes that result in poor health. It impairs memory and increases the risk of depression, lowers immune response, elevates blood pressure and the risk of cardiovascular disease and affects hormonal systems. People who are already vulnerable because of poor health are especially liable to experience poorer mental health and cognitive outcomes due to increased stress. Chronic stress sometimes leads to negative coping behaviours, such as smoking, alcohol abuse and other addictions. That is, chronic stress may account for much of the variance in health and social outcomes associated with the harmful aspects of lower social status.[12]

Unlike material deprivation, which might be expected to

disappear as income increases, chronic stress exists along a continuum. One particular factor associated with chronic stress is economic insecurity, which can affect individuals at any income level. A young mother who relies on provincial income assistance suffers from income insecurity, but so do low-income workers facing economic insecurity because they have no idea how many hours they might be able to work or whether their contract will be renewed, as well as entrepreneurs whose income insecurity is related to market conditions beyond their control.

## Economic Insecurity

Economic insecurity is not the same thing as low income. People with very low, but stable and predictable, defined-benefit pensions do not suffer from economic insecurity. They may suffer from low income and, sometimes, material deprivation. By contrast, people with moderate incomes live with income insecurity if their jobs and incomes are subject to sudden and unpredictable changes. Economic insecurity exists when a family fears that its income might fall dramatically without advance notice and without the resources necessary to ride out the risk. Economic insecurity is a state of mind rather than a characteristic of an income flow. It can be offset by insurance, such as Employment Insurance, or by sufficient savings to deal with unexpected shortfalls. Economic insecurity can persist even when income is stable if people fear changes in their economic situation. Someone who works on a short-term contract might earn a relatively high income, but if the contract itself is subject to cancellation, and there is no insurance or wealth to fill the gaps between contracts, then that individual would suffer from economic insecurity. The fear of job loss is the greatest cause of economic insecurity but not the only cause.

There is a deep literature on the causes and consequences of economic insecurity. The new economy has been revealing itself for many years, but since the 2008 financial crisis, it has become increasingly impossible to ignore the growing numbers of workers who spend many years or their entire careers working on insecure, short-term contracts. All of this contributes to chronic stress, which itself leads to poorer health.

## Income Inequality

Within any given country, some people do much better than others. Richard Wilkinson and Kate Pickett argued in *The Spirit Level* that there is a strong causal relationship between inequality and a wide variety of population health outcomes observed in different settings over a number of years. More equal societies do better than less equal societies. Violent crime rates are lower, and people live longer. Very early births are less common, and children are more likely to finish high school on time. Prevalence of chronic disease is lower, and when people do get ill, they are less likely to suffer secondary effects that reduce the quality of their lives. Not only do people live longer, but they spend more years in good health. Children also have better health in more equal societies and do better in school.[13]

Income inequality, like economic insecurity, might also affect health outcomes through increases in chronic stress. Large income differences between rich and poor seem to worsen most of the problems associated with low income. Health outcomes that are strongly related to social status, such as poor birth outcomes, are particularly vulnerable to rising income inequality. It may be that inequality leads people to constantly compare their aspirations and achievements with others', and to suffer stress when they fall short.

However, income inequality has an effect that goes beyond the individual. Income inequality is a collective measure; it measures how equally a society's resources are shared, and when these resources are shared more equally, everyone is better off. In more unequal US states, people score lower on "agreeableness," which measures how concerned they are about getting along with others. In European countries that have higher income inequality, people show less solidarity and less willingness to help others. More equal societies may be healthier because they are more cohesive and enjoy better social relations, both of which are associated with better population health.[14]

Particularly worrying is a growing gap in aspirations and lifestyles between those who graduated from high school and completed some higher education, and those with a high school education or less. This perceived gap is fed by the greater role played by social media in our lives. The feeling of being left behind is enhanced by the flood of achievements and possessions posted by others, and the sheer speed at which perceptions occur in this realm does not encourage critical appraisal. Even old-fashioned media has been overwhelmed by reality TV that encourages interpersonal comparisons. This focus on personal achievement and personal possessions creates the impression that everyone else is doing better than we are and living happier and more productive lives. This perception of growing social disparities may be less real than perceived, but it still causes chronic stress among those struggling to keep up. It also fractures the sense of solidarity that is essential to social well-being.

## A Decline in Social Solidarity

The growth of income inequality is much stronger in the US than elsewhere in the industrial world, and the manifestation of inequality in terms of social divisions is also starker. This decline in social solidarity affects population health in dramatic ways. Richard Reeves argues that the essential divide in US society is not the perceived gap between the top 1 per cent (or even 0.01 per cent), who benefit from economic change, and the rest of society facing stagnant incomes, but rather the gap between the top 20 per cent — the upper middle class — and the rest of society. The growing divergence is apparent in where people live, how they form families, their lifestyles and, especially, their attitudes. Reeves argues that members of the upper middle class are becoming more effective at passing their status along to their children through the use of zoning laws that encourage homogeneous neighbourhoods and schools, college application processes and the allocation of internships. This reduces overall social mobility and hardens attitudes among the privileged against efforts to enhance equality and broaden opportunities. These entrenched attitudes mean that political efforts to reduce the gap will be met by vocal opposition.[15]

The decline of social solidarity is especially associated with a variety of negative mental health outcomes. Since 2005, the World Happiness Report has published the results of a series of surveys designed to measure how people in countries all around the world felt about their lives. One of the most surprising results was the sudden and steep decline in American well-being. Between 2006 and 2016, the United States fell from number three (of thirty-three countries) to number nineteen (of thirty-four countries).[16] In the 2020 report, the United States was at number eighteen.[17] This was not the result of a declining economy or even declining physical health outcomes. On average, the US did well economically, but the gains were not equally distributed across the population, and this disparity is reflected in the other four factors that measure social solidarity: social support; perceived corruption of business and government; freedom to make life choices; and generosity of donations.[18] Social well-being cannot be improved through economic growth alone. If the US scores were returned to their 2006 levels for these four factors, well-being would increase dramatically. To achieve the same increase in well-being through economic growth alone, GDP per capita would have to increase from $53,000 to $133,000. Canadians shouldn't be complacent; Canada fell out of the top ten for the first time in the 2020 report. The social solidarity of the Nordic countries has cemented their position at the top of the list.

The decline in social well-being in the United States shows up in various ways. Economists Anne Case and Angus Deaton have spent a lot of time in the past decade investigating the US malaise, and they make an even bolder claim. Other studies largely corroborate their results while challenging some of the details.[19] Case and Deaton identified a series of deaths that they label "deaths of despair" — that is, death by suicide, drug poisoning and alcohol — that they believe increase as social well-being declines. They documented an increase in the death rate associated with these causes over the past two decades among white fifty- to fifty-four-year-olds with a high school diploma or less and argued that growing economic disparities are responsible. Case and Deaton suggested that it is the "crushed aspirations" of poorly educated, white workers struggling to find and keep jobs in a changing economy that have led them to replace stable marriages with serial monogamy, to drop out of the workforce and to replace their participation in traditional communal churches with attendance at "prosperity gospel churches" that emphasize individual identity. Low-income minorities have fared even worse in absolute terms but there is no similar increase in the death rate associated with these causes, possibly because their expectations were more modest to begin with. While white workers watched in despair as jobs they considered their birthright disappeared, other workers have always been more skeptical that the American Dream was within reach. These are all aspects of an unhealthy, and increasingly unequal, society.

Case and Deaton found similar but not nearly as dramatic results in other countries that have faced similar economic challenges in recent years. In Canada, for example, the death rate due to drugs, alcohol and suicide among this age group is also increasing, but very modestly. Case and Deaton attribute these different international experiences to the fact that most of the other countries they investigated still have reasonably functional social safety nets, including at least basic welfare and social medicine, unlike the social welfare system in the United States.

I am struck by the realization that Case and Deaton's despairing fifty- to fifty-four-year-olds are exactly the same age as the many young men from Dauphin who were permitted, by Mincome, to finish high school. Even though Case and Deaton did not find the same stark empirical evidence for Canada that they found in the United States, there is no doubt that young men who were encouraged by family poverty to leave school early struggled in their later lives as compared to their lucky contemporaries who had different opportunities because they finished high school.

It is easy to focus on the health consequences of income inequality because income is relatively easy to measure, but the divisions in society go beyond mere income. As Reeves and others have suggested in the US case, it may be the decline of social solidarity that leads to the mental health outcomes that Anne Case and Angus Deaton capture in their deaths of despair. Social solidarity is threatened by growing income inequality, but it also worsened by gaps in education and opportunity, which extend far deeper than income.

Basic income alone will not and cannot eliminate the growing income inequality that seems to be a feature of the changing economy. Basic income provides resources at the bottom end of the income distribution; it allows people who haven't accumulated resources of their own to withstand unexpected events, such as a sudden job loss or an illness or accident, and to develop the resilience necessary to recover and to reclaim their previous lifestyle. High incomes, however, have been increasing much more quickly than average incomes and, over time, more and more resources are being accumulated by smaller numbers of people who are lucky enough to possess the necessary skills to benefit from the changing economy.

## There is Nothing like a Pandemic to Remind Us That We Are All Connected

If we needed a reminder, in the starkest of terms, that health depends on income, the COVID-19 pandemic furnished us with one. Canadian policymakers shut down access to remote northern settlements so the infection would not take root in crowded and substandard housing and overwhelm rudimentary health care systems. Homeless shelters struggled to enable clients to practice physical distancing. Tent cities in Vancouver, and then across the country, were removed and their inhabitants resettled in empty hotels and residences. Public health physicians feared that if the infection established itself among the poorest, the pandemic would be prolonged and all of society would feel the consequences.

As mortality soared in personal care homes and retirement residences, the poor working conditions of those charged with caring for seniors was quickly identified as an important source of risk. Careworkers spoke of washing and dressing frail and vulnerable patients at several different institutions, commuting between them by public transportation. They documented the absence of personal protective equipment and the time pressure that made hygiene challenging. Health care aids were offered part-time positions with no benefits for $14 to $16 an hour — $1,960 a month if they can work thirty-five hours a week — to put their lives and families at risk.[20] The temporary employment agencies that supplied much of this labour charged the institutions $35 to $40 an hour. These frontline workers were lauded as heroes and many provinces offered temporary wage top-ups during the worst of the pandemic, but the base pay they received remained lower than the $2,000 a month that the federal government offered workers who lost their jobs due to COVID-19.

It is easy to see how the conditions of work in this sector spread disease and prolonged the epidemic. In the context of infectious disease, it's hard to ignore how the poverty and poor working conditions of one person affects others. In high-income countries, however, we are much more likely to face the consequences of poor mental health and chronic conditions than we are to confront infectious disease, which makes it easier for us to imagine that someone's poor health is the consequence of decisions they've made about how to live their life. If we believe that everyone's health is the consequence of their own choices and behaviour, then we don't have to worry about how their health affects us. However, mental as much as physical health has consequences that go beyond any one individual. We are, to use the cliché that public health officials around the world repeated during the pandemic of 2020, "all in this together."

## Basic Income Can Help

Basic income alone cannot eliminate all the growing divisions in society. It can, however, address such fundamental issues as material deprivation and income insecurity. A basic income is designed precisely to reduce the debilitating chronic stress associated with these factors. Moreover, a basic income may address some of the social exclusion associated with poverty. People with the resources to allow their children to participate in low-paid internships or to attend university can give their children a fair chance to benefit from opportunities that high-income families take for granted. All of these outcomes lead to better individual and population health. Basic income extends these opportunities to other children.

There is a monetary return on these benefits to population health. Canada spends an inordinate amount of money on the provision of health care. Hospital care alone costs more than seventy billion dollars every year. Basic income recipients are less likely to need to be hospitalized compared with similar individuals who do not receive a basic income. Does it not make sense to invest more money upfront in a basic income program that gives individuals and families the resources they need to live better, more fulfilling lives? That investment would pay off in a need for fewer hospital beds and lower demands placed on family doctors, who too often find themselves prescribing antidepressants and anti-anxiety medications to people living with the stress of chronic poverty and economic insecurity. Poverty and economic insecurity are extremely expensive, and nowhere are the costs more apparent than in our overburdened health care system. If we want to make health care sustainable in Canada — to get the costs of delivering health under control — then we need to do a better job of addressing the factors leading to poor health.

# Chapter 4
# The Future of Work

"There is a pretty good chance we end up with a universal basic income or something like that due to automation."

— Elon Musk[1]

"A lot of exciting new innovations are going to be created, which will generate a lot of opportunities and a lot of wealth, but there is a real danger it could also reduce the amount of jobs. This will make experimenting with ideas like basic income even more important in the years to come."

— Richard Branson[2]

"We should have a society that measures progress not just by economic metrics like GDP, but by how many of us have a role we find meaningful. We should explore ideas like universal basic income to make sure everyone has a cushion to try new ideas."

— Mark Zuckerberg, in a May 2017 Harvard University commencement speech[3]

"If machines produce everything we need, the outcome will depend on how things are distributed. Everyone can enjoy a life of luxurious leisure if the machine-produced wealth is shared, or most people can end up miserably poor if the machine-owners successfully lobby against wealth redistribution. So far, the trend seems to be towards the second option, with technology driving ever-increasing inequality."

— Stephen Hawking[4]

Tech industry insiders were championing basic income long before COVID-19 came along. They believed that technological change and, especially, developments in artificial intelligence would permanently reduce the need for human labour. There is little evidence, historical or otherwise, to support the idea that technology will do away with the need for human labour, but there is ample evidence that it has already transformed the nature of human employment, and made it much more precarious.

The economic disruption caused by COVID-19 and the Canadian government response to it both revealed and amplified changes that were already well underway. Many people discovered that there was little need to go to a place of employment every day for a fixed number of hours in order to do their jobs. Online shopping and delivery options were already in place, but COVID-19 encouraged their widespread acceptance by consumers. Some workers no longer needed to risk their health in crowded public transportation. For many, the line between work and life became increasingly blurred, with all the benefits and costs that entailed. Other workers will always be required to do their work on site — the careworkers, shelf stockers at supermarkets, cleaners, delivery truck drivers and frontline health system employees, among others. The pandemic emphasized the diversity of workplace experiences and possibilities, and also drew our attention to the circumstances that many of the lowest-paid workers contended with on a regular basis.

Some of the jobs lost during the economic disruption may never return or might return in ways that make them unrecognizable. Interest-free loans have facilitated the adoption of new technology that could change the nature of employment, creating new, skilled jobs and eliminating other kinds of work. These changes were already occurring before the pandemic and even before the 2008 recession, and each economic disruption has accelerated their impact. When it is possible to measure and value work in ways other than the number of hours on-site, employers can invest far less in commercial real estate and more in online visibility. New technology has allowed employers to break a job into its attendant tasks and hire those tasks out on an as-needed basis, reducing their production costs and their long-term commitment to workers. Workers could increasingly begin to bear the risk and freedom associated with being independent contractors. The difficulty of organizing labour under such circumstances further undermines private sector trade unions that have been losing ground for decades.

When Mincome and the other experiments of the 1970s were designed, many critics worried that giving people money for nothing would discourage work. In all honesty, most taxpayers worried less about the psychological effect this might have on the workers than about its effect on the economy. Who would grow our food and drive the trucks and teach our kids and build our houses and make our cars? If fewer people worked, what would happen to the economic growth that supports our standard of living? Fewer people working, they reasoned, meant less for all of us.

One indication of how much the world has changed is that one of the justifications for some of the basic income experiments introduced after the 2008 stock market crash was a set of beliefs widespread among many in the technology field. They claimed that, whether we are ready or not, advances in robotics and artificial intelligence mean that many of us will be working less in the very near future. Silicon Valley entrepreneurs who invest in disruptive technologies and watch their incomes grow were the first to sound the alarm: if machines can do the hard and dirty work of production — and do it faster, better and cheaper — then we don't need people to perform these tasks. To be sure, they recognized that human labour would still be necessary to program the machines and develop the new technologies (although, they pointed out, advances in machine learning are calling even that into question), and probably to provide some kinds of work in hospitals, daycare centres and nursing homes (although advances in robotic technology are rapidly changing some kinds of surgery, and robots are providing companionship for frail seniors). However, they argued, the total number of person hours required to perform these tasks would be much smaller than we now employ in production. And the workers that would be required by this new economy are not the same people we are used to employing; miners can't be transformed into nursing home attendants overnight, and truck drivers do not easily become programmers. The problem, from the point of view of people like Elon Musk, was not how we can get people to work, but how we can get money into the hands of people who are not required to work. If we don't solve that problem, they noted, governments would be facing social unrest beyond anything they have witnessed so far. Displaced workers need to eat, and — at least as important from the perspective of people whose large incomes depend on these technologies — someone needs to buy all the new goods and services created by the machines. Basic income seems like an obvious solution.

There are two very distinct views about the future of work, neither of which is very convincing. Some side with the Silicon Valley utopians and imagine that technology will reduce the demand for human labour while simultaneously creating unimaginable wealth. Others focus on the aging population and argue that we are heading into a period of labour scarcity. Simply maintaining our existing quality of life will require everyone to work longer and harder in order to support a much larger dependent population of people too old to work. The correct view is, as usual, somewhere in between.

There will always be plenty of work for humans to do, but the ways in which that work is organized have changed and continue to change. Consequently, technology is not eliminating jobs as much as making them ever more precarious. Basic income is essential, not to distribute money to people whose labour is no longer needed, but rather to offset the consequences of growing precarity.

## The Old View of Productivity and Growth

Not everyone shared the sweeping visions emanating from California. Traditional policy advisors in the Bank of Canada, the Department of Finance and international agencies such as the Organisation for Economic Co-operation and Development (OECD) imagined the future unfolding much like the past. From their perspective, the problem was just the opposite of the Silicon Valley prediction; they worried about an emerging labour shortage. All the goods and services we use in our daily lives, they pointed out, are the product of labour. All the social programs that support our children, the elderly and people with disabilities are paid for by taxes on people who work. Without workers, nothing would be produced. If we pointed to automation, they reminded us that someone needs to create the robots, to program them, to oversee and repair them and to record the value of what they produce. If we talked about self-driving vehicles, they pointed to the massive investment of human effort that created such vehicles and the human ingenuity that will be required to repair them and to design the next technological breakthrough. Sure, factories produced with smaller workforces than ever because of automation, but there were so many more firms out there. Economic growth, they believed, would create new jobs more quickly than automation would eliminate them.

Their policy priority was to increase the proportion of people working, because these workers would be the source of tax revenue that would pay for the pensions and healthcare required by the massive baby boom generation just moving into retirement. We had to invest in policies that encouraged people to work for pay: for example, offer daycare to keep parents of infants working and increase immigration so that a steady flow of younger immigrants could backfill the aging labour force. Not very long ago, the federal government attempted to increase the age of entitlement for Old Age Security from sixty-five to sixty-seven to encourage people to work for more years and to draw pensions for fewer years. According to these traditionalists, offering a basic income to people living in an economy on the brink of labour shortages is foolish; it would encourage people to work less just when what we need desperately is for everyone to work more.

This story is based on enough fact that it seems credible. The Canadian population is undeniably aging, but this generation of old people in high-income countries is among the richest and healthiest that has ever lived. The poverty rate among those over sixty-five was half that of younger people in 2019, and not only because of their government pensions. Canadians over sixty-five have benefited from the rapid expansion of the economy in the 1950s and 1960s, from the investment opportunities that saw modest savings expand and from the housing boom that created millionaires of ordinary workers. The fear that an aging workforce would place more demands for support on the smaller working-age populations that followed was based on the assumptions that the aged are a net draw on social resources and that the only way to finance new programs is by imposing taxes on workers. Seniors do collect pensions and draw on health care, but they also pay income taxes on dividends and taxes on capital gains. The amassed wealth of seniors today is considerable, which lessens their reliance on Old Age Security and, especially, the Guaranteed Income Supplement. They are healthier than past generations and entering medically intensive personal care homes at lower rates.

There is something a little archaic about this story of looming disaster. To generate economic growth, this story claims, more and more people must work ever-longer hours for many more years. This depressing story of scarcity, unending toil and limited options flies in the face of the unbounded optimism of Silicon Valley, many of whose denizens regard it as unimaginative, backward-looking and more than a little mean-spirited.

## Silicon Valley Utopianism

A venture capital accelerator that supports tech start-ups, Y-Combinator undertook the task of developing a basic income experiment in two as-yet-unnamed US states. Sam Altman, its CEO, argued that it would take somewhere between ten and one hundred years for advances in artificial intelligence to induce governments to start giving handouts to avoid mass riots. In a January 2016 blog post, he wrote, "Fifty years from now, I think it will seem ridiculous that we used fear of not being able to eat as a way to motivate people. I also think it's impossible to truly have equality of opportunity without some form of guaranteed income."[5]

These speculators argued that the first industrial revolution, which took place in the middle of the nineteenth century, relied on the steam engine and the creation of large factories. The second industrial revolution, early in the twentieth century, exploited the power of electricity and the internal combustion engine. The third automated production through electronics and information technology in the mid-twentieth century. The fourth, or digital, revolution has been underway since the middle of the twentieth century. Billions of people linked by mobile devices with unprecedented access to knowledge and processing power, accompanied by disruptive technological changes in artificial intelligence, robotics, the internet of things, 3-D printing and nanotechnology, are remaking the world and the economy.

So far, the chief beneficiaries of this new economy have been consumers with enough income to access the digital world; they can stream music, play games, order a ride or dinner, work and watch a film in ways unimaginable a few years ago. This world also holds the promise of more efficient production lines and lower-cost transportation and communication. Economic growth no longer means more people working at traditional jobs for more years, but fewer and fewer humans working to produce ever-larger quantities of the goods and services that we already consume and other commodities we can scarcely imagine.

If we can produce more and more with less labour, why encourage work? Jobs, they argue, will be scarce and workers plentiful. We could all share existing jobs by working fewer hours or, alternatively, some people could continue to work while others withdraw from the workforce and occupy their time any way they like. They can draw pictures, take care of their aging parents or young children, write bad poetry (or literary masterpieces), volunteer, spend the summers canoeing and winters skiing or snuggle down in cafés inventing new apps and new games to occupy their fellow humans in their growing free time. The only challenge is who will buy the output created by the machines?

This story, as engaging as it is, is also too simple. Even though it sounds like something from science fiction, it is an old story that we've told ourselves many times throughout history: "rapid technological change is just over the horizon, and we are just on the edge of fifteen-hour work weeks and massive unemployment." Or, depending on the writer, "technological change is just about to transform society by freeing us from labour and giving us all time to become poets and philosophers." It is, in fact, a kind of zombie economics: an old idea that keeps struggling back to its feet no matter how many times history tries to kill it off.

## Disruptive Technological Change Is Not New

This is not the first time in history that we have faced massive technological change. Some reports breathlessly forecast a future in which self-driving cars and trucks displace from the US workforce 1.6 million truck drivers, 800,000 delivery truck drivers, 180,000 taxi drivers, 160,000 Uber drivers, 500,000 school bus drivers and 160,000 transit bus drivers, not to mention the 445,000 auto body repair shop workers who will no longer be required to repair the consequences of higher accident rates associated with human driving error, the hospital workers no longer required to patch up human victims and the many associated jobs — in total, well over four million US jobs lost to just one foreseeable change.[6] In Canada, a study published by the Conference Board of Canada estimated that 560,000 people working in the transport, truck and courier service industries may lose work along with 50,000 taxi drivers and chauffeurs.[7]

What would a similar article written at the turn of the twentieth century have foreseen? Would it have reported that a massive new industry made feasible with lower-priced internal combustion engines would soon create millions of jobs worldwide not only for truck drivers, but in supporting industries, or would people have mourned the loss of horses, drivers, buggy manufacturers, farmers, train makers and engineers and others who would soon be displaced? In the nineteenth century, 80 per cent of Canadian jobs were in agriculture; today about 2 per cent of jobs are in agriculture, largely because of technological change that has substituted machinery for human labour. One tractor can do the work that previous generations relied on a dozen children to provide. Closer to our own time, is there focus on the new jobs in communications that computer software makes possible, or do people mourn the downturn in pulp and paper and the demise of local newspapers?

The original Luddites were nineteenth-century British weavers and textile workers who objected to the use of automatic looms and knitting frames in textile factories. The first computers were developed and implemented in nineteenth-century textile mills. Most of these workers had spent years learning their craft, and they feared (correctly) that the new equipment could be operated by unskilled operators who were robbing them of their livelihood. When their petitions to the government were ignored, some began breaking into the mills to destroy the machinery. They called themselves Luddites after the mythical Ned Ludd, who was supposed to have been an eighteenth-century saboteur who, like Robin Hood, had been rumoured to live in Sherwood Forest. The Luddites wrote letters and petitions signed King Ludd or General Ludd.

The word "saboteur" has an interesting history. In English, it has been used from early in the nineteenth century to mean someone who deliberately destroys machinery or bridges to thwart an enemy. However, in French, it was common much earlier to liken a slow and clumsy worker to someone wearing wooden shoes, or sabots. In 1897, French anarchist Émile Pouget recommended that workers engage in a work slowdown, which he called "sabotage," to protest the use of labour-saving technology.

When Gutenberg introduced his press, there were no doubt people mourning the loss of jobs for scribes, and the invention of the wheel probably caused consternation among the bearers who would no longer be in such demand. The speed of technological change has increased dramatically, but its effect on the number of jobs has not changed. Technology changes over time, and each technological change has brought more jobs, new opportunities and economic growth than it destroyed. Those displaced by the changes suffered; it has never been easy to switch from old ways of doing things to embrace new opportunities. In every instance, the people who mourned the loss of a way of life resisted the changes and imagined that the world was ending. And in every case, there was still plenty of work for humans to do.

As a species, humans are not very good at imagining the real changes that the future will bring, and we have always focused more on what we are losing than on what we are about to gain. There will be changes, but one change we need not fear is the elimination of work.

## Imagining a Future without Work Is Not New

John Maynard Keynes is well-known today for championing a set of policies that highlighted the important role that a government can play in ensuring that the economy does not fall into a prolonged depression. He is less well remembered for an essay he published in 1930, titled *Economic Opportunities for our Grandchildren*. In it, he predicted that within a hundred years — that is, by 2030 — living standards in industrialized countries would be between four and eight times higher than they were when he wrote the book. And, in fact, his estimate was modest if anything. Productivity grew far more quickly than he imagined. Where Keynes went spectacularly wrong was in how he expected us to adapt to our greater wealth. He predicted that we would reduce our work week to perhaps fifteen hours and share the necessary labour required to produce what we consume. The rest of our time we would spend improving ourselves through education, art and friendship.

Instead, we decided that we'd rather just consume a whole lot more. North American working hours have remained more or less steady for decades, and we work 30 per cent more than Europeans. Workers can't be convinced to take their full vacation entitlement. European workers are now under increasing pressure from their governments to increase the hours they work, and efforts are underway in many countries to raise the age at which a worker can receive a state pension.

Nineteenth-century philosopher and economist John Stuart Mill is best remembered today as a reformer and a classical liberal. He championed free markets but recognized that the state had a role to play in limiting working hours and ensuring that workers were protected on job sites. He fought successfully to extend the vote to working men and, less successfully, to all women. He championed a woman's right to own property, to work and to divorce, and was active in antislavery circles.

Mill also imagined that capitalism was a necessary, but not ideal, stage in historical development. He believed that only capitalism could have generated the wealth that Britain had achieved by the nineteenth century, but he was well aware of its limitations. He imagined that the end of capitalism as it existed in the nineteenth century was just beyond the horizon and that, having worked so hard to create an economy that could generate such wealth, people were just about ready to enjoy their reward in the form of increased time to spend on the finer things in life. In *Principles of Political Economy*, he wrote, "I confess I am not charmed with the ideal of life held out by those who think the normal state of human beings is that of struggling to get on; that the trampling, crushing, elbowing, and treading on each other's heels, which form the existing type of social life, are the most desirable lot of human kind, or anything but the disagreeable symptoms of one of the phases of industrial progress."[8]

Mill recognized that economic growth was not endless and believed that the real problem facing nineteenth-century Britain was that existing wealth should be better distributed: "I know not why it should be a matter of congratulation that persons who are already richer than anyone needs to be, should have doubled their means of consuming things which give little or no pleasure except as representative of wealth."[9] Economic growth for its own sake was unnecessary. A far better alternative would be to focus on the "art of living" — education, philosophy, music, friendship — which would be more easily pursued when less energy was devoted to work.

Even the father of modern economics, Adam Smith, recognized the dangers of overwork. He wrote *On the Wealth of Nations* in 1776, and one of his most well-known passages involves a description of the division of labour in a pin factory, in which one man straightens the wire, another cuts it and so on. Through the co-operation of labour within the factory system, efficiency increases and output increases dramatically. But even Smith recognized the consequences of too great a reliance on the division of labour. When every worker has only a simple task to perform, he has no time or inclination to consider any ideas beyond those immediately connected to his employment. According to Smith, this leads to poor outcomes for the individual as well as society at large.[10]

The post-work utopia imagined by Silicon Valley executives may seem like science fiction, but most good science fiction is rooted not solely in imagination, but in the ideas of the present and the past. So, too, are the ideas that technology is disruptive, that it will lead to a world beyond work, and that this post-work world might be a significant improvement over the current situation.

## A More Realistic Story

So: is society heading into a period of labour shortages in which policies to force as many people as possible to work longer and harder will be adopted, or will it be a world where jobs are scarce because machines produce all anyone can possibly need or want? As it has throughout history, technology will disrupt the current state of society. It will cause shortages of some kinds of labour while other workers struggle to find jobs. In fact, technology will create more jobs than it will destroy. The real issue is one particularly suited to basic income: technology will affect the quality of the jobs available, and the rise of precarious labour will force a discussion about how to deliver social policies.

Without question, there will be labour shortages for particular kinds of labour. There are skill mismatches in some high-technology areas, which tend to drive wages in these sectors very high, effectively turning the market for highly educated labour international and this kind of labour into a highly prized (and highly priced) commodity. No amount of legislation designed to keep sixty-five-year-olds working for a few more years as Walmart greeters, and no rules requiring the unemployed to show that they have actively searched for work, will solve this problem. It is a matter of the supply of these kinds of labour lagging behind demand in rapidly evolving sectors. One obvious solution is to raise wages to attract people and encourage them to gain the necessary skills. And this is what markets do — and do very well. We don't need social policies or government regulations to address labour shortages for highly skilled and highly priced workers.

At the other end of the wage scale, there are also labour shortages. It is increasingly difficult for firms to find Canadians willing to do hard physical labour at low wages in agriculture, to find minimum-wage workers for the service industry (especially in locations where the housing market is booming), or to hire unskilled workers in the low-wage, non-unionized construction sector. One response would be to offer higher wages and better working conditions which might attract workers, and this is how a market would work. Automation is an increasingly feasible alternative. Again, left to itself, the market does a pretty good job of eliminating labour shortages by allowing wages to increase and encouraging automation when it would pay off.

And yet, some aspects of current economic change are profoundly different from the past. Although technological change brings new opportunities, it also will cause significant disruptions. While there is no shortage of jobs, the kinds of jobs that are on offer are rapidly changing and will not necessarily match well with the skills of the people who need work. It is no easy task to turn the pharmacists displaced by pill-counting robots into app developers, and it is even more difficult to re-employ the people laid off from factory work or resource industries as caregivers. Increasingly, the new jobs that are created will not look anything like the jobs of the past and will require significant and extensive retraining.

Even when the work to be done is unchanged, the ways in which people are hired to do that work have changed. Instead of hiring someone into a career position and committing to that person for the long term, employers are more likely to seek contract workers who can be hired and let go on demand. The trend towards precarious and contingent employment is already well entrenched, and technological changes will enhance this shift. Global competition has heightened the desire on the part of Canadian firms to reduce labour costs. At the same time, new technologies make feasible new types of contingent work. In 2013, Carl Benedikt Frey and Michael A. Osborne suggested that 47 per cent of US employment is at high risk of being automated in the next twenty years.[11] Creig Lamb replicated Frey and Osborne's study for the Canadian economy in 2016, and estimated that 42 per cent of employment in Canada is at high risk.[12]

A report by the federal government documented the range of job types in existence and the general movement towards less and less stable types of work contracts.[13] In the past, unskilled and semi-skilled workers such as taxi drivers and food delivery personnel have been especially vulnerable to work outsourcing through online platforms such as Uber and SkipTheDishes, but the rise of new virtual platforms threatens even middle-class jobs. As technology becomes increasingly integrated into our work, complex careers such as accounting, law or pharmacy require less skill on the part of those who undertake some of the work. Large parts of the work of community pharmacists can be replaced by pill-dispensing robots. As the software becomes more sophisticated, larger parts of many professional jobs, such as law, become less demanding.[14] Professional careers increasingly turn into lower-skilled full-time or part-time jobs undertaken by legal assistants and paralegals, bookkeepers and pharmacy technicians. A firm with a new contract might hire freelancers as contractors for a fixed term and then release them when the project is complete. Potential contractors face competition not only from Canadians, but from workers all over the world who can access the new online platforms. This competition has dramatic effects on international income distribution. Skilled workers from low-wage countries can now access higher-paying jobs offered by firms located in high-income countries while workers in high-income countries face new competition for work they used to assume was theirs by right.

Translators, for example, who used to have relatively good access to permanent jobs with reasonable incomes, now find themselves in competition with contractors from all over the world, not to mention machine translations that are improving rapidly. Newspaper columnists are a dying species, and journalists of all types find themselves cobbling together an income from a series of less secure contracts and jobs. A variety of online platforms (or websites) bring together those who have projects to be completed with those eager for work, and the number of platforms as well as participants is staggering. In 2020, for example, Upwork boasted twelve million freelancers and five million clients; Freelancer had twenty-one million users; ProZ listed 1,086,207 translators and translation companies; Catalant, formerly known as Hourly Nerd, boasted over 70,000 "elite, independent experts."

There are also websites for those willing to take on even shorter-term, less demanding tasks for much less money. Workers can supplement their incomes by completing microtasks — anything from accessing a website to completing a survey to tweeting in response to key words — that pay as little as five cents a task through online platforms like Amazon's Mechanical Turk.

As long as decisions to participate in such activities are a choice and not a necessity, they provide a valuable opportunity for potential employees. These platforms offer opportunities for creatively balancing the necessity of work with the freedom to allocate time to other activities such as travel, education, creativity or leisure. Many platform workers are young people who are also engaged in education, and these work arrangements allow them the flexibility to combine their various commitments. However, for some people, part-time work or platform work is oppressive. They would prefer full-time, standard jobs that, because of the rapidly changing job market, they cannot find or cannot keep.

Technological change is disruptive, and it will have important consequences that basic income solves very well. Basic income can make life easier for people whose jobs have disappeared and who cannot easily retrain for new opportunities. Basic income can supplement the incomes of people whose jobs have been transformed by technology from full-time careers into contingent and low-paying piecework. However, technology will not eliminate the need for human labour.

# Chapter 5

# Work and Human Dignity

Mincome hired dozens of young graduates from the Universities of Manitoba and Winnipeg to interview recipients and collect data. As I began to work through the data collected during the Mincome project, I spoke with a well-respected Canadian sociologist who told me that he'd had his first exposure to social science research as a Mincome interviewer. He told me a story that still moved him almost forty years later. He went to visit one of the Mincome families living in the rural municipality surrounding Dauphin and pulled up in front of a small house on a very marginal farmstead. Used to deprivation by this point, he steeled himself for what he might find within. He was welcomed and ushered into the front room to wait for tea and dainties.[1] Taking pride of place, a polished, oversized wooden stereo console occupied one long wall, sur-rounded by shelves and shelves of records — the largest classical music and opera collection he had ever seen. Noticing his interest, the owner began to explain how the collection had been gathered and cared for over many years, and how she and her husband had raised their children in a home poor by many standards, but always rich in music and literature. She laughed as she told him how every-thing stopped at noon on Saturdays so they could listen to the radio together — *Saturday Afternoon at the Opera* on CBC.

One of the reasons that story resonates is because it is a reminder of the richness and variety of human experience. People do their best to live their lives in ways that affirm their individuality. Any "rational" consideration of that story might suggest that indoor plumbing should have been a greater priority than a music collection, but it would be hard to argue that the family had made an uninformed decision. Yet we often do a very poor job of recognizing human variation, and, as a result, our analysis of how a basic income might affect our lives is quite naive.

## Why Do People Work?

One of the great fears that many critics bring to a discussion of basic income is that people will work less if they can get money from a basic income for doing nothing. This is an important con-sideration because if enough people work less, the cost of running a basic income program, and the burden on taxpayers, will be greater than expected. At the same time, a significant reduction in work effort will also reduce the growth of Canadian productivity and, consequently, the growth of tax revenue that could be used to pay for the program. That is, if people work less, basic income becomes more expensive at the same time that our ability to pay for it is con-strained. There is also a moral issue involved: most people believe that working is good for everyone.

Economists like to talk about "incentivizing labour" — making work pay. This is based on the assumption that the only reason anyone works is because they are bribed with money to do something they would not otherwise choose to do. They will work harder only if they are offered higher wages. If their take-home pay is cut through higher taxation, they will work fewer hours or work less hard and produce less during the hours they do work. If they are offered money without needing to work, they will not work. There is, however, very little evidence to support this claim, and a great deal of evidence to suggest that the reasons people work are as varied as the people themselves.

This might seem contrary to recent experience with the Canada Emergency Response Benefit, but the CERB differs from a basic income in important ways. When the benefit was first rolled out, it was offered only to people who were quarantined, who had lost their jobs due to COVID-19 or who had children to care for after the schools were closed. At the outset, people whose hours were reduced but who still had a job were ineligible, so the criteria were changed to allow people to earn up to $1,000 a month while receiving the CERB. Wage subsidies for firms — the Canadian Emergency Wage Subsidy (CEWS) — were rolled out a few weeks later; the rationale was that firms could use the subsidy to keep workers on the payroll even though revenue might have dropped, which would allow the firms to survive and to ramp up more quickly when the economy restarted. Almost as soon as the applications were available, some employers complained that they couldn't convince the workers they had laid off to come back to work because these workers would rather stay at home and collect the CERB. Some lawyers advised employers that they should ensure such workers were ineligible for the CERB by declaring on their record of employment that the employee had voluntarily refused to work.

Of course, there are many reasons for workers refusing to return to work, none of which has to do with an epidemic of laziness. Some employers were unable to provide a safe workplace for employees by ensuring social distancing or providing protective equipment. Workers worried that returning to work would bring the virus home to their families. In some provinces, the decision was made to allow firms to re-open without thinking about how children were to be cared for. If the elementary schools, day camps and daycare centres remained closed, no parent was free to work no matter how profoundly an employer might need labour. But labour compensation also played a role, although it was more complex than many employers suggested.

The CERB was not designed as a basic income. A targeted basic income would gradually decline as work income increases, which ensures that it always pays to work an additional hour. If, for example, the benefit was to decline by fifty cents for every dollar earned, workers would always be financially better off by working an additional hour. By contrast, earning up to $1,000 a month made a worker better off but as soon as she earned $1,001 she lost the entire CERB. If an employer could not promise a returning worker a set number of hours, all the risk associated with an uncertain recovery fell on the worker. Anyone who agreed to work under such circumstances faced the real possibility that they would earn more than $1,000 a month thereby losing the CERB, but less than the $2,000 guarantee the CERB provided. As a consequence, there were proposals to make the CERB work more like a basic income, by reducing benefits gradually as income increases.

For almost everyone, whether or not people choose to work depends at least as much on the terms and conditions of employment as the wage. Consider the very different decisions that two low-wage workers make about whether to work or to receive the CERB and how they might react to a basic income.

The daycare where Julieta works is a happy place. Three little girls with microphones fashioned out of toilet paper rolls are belting out a slightly off-key but very enthusiastic rendition of "Jolene" as Dolly Parton plays in the background. Jack, a slightly tearful new boy, is sitting quietly with one of Julieta's colleagues listening to a story about bears, and Spiderman and Ariel are in the playhouse caring for their new baby. Julieta makes $14.71 an hour — the median salary of daycare workers in Winnipeg in 2020. If she works 35 hours a week, she earns $2,059.40 a month out of which she pays for a bus pass to get to work and fees for her own son to attend an after-school program until she can pick him up. She loves her job but is clearly better off financially if she receives $2,000 a month as a basic income. What would she do, I asked, if she were permitted to collect $2,000 and earn up to $1,000 with no penalty? She loves her job, she tells me, but would cut her hours in half because she and her son could live so much better on $3,000 a month than $2,000 a month. What if she got $2,000 a month, but that would be reduced by fifty cents for every dollar she earns from the very first dollar? That is, if she doesn't work, she gets $2,000. If she works full-time, she gets $2,059.40 wage income plus $970.30 from the basic income ($2,000 minus 0.5 X $2,059.40) for a total of $3,029.70. If she works half-time and earns $1,000, her total earnings would be $2,500 a month. She would work full-time, she tells me, because she's better off with $3,000 than $2,000 or $2,500 and, besides, she really likes her job. She loves the kids and she's proud to help the parents. The economist in me points out that if her basic income is reduced by fifty cents for every dollar she earns, that's equivalent to working for $7.35 an hour — less if you take into account other deductions. She shrugs and tells me that she likes her work and wants to give her son a good life.

Marcus works in southwestern Manitoba as a pork production technician. That job pays $14.40 an hour, and comes with benefits that include a company pension, paid vacation and life insurance. He works with many temporary foreign workers, and his employer often hires formerly incarcerated people like Marcus. At thirty-five hours a week, the job pays $2,016 a month. Since he needs a vehicle to drive to work, he is clearly better off financially if he receives a basic income of $2,000 a month. He says he'd quit in a heartbeat. What if he were permitted to earn $1,000 a month and still receive the basic income? He wouldn't work. He says he can live on $2,000 a month and if he isn't working at that plant, he can look for a less soul-destroying job. What if he were offered a basic income of $2,000 that would fall by fifty cents for every dollar earned? He still wouldn't work at this job. When I ask him what he would do if he weren't working here, he replies that he would look for something else, even if it paid less. He likes to keep busy he says. It keeps him out of trouble.

Concerns about the food supply chain were raised during the pandemic when Cargill, the largest federally regulated slaughterhouse in the country, which processes 36 per cent of all Canadian beef, closed after almost half its employees tested positive for COVID-19. The employer said it couldn't keep its employees safe, pointing to crowded housing and carpooling on the sixty-mile commute from Calgary as risks outside its control. A cynic might point out that the income earned by its workers almost certainly had some role to play in the housing and transportation decisions they made. Most of its employees, Cargill noted, were temporary foreign workers or new immigrants. Fish plants in the Maritimes similarly struggled to stay open, and farmers worried about labour shortages. Canadians enjoy very low food prices, but these prices are possible only because everyone from employees in fast food restaurants, grocery store shelf stockers, slaughterhouse employees to agricultural workers is asked to do physically and mentally demanding work at wages that don't allow them to rise out of poverty. If employees like Marcus had access to a guaranteed livable income, many might choose not to do this backbreaking work.

Critics of basic income argued that these are important jobs and someone needs to do them. However, there is a choice. The terms and conditions of employment for these essential jobs could be improved, recognizing that it would mean higher prices for consumers. Some of the jobs might disappear if employers, faced with higher costs to employ labour, choose to invest in labour-saving technology instead. This would be a positive outcome because people like Marcus could work elsewhere while machines do the jobs that have, until now, been done by humans who have been coerced and threatened with starvation and homelessness if they refuse. "But what about the poor?" critics ask. "Wouldn't the poor be hurt most by higher food prices?" It seems too easy to argue that a basic income and better wages would mean fewer poor people to worry about. If employees earned higher wages, they would pay more in taxes, which would support higher basic incomes and food prices that cover the actual costs of production without exploiting workers. For the past several decades, the opposite path has been followed. The price of food has been driven down to compete with cheap imports and then the costs of cheap food have been off-loaded on to the labour that makes these products available. Their poverty puts pressure on merchants to lower prices even more, so that consumers can afford their product. If workers balk, temporary foreign workers are used to keep wages low. All the while, consumers become more and more dependent on the efficiency of centralized agricultural production that simultaneously drives down wages and puts our health at risk. They turn to fast food restaurants for cheap prepared food made possible by the terms and conditions of work — conditions that the pandemic made it impossible for us to ignore.

Even though there are some employers that struggle to find workers, it is undeniable that most people value work. In the *World Happiness Report*, which appears regularly, a group of economists and psychologists have surveyed people from all over the world to find out how happy they were — whether they believed themselves to be happy or depressed, and how they evaluated their lives overall.[2] The reports have consistently found that people who were employed scored higher on "positive affect,"[3] lower on "negative affect" and higher on overall "life evaluation"[4] than people who were not employed. The first response might be to dismiss these results; after all, people who are employed are more likely to have money than people who are unemployed and, with money, they can afford to build more comfortable lives. However, even when comparing people who were the same age and sex and had the same family income, the unemployed still reported significantly less well-being than those with full-time employment. It was not just the money associated with employment that seemed to bring satisfaction. These results are important because how long we live, how well we function and how healthy we are overall is associated with how satisfying we find our lives.[5]

Not all jobs are equal, to be sure. The report identifies some characteristics of jobs associated with improved well-being: higher wages, job security, autonomy, the opportunity to learn new things, support from others on the job and opportunities for advancement. Other characteristics reduced perceived well-being: job insecurity, dirty or dangerous work, lack of control, jobs that interfere with family time and worry about work outside job hours.

In general, people who found the kind of job arrangement that they wanted were happiest. For example, in high-income countries, self-employed people were happier than those with full-time employment. Presumably, self-employment gave them the opportunity for greater autonomy and control over their time. In low-income countries, however, self-employment was often less about controlling one's own life than about survival; it was often the employment of last resort, and it's not surprising that many people in such circumstances would prefer a regular, full-time job. All employment variables mattered more for men than for women. Women who voluntarily worked part-time were happier than those working full-time. Involuntary part-time employment and being out of the labour force were associated with lower levels of happiness, especially for men.

On a less theoretical level, some people work very hard to find a job when there is no material advantage to doing so. For example, most food banks in Canada rely on volunteer labour, and the volunteers are disproportionately people with lived experience of poverty. Many are not in the labour force because of disabilities or mental health issues that make it difficult to keep a job even though they might not qualify for disability support. Working at the food bank does not increase their entitlement to a food basket; they get one whether they work or not. It does not earn them any other material rewards except, perhaps, a modest lunch and a bus ticket. The work can be hard and dusty; there are not many opportunities to perfect high-level skills. However, no food bank has difficulty attracting volunteers from among its clients. People value the job. Their reasons vary: some like the social aspects of work while others want to feel useful.

Work helps to structure our lives. People feel better about themselves and about their lives when they work, and this is true not only of high-paying professional jobs with autonomy, but also of many low-skilled and physically demanding jobs. Most people like to work. A 2014 meta-analysis found strong evidence that employment protects individuals against depression and reduces psychological stress. Employment is associated with better mental health.[6] These results are consistent with all we know about the positive effects of work on human well-being.

Some people have the opportunity to decide how many hours they want to work. For those in standard jobs, there is often little choice: many jobs do not allow workers to voluntarily reduce their hours (and pay) without losing benefits and opportunities. Some jobs allow overtime, but whether to accept it is often not entirely under the control of the worker. However, the labour market is changing in such a way that many people can find a second job or "side hustle" that offers them the opportunity to work a few more hours for more money. How do people decide how many hours to work? Whether they realize it or not, they probably weigh the benefits of working an additional hour against the costs of working that hour. The benefits include how much more money they will bring home after taxes, and costs include things such as additional child care, transportation, and so on. Many of the benefits and costs, however, are not monetary: costs include time away from family and reduced opportunities to engage in unpaid volunteer, creative or care work. A non-monetary benefit might include the opportunity to learn particular skills, or to build relationships with colleagues or contacts. The satisfaction of doing a job someone considers important and meaningful will influence how many hours they want to work, as will the praise received from a skilled employer. People are different and will be influenced by different factors.

Dan Ariely is a behavioural economist at Duke University and the author of *Predictably Irrational*. In a series of laboratory experiments, Ariely explored how people make decisions and showed that human beings are often less rational than economists sometimes assume. He investigated the question of what motivates people to work, and, using two ingenious experiments, demonstrated that work is not motivated solely by money, but it isn't motivated by the pleasure of the work itself either. In one experiment, participants were given a simple building task using Legos and asked if they were prepared to undertake the task for $3.00. If they agreed, the experimenter accepted the result, set it on the table and offered the participant a second opportunity to build for $2.75. If they agreed, they were offered a third opportunity at a lower price, and so on. Then the experiment was repeated with different participants, but this time the experimenter disassembled the product of the first round as the builder was completing the second. The participants were prepared to build more creations at a lower price when the experimenter accepted the result than when the experimenter destroyed the result. The pay offered to the participant was unchanged, but the futility of the task was made much clearer in the second case. In a second experiment, participants were given the opportunity to make origami creations. In one trial, participants were given good instructions, and then they were given the opportunity to "buy" the results of their labour. The participants valued the products they created more than did others who, presumably, had a more objective view of their quality. In a second trial, the participants were given poor instructions. The results were objectively worse than in the first trial, but participants valued the results even more — presumably because of the extra effort required to complete the task.

Most humans, Ariely concluded, work harder and longer when we can see that we are making constant progress and feel a sense of purpose in our work.[7] Focusing too narrowly on take-home pay often leads to unwarranted conclusions.

Notwithstanding all of these insights, the debate about whether people offered a basic income would work fewer hours tends to ignore everything except money.

## The Effects of a Basic Income on the Amount of Work People Do

Experiments were conducted in North America during the 1970s precisely to understand whether people would work less. However, these were short-term experiments, and all participants knew they were temporary. People might behave differently when a program is generally available and expected to be permanent than when they participate in a temporary experiment. We do know that when offered a basic income in a temporary experiment, the reduction in work effort was quite modest.

Five negative income tax experiments took place in North America in the 1970s — four in the United States and Mincome in Canada. The first American experiment was conducted on urban populations in New Jersey and Pennsylvania between 1968 and 1972.[8] A second experiment was conducted in Gary, Indiana, to examine the effect of a basic income on single parents.[9] A third took place in North Carolina and Iowa to look at the effects on rural populations.[10] The final experiment was the Seattle-Denver Income Maintenance Experiment (SIME/DIME), which had access to a much larger experimental population.[11] The four US experiments used a carefully selected experimental sample and assigned participants randomly to one group that would receive the basic income and another that would not. They collected quantitative and qualitative data from both subjects and controls, and experimenters hoped that comparing the experiences of those who received the basic income with those who did not would allow them to determine the effects of a basic income on a wide variety of social behaviours. The Winnipeg site of the Canadian experiment followed the same structure, but the Dauphin site was the only saturation site in any of the North American experiments that offered a basic income to all qualifying participants in the site.

Details of the experiments are summarized in Table 5.1.

Table 5.1 Summary of the Features of the North American Income Maintenance Experiments

| Parameter | New Jersey | Rural (RIME) | Seattle-Denver (SIME/DIME) | Gary | Mincome |
|---|---|---|---|---|---|
| Site | Trenton, Patterson-Passaic, and Jersey City, N.J.; Scranton, Pa. | Duplin County, N.C; Pocahontas and Calhoun Counties, Iowa | Seattle, Wash.; Denver, Colo. | Gary, Ind. | Winnipeg and Dauphin, Manitoba |
| Eligibility | Intact households headed by able-bodied males 18–58 with at least one dependent and incomes < 150 per cent of poverty line | Families with at least one dependent and incomes < 150 per cent of poverty line | Families with at least one dependent and incomes < $11,000 (singleheaded) or $13,000 (double headed) | Black households, head 18–58 with at least one dependent and income < 240 per cent of poverty line | Families with able-bodied heads under 58 years old, incomes < $13,000 (family of four) |
| Sample Size | 1,357 households: 725 experimentals, 632 controls | 809 families: 587 non-aged male-headed, 108 non-aged female-headed, 114 older heads | 4,801 families (Denver 2,758, Seattle 2,043) | 1,800 black households, 60 per cent female-headed (125 households added with incomes above 240 per cent of poverty line) | 1,300 families and single individuals |
| Plans [not all $t$, $G$ combinations included in each experiment; more generous plans (high $G$, low $t$) typically excluded] | 8 plans; $t = .3, .5, .7$; $G = .5, .75, 1.0, 1.25$ of poverty line ($5,000 for family of 4) | 8 plans; $t = .3, .5, .7$; $G = .5, .75, 1.0$ of poverty line | 11 plans; $t = .5, .7, .7^*, .8^*$ (* indicates tax rate declines per .025 per $100 income); $G = .95, 1.2, 1.4$ of poverty line; training counselling, training subsidies (50 per cent, 100 per cent) | 4 plans; $t = .4, .6$; $G = .75, 1.0$ of poverty line, social services counselling, day care subsidies (35 per cent, 60 per cent, 80 per cent) | Winnipeg; 7 plans; $t = .35, .5, .75$; $G = $3,800, 4,800, 5,800 (family of four in 1975) Dauphin: 1 plan (saturated site); $t = .5$; $G = $3,800 |
| Duration (start-up date) | 3 years/1968–69 | 3 years/1970 | 3, 5 years, 20 years (Denver only)/1969 | 3 years/1971 | 3 years/1975 |

Note: $t$ refers to the experimental tax rate; $G$ refers to the experimental income guarantee rate.

Source: Derek Hum and Wayne Simpson, "Economic Response to a Guaranteed Annual Income: Experience from Canada and the United States," *Journal of Labor Economics* 11, no. 1, part 2: U.S. and Canadian Income Maintenance Programs (1993): S275.

The researchers hoped that the experiments would throw light on all kinds of social behaviours, but the experiments were designed specifically to illuminate one set of decisions. The fundamental purpose of all these experiments was to determine whether a basic income would induce people to stop working and live on the basic income instead. Would those who continued to work choose to work fewer hours? Overall, the results of the experiments were remarkably consistent. The results are summarized in Table 5.2.

Table 5.2 Annual Change in Hours Worked During North AmericanIncome Maintenance Experiments

| Experiments | Husbands | Wives | Single Female Heads |
|---|---|---|---|
| Mincome | -20 (1 per cent) | -15 (3 per cent) | -56 (5 per cent) |
| | | | |
| New Jersey | -57 (3 per cent) | -62 (28 per cent) | |
| Rural | -93 (5 per cent) | -180 (28 per cent) | |
| Seattle-Denver | -135 (8 per cent) | -129 (20 per cent) | -134 (13 per cent) |
| Gary | -76 (5 per cent) | -18 (6 per cent) | -84 (23 per cent) |
| Overall US Results | -69 (6 per cent) | -70 (19 per cent) | -85 (15 per cent) |

Source: Derek Hum and Wayne Simpson, "Whatever Happened to Canada's Guaranteed Income Project?" *Canadian Public Administration* 36, no. 3 (1993): 448.

The second column in Table 5.2 represents the effect of basic income on the number of hours worked by those most attached to the labour market — adult men. These were primary earners and their reaction to a basic income was, overall, quite modest. Men, for the most part, did not quit their jobs although the average number of hours worked did fall a small amount. The smallest average results occurred in Manitoba (an annual work reduction of less than half a week) and the largest in Seattle-Denver. However, these results represent average reductions in hours worked. Among men, the largest effects were on adolescents in all of the experiments. If we look at the results a bit closer, interesting effects become apparent. For example, Seattle-Denver had a combination of experimental designs underway, some of which included heavily subsidized or free job training. One of the significant results in that experiment was a positive effect on adult education. Did these men reduce their work hours because they received a basic income and they preferred not to work, or did they reduce their work hours to engage in job training or, as the researchers labelled it, to accumulate human capital? Certainly in Dauphin, reduced work effort among young males was associated with increased education.[12]

Basic income was associated with a larger reduction in work effort for women, but both the design and the context in which these results are produced needs to be taken into account. In the Canadian case, the results were very small overall with the largest reduction in work effort associated with single mothers. Women in all five sites, whether they were married women or single mothers, worked significantly fewer hours if they received a basic income. The percentage change is large, but what is most notable is how few hours married women worked even before the experiment began. For example, in New Jersey, a 28 per cent reduction in work hours resulted in sixty-two fewer hours worked per year, which means that on average, these women were working about four hours per week before the experiment began. These experiments took place during the 1970s, when few women expected to work their entire lives. Women were just beginning to enter the workforce in large numbers, and many still did not consider their jobs an important part of their identity or even an important source of income for their families. If they did work out of necessity, it is unlikely that they had the training or the opportunity to access good full-time work. A reasonable response, under the circumstances, was for many of these women to opt out of paid work or reduce their hours to take care of their children. Most women today do not consider their earnings either secondary or expendable. They work for the same reason that men work — to pay their bills.[13]

These numbers illustrate a much more fundamental change in the ways that women and men and families organize their lives. These experiments took place at the beginning of a period of profound change in family organization. Men were still primary earners, and both spouses expected them to be. Lone mothers were more often widows than divorced or never married. Mothers of young children received income assistance, but there was little support for widows with grown children beyond savings or, in exceptional cases, survivor's pensions attached to their husbands' previous employment. During Mincome, especially in the Dauphin site, widows were in a particularly difficult position. There was no Guaranteed Income Supplement at that time, and many would have been too young for Old Age Security. There was no mature Canada Pension Plan in place, and many of their husbands would have been self-employed with little capacity to leave a large pension or insurance policy. When their husbands died, they found themselves with grown children but too old and unskilled to compete for a job and too young to collect a pension. They had never trained to work and never expected to do so. The introduction of a basic income for these women alleviated a great deal of hardship. Younger women were beginning to move into the labour market and to regard their work as more than a temporary period before motherhood or an opportunity to buy extras for their families. Yet older women were still living with a set of values and expectations forged in a period of male breadwinners and stay-at-home wives.

Overall, the results of the 1970s experiments suggest that people will not substantially reduce their hours worked. However, these experiments all had a definite end date that was known to participants. Those most likely to curtail their work in the experiments were precisely those making short-term decisions: the older worker coasting into retirement, the young worker who knows that eventually a real job will be necessary but perhaps not quite yet, and the mother with preschool children who will not be infants forever. Those with longer perspectives had virtually no reaction. There is a problem with generalizing about human behaviour from temporary experiments. We do not know how people will change their work behaviour if basic income becomes an established program. We can guess that those used to living a richer lifestyle will be hesitant about trading it for a modest basic income. We can assume that people who derive satisfaction and pleasure from their work will continue to work. We cannot, however, know with certainty how low-wage workers will behave when basic income is fully institutionalized — and no experiment can produce that knowledge with certainty.

There are other kinds of data we can look at to get some idea of how people would behave if a basic income were introduced. Czech economist Jitka Specianova looked at different kinds of data to determine whether people might stop working when they received money without working. The largest results were among lottery winners who received their winnings as an annual or monthly income, in almost all cases significantly larger than any proposed basic income. In general, lottery winners were likely to decrease the amount they worked, but the overall size of the effect was still small. The size of the response depended on the amount of the lottery winnings, the satisfaction people had with their current job, whether they perceived the job as a part of daily life, their age, education, gender and status. That is, Jitka's results confirm the findings of Dan Ariely and others: many factors other than wages and taxes influence whether and how much people choose to work.[14]

Of more relevance to Canadian decisions, Kourtney Koebel amd Tammy Schirle examined how women responded to the introduction of the universal child care benefit (the forerunner of the Canada Child Benefit), which is similar to a basic income for families with dependent children. They discovered that married mothers were slightly less likely to work, but divorced mothers were significantly more likely to work. There was no effect on single mothers or those in common-law relationships.[15] These results hardly suggest a flight from paid work.

There is little evidence that the introduction of a basic income will cause people to work substantially less overall, but there is some merit to allowing individuals the right to choose how much to work without coercing them to take whatever job they can find. Some people, particularly those in low-paid and unpleasant jobs, may choose to work less if they have access to a basic income. If the work they abandon is necessary work that must be done, their refusal to work will encourage employers to improve the terms of employment. If consumers will not buy the products at a price sufficient to hire enough labour to produce it, then those consumers will have made the decision to do without the product.

The ability of poorly paid and badly treated workers to reject demeaning work is not a problem to be solved; it is a benefit of basic income.

## The Social Benefits of Working Less

It is not very likely that a basic income will cause people to work significantly less. However, it is worth considering whether a reduction in work hours is necessarily a negative outcome. North Americans work many more hours than people in most European nations, and since the 1970s, the increase in hours worked by women has broadened the gap.[16] We have begun to transform other social policies to reflect growing evidence that overwork is not necessarily beneficial. In Canada in the 1970s, the entitlement to maternity leave was four weeks. Since then, we have substantially increased paid and partially paid parental leave because we recognize the evidence that families benefit from the opportunity to spend more time together and to forge deeper bonds with newborns. Moreover, the leave is extended to men as well as to women because it is more than just an opportunity to heal from the physical trauma of birth. Young people are encouraged by all kinds of social policies to stay in school longer, to engage in training and to take their first jobs at a later date. More and more private firms are offering opportunities for sabbaticals, recognizing the benefit that comes from productive leisure. Is it necessarily a negative outcome to find that families will take some of their income — especially if their income is enhanced through a basic income — in the form of greater flexibility in their use of time? Some will engage in training and education; others will spend more time taking care of their own family members rather than paying others to provide necessary care. Some people might choose to spend time in creative or voluntary pursuits or to engage in innovative entrepreneurial activities. Others may just read more novels or go for an additional hike. The point is that wealthy societies can afford to take some of their wealth in the form of a greater quality of life associated with time away from paid labour.

Some work is important to the well-being of society but is not part of the paid labour market. Caregiving has never fit well into a formal labour market. Nursing homes are rarely preferred by patients over care provided by a family member. A mother at home with preschoolers today faces social pressure to justify her decision not to use daycare, but no one would argue that a society can survive and flourish without someone undertaking these activities. These services might be provided by someone we pay to do the work, or they might be provided by a family member for no pay, but society does require that this kind of work be done. A basic income is a way to value the unpaid work of caregivers. Similarly, creative work is essential to social well-being, but the market does a poor job of encouraging it. Long before the Industrial Revolution, artists required the income and support of patrons to assure their continued production. More recently, the state has provided pensions or grants to a small number of applicants. Both institutions recognize how significant creative work is, but neither encourages widespread creativity or supports all those who believe they have something worthwhile to say. Some artists and some caregivers may choose to subsist on a basic income and dedicate themselves to what they consider their important work rather than taking a job for pay. Whether we want to support a more robust creative sector and the freedom to choose whether or not to work for pay depends on the kind of society in which we want to live. If the cost of a basic income is the production of a little more poetry than the market would support, is that a bad thing?

There will no doubt be some people who choose not to engage in non-market production, volunteer labour or work for pay. If a basic income is provided without conditions, some people will do very little. Some will fish all day or daydream under an apple tree. This decision is a difficult one for people living in industrialized countries to accept, but the great philosophers of the past recognized the importance of leisure. Economists tend to identify leisure as any period not devoted to work for pay in the market, but philosophers have always had a more nuanced view. Aristotle pointed out that as soon as society had reached a level of output that would allow it to provide the necessities of life for everyone, people began to think about science and art. It is no accident, he claimed, that scientific progress occurred first in places where people had a reasonable amount of leisure time that they could use to think rather than simply work. Egypt, for example, is where mathematics first began to flourish, and it began among the priestly caste that was allowed time for leisure.

Almost all of the great achievements of past centuries in the arts, sciences, music, philosophy and scholarship were created by people who had, for all intents and purposes, the equivalent of a basic income. They were not people who worked for a wage, but rather members of aristocratic families who did not need to work for money, or talented individuals who had attracted a patron who could finance their leisure, or employees of the Church for (some of) whom "holy leisure" had always been part of a balanced life. Leisure — not mere relaxation or entertainment, but time and the ability to contemplate — is essential to the well-being and advancement of societies.

Contemporary philosopher Martha Nussbaum wrote *Creating Capabilities*, in which she argued that leisure is at least as unequally distributed in our world as is wealth and is at least as important for social progress. She imagines a young girl named Vasani in rural India, and wonders whether she ever has access to time just to sit and think, to enjoy something beautiful or to share tea with her friends. We might ask the same question about a harried single parent, rushing between daycare and two different jobs: what is the value of leisure?

Basic income not only offers everyone access to the resources to live a modest life; it offers to everyone the opportunity to participate in leisure. Not everyone will spend money the way I believe they ought to, and not everyone will spend time the way I think it ought to be spent. But I am not in a position to judge the priorities of other people. The fundamental characteristic of basic income is that everyone becomes the judge of how to spend their own time and money without the help and assistance of people who believe themselves to know better. In our culture, leisure may be the most difficult good to obtain. We are rich in money and resources. We struggle with too much food and too much waste. We are brought up from infancy to achieve, to make, to do. We are not encouraged to be visionaries and dreamers.

## Reconsidering Our Attachment to the Labour Market

Not everyone is a caregiver or an artist, and not everyone aspires to be. With no work requirement, some people will nonetheless choose to work for pay because that is how they find human contact and satisfaction in their lives. Some will work for a wage or the inherent value of the work itself while others will work because they enjoy their colleagues or the routine of work. A few will decide that, on the whole, the job they are offered is not worth the low wage attached to it. They will either seek a different job, volunteer or do something else with their time. The job will then be done by someone who makes a different decision about the value of the wage and the nature of the job. If no one chooses to take the job at the wage offered, then either the wage will have to increase, or the job will not be done.

As economies grow and develop, many previously necessary jobs do disappear from the local labour market. Few people in North America or Europe have the households full of servants that earlier generations "needed" and that are still considered essential to middle-class life in places like India or Indonesia. Even the well off survive without the footmen and butlers that used to facilitate genteel lives. Farms in Europe and North America today do without much of the low-paid farm labour that characterized earlier agriculture. The very low-wage child labour that was essential to nineteenth-century textile factories that drove economic growth during the first industrial revolution is not a feature of high-income industrialized economies today. As certain types of labour become more expensive, either technology (such as washing machines and dishwashers) replaces formerly necessary workers, or we choose to do without the product of these labourers as we now do without small appliance repair. At some point, it becomes cheaper to replace the toaster than to hire someone to fix it.

A basic income encourages us to ask important questions about how we want to live our lives, how we value ourselves and each other, and how we will know whether our society is developing in directions that lead to better lives and greater opportunities. A basic income is not simply about eliminating poverty, but about extending the freedom to each of us to make these decisions for ourselves based on our own set of values.

# Chapter 6

# Women and Basic Income

When public health measures designed to reduce the spread of infection were introduced, women and men were affected very differently. While men usually bear the brunt of recessions because heavy construction and the resource sectors are often the first to decline, women were the first to lose their jobs this time. Retail stores and restaurants closed before the pain spread to other areas of the economy. Not all women were affected, of course. Women are disproportionately employed in retail and restaurants, but they are also more likely to be employed as teachers, caregivers and in the civil service — sectors that escaped some of the worst economic consequences of the closure. Some continued to leave home to work — personal support workers in care homes, for example — and worried about the impact of their work on their families. Others balanced work and caregiving, as they attempted to work from home while caring for young children. Young families were the most affected, because as soon as schools closed at least one parent was required to provide care. The importance of gender was highlighted, but so was the diversity of women's lives. All women are not all alike. Women's lives vary, as do their experiences, their opportunities, their needs and their ideas.

For most of recorded history, women have provided most of the unpaid work that society relies upon, such as caring for children and others who need extra help. Unpaid work makes women's lives and their participation in the paid labour market less predictable than those of men. Anyone providing care for others knows that we all face times in our lives when help from others and support from social programs becomes vital. Women's voices were instrumental in the introduction of Family Allowances in Canada in 1943. Women were visible in the fight for medicare in the 1960s and are still central to the expansion of supports for people with disabilities and pensions for older people. Women have always been primary advocates for the welfare state, in Canada and around the world. They continue to fill most of the frontline positions in publicly provided services as caseworkers and careworkers, and they are more likely than men to benefit from public support at some point in their lives. And yet the welfare state, which is so central to the lives of women, has also been complicit in regulating women's lives. This is especially the case for women whose lives do not conform to the dominant culture.

Social and gender roles have changed dramatically over the past forty years, opening up new opportunities for women in the workforce. Women who have benefited least from these changes are most likely to see the advantages of a basic income. Indigenous women have taken a leadership role in advocating for a basic income in Canada. On the third of June 2019, *Reclaiming Power and Place: The Final Report of the National Inquiry into Missing and Murdered Indigenous Women and Girls* was published. Among the calls for justice was for "all governments to establish a guaranteed annual livable income for all Canadians, including Indigenous Peoples, to meet all their social and economic needs."[1]

By contrast, some women who came of age in the 1970s and now hold positions of influence benefited disproportionately from the rapid progress of women in the workforce. They took advantage of new educational opportunities and trained for careers that offered promotions and paid them far more than most women of earlier generations could expect to attain. Some of these women are keen to ensure that all women benefit as they have done, and remain skeptical of a basic income that, they believe, would undermine hard-won progress by allowing women to take time off work to care for young children or other family members. They note that career interruptions can have consequences, not only on immediate income, but on lifetime earnings and even pension entitlements. However, while professional women obsess about career trajectories and pension entitlements, other women struggle to feed their families and pay the rent. The struggle to create greater opportunities for all women, including the most marginalized, must be accompanied by a recognition that not everyone is now in a position to make equal use of them.

Basic income is vital to those who have not yet shared in the benefits of the social change. With the economic security offered by a predictable basic income, some of these women will also be able to take advantage of education and career opportunities. Others will raise daughters, nieces and granddaughters who benefit from social change. Basic income gives women the freedom to make all kinds of decisions — decisions that someone without a predictable, livable basic income cannot make. A basic income gives a woman the resources she needs to work on her own issues, on her own timetable and in her own ways. She can leave a toxic relationship, even when there are no nearby shelters or if the police are less than helpful. It gives her the ability to feed her kids, even if she is not ready to benefit from job training or paid work. Women who have experienced trauma in their lives are often nowhere near ready to get a job, no matter how beneficial a caseworker believes it would be for them. A basic income allows a woman to move — to rent an apartment in a different part of town or a different town altogether. A woman fleeing domestic violence needs the means to buy a bus ticket, but she also needs to have public transportation available. Services are important — essential even — but they must not be a replacement for income that a woman can spend any way she wants to in order to meet her own needs, without seeking the approval of anyone.

Giving people real freedom to make their own decisions is challenging for everyone. When people have freedom, they don't always make decisions that win the approval of others. Some women might indeed decide to care for young children at home even when they understand fully the financial consequences of taking a year or more out of the workforce. Others will use a basic income to provide appropriate care for their children so they are free to work at a demanding job, but the care they choose might be different from the care that others think is most appropriate. Basic income validates all these choices, because it is only with a guaranteed livable income that some women have the opportunity to make any choices.

## Women in the Paid Labour Market

Canadian social programs were created at a time when there was a widely shared story about how the world worked. Women and men played distinct roles, with men taking primary responsibility for supporting a family financially and women at home raising children, taking care of older or disabled family members and keeping a house. If this were ever true, it is no longer the case and dramatic social change never comes without anxiety. Some women worry that the gains women have made in the labour market are fragile, and it would take little to reverse recent progress. Others fear that rapid change has costs that we have not taken into account, and that women still bear a disproportionate burden. Basic income acts as a magnet for such fears because it can affect our decisions about whether and how much to work for pay.

Labour economists such as Barbara Bergmann recognize the gains women have made in the labour market over the past fifty years and worry that the labour force participation rate of women seems to be stalling at levels lower than their male counterparts, suggesting that full gender equality is still elusive.[2] Others argue that women's lives are about more than their jobs and gender equality involves more than pay scales and professional opportunities. A basic income, they argue, could help to eliminate the power differentials between men and women that still subject too many women to poverty and violence.[3] Nested in the middle of this debate is a concern about caregiving: in Canada, as elsewhere in this world, women provide most of the unpaid caregiving for children and the aged.[4] A basic income would compensate women for their work outside the market and provide the resources necessary to leave coercive personal relationships. But is the cost too high? Will a basic income encourage women to work less, and will this damage their lifetime earnings, their pension entitlements and their job achievements?[5]

Previous experiments can't contribute much to a discussion of gender today. The North American experiments took place during the 1970s — neolithic times insofar as gender relations are concerned. Middle-class mothers of preschoolers stayed at home except in the direst of financial circumstances, and even many school-aged children lived with stay-at-home mothers. Lone female parents were exceptional and usually the result of the early death of a spouse rather than divorce or unmarried parenthood. Male wages substantially exceeded female wages, so that even if a couple chose to make a "rational" decision about which one would work outside the home, there would be little to discuss. Similarly, generalizing from experiments in low- or middle-income countries with very different social expectations poses difficulties.

A basic income will have a profound effect on the lives of women just as it will transform the lives of men. However, different women will have distinct needs, expectations and experiences. There are immense differences among the experiences and opportunities of Canadian women, and understanding the impact of a basic income on women requires the use of enough imagination and empathy to recognize that education, culture, social class, ethnicity, race and geography matter at least as much as does gender. Basic income, however, works by offering people security and independence. While each will experience the effects of basic income differently, no adult can be made worse off by greater security and independence.

## Basic Income, Work Gaps and Lifetime Consequences across the Income Spectrum

In 2019, 83.6 per cent of working-age women were in the paid labour force (including 70 per cent of women with children less than three years old), compared with 91.3 per cent of men. Both adults reported income in 96 per cent of two-adult families. Only 50.7 per cent of husbands earned more than their wives, while 32 per cent of couples relied equally on the earnings of both spouses, and 17.3 per cent of wives earned more than their husbands. As recently as 1985, 71.3 per cent of husbands earned more than their wives.[6] The increased participation of women in the paid labour market is accompanied by a smaller increase in the participation of men in household tasks. In 1986, women provided 75 per cent of household labour; thirty years later, they still provided 61 per cent of household labour and 65 per cent of the hours spent caring for children.[7]

However, women have a variety of experiences inside and outside the workplace. Choosing to stay at home with a young child has different consequences for a single mother than for a married woman. Someone with only a high school diploma or less will face different consequences than someone with a graduate degree. Consider, first, the highly educated worker. According to Statistics Canada, approximately 300,000 mothers with a university degree who have children less than five years of age were not working for wages in 2017.[8] Of these, 200,000 were living with an adult partner. The decision to work or not to work depends on many factors, but the availability of good quality daycare is no doubt one of them.[9] Another is the existence of a high-earning partner to subsidize the family during a period out of work. Women who take time off work will consider the consequences of time outside the labour market, and these consequences will depend on the kind of job the mother might have held. For example:

Yang is a university professor. Time off from work means slower career progress in the form of delayed tenure and promotion. The delay of a single year in promotion can have a dramatic impact on lifetime earnings. A professor is likely to have access to a pension plan. Time out of the work force reduces pension accumulation. When Yang returns to work, she will face colleagues on her promotion committee who will examine her publication track record, and some of them will wonder why she didn't use her parental leave to write a book or attend a conference while caring for a young child with no salary and no institutional support. In any case, her promotion will be delayed until she publishes enough to meet the promotion criteria. However, professorial work has many benefits, including sabbaticals and the opportunity to negotiate unpaid leaves. Most professors have access to generous paid parental leave, although studies show that mothers who take parental leave have slower subsequent career progress while fathers who take parental leave seem to find the time to write books and articles that enhance their careers.[10] Professors have more control over their time than do many workers. Most universities have daycare centres that prioritize staff and students; daycare might be costly, but it is an investment. A professor facing the decision about whether to continue to work or take time off to care for young children is in a very privileged position relative to most women, and few would argue that she is not capable of considering the consequences and making an informed decision.

Tooba, by contrast, is an associate at a top law firm. She is gunning for partner but finds the hours she is expected to bill incompatible with her child care responsibilities. If she leaves the workforce, even for a short period, she will be penalized in terms of her career prospects when she tries to return. If she looks around for other opportunities, she will find that some legal jobs are far less demanding than the one she holds. She may well decide to take a salaried job in a corporation, or to become a professor at a law school or to otherwise move to the "mommy track" that affords her lower career horizons. Her lifetime income will be much lower than it might have been had she stayed at her previous job, as will her retirement savings. Her family life would certainly be less stressful. The decision she will make is not obvious, and it is certainly a conflicted choice for many women. However, few would argue that this woman is incapable of making an informed decision.

Lindsay is an administrator in a firm. Her diploma affords her a reasonable salary and good benefits. Government and firm-level parental benefits offer her generous leave when her child is born, and her employer offers a few days each year for health and family care responsibilities. The cost of daycare may be significant and cause her to reconsider her job at times. If she does choose to leave her job, she is confident that her documented skills and good references will find her a new job when her child is a few years older. After all, many women work in this kind of job, and parental decisions, stressful as they are for individual families, are a well-understood part of career progress. Time off work with a young child will have an impact on her lifetime earnings and ultimately her pension, but she faces a fairly flat career path. Not many people become vice-president, so delayed promotions will matter less to her than to some women in different kinds of jobs. Again, there is no reason to assume that she is incapable of considering the consequences and making a decision.

These three well-educated women might make different decisions about continuing to work when their children are young because their careers are very different from one another. Their personal lives might also be quite different. An educated mother with a similarly well-educated partner has additional support both for the direct work of parenting and in financial terms. A university degree is no guarantee of economic well-being, but most married women with university degrees will be living with a partner who also has a good salary.[11] Whether she takes time off work to stay home with a young child or not, her decision will not be affected by basic income because her family income will be too high to qualify. The decisions these families make will depend on how each partner values his or her work, their relative wages and job circumstances, and the particular value that each partner places on the opportunity to spend more time with a young child. Either parent might decide to spend more time with a young child, and, depending on particular circumstances, either parent might have greater flexibility on the job or face fewer costs associated with time off work.

One thing that we can be fairly certain about is that a basic income will have little impact on the decisions of these highly educated women.

Now, think about Chantal. She doesn't have a university degree or even a college diploma. Nevertheless, she has a good job at a manufacturing plant with a moderate salary and a union to negotiate benefits. Again, her parental benefits will allow her a long leave when her baby is born and adequate time off for family issues. Daycare will be a concern; is high-quality daycare at reasonable prices available? She has no partner to share child care responsibilities. Depending on the availability of child care, she might decide to stay home with her child or to continue to work. If she stays home, her future prospects are not likely to be much affected. During her period at home, she will benefit from the basic income. When she decides to go back to work, her future income and job prospects will not be much affected by the gap in her résumé.

Finally, imagine Darlene's life as a minimum-wage worker. Her job is not professional; it is not even full-time. She works two jobs with unpredictable hours, and, in the absence of a union, she has no access to generous leave policies or other benefits. She may or may not qualify for parental leave from Employment Insurance when her child is born; much depends on how many work hours she can get in the coming months. If she chooses to work, she will leave a very young infant to work at a job in which the hours do not coincide with those of most daycare centres. She might be forced to use private daycare, the quality of which varies. She has a partner, but he does not earn much more than she does, and his hours are equally unpredictable. If she were offered a basic income, she might well decide to stay at home. She would be better off financially than she would be in a minimum-wage job that requires her to pay for daycare. When her child goes to school, and she goes back to work, the gap in her work history will not hurt her prospects. She was not headed to the corner office before she decided to take time off work, and she is not likely to get there afterwards.

If we consider the variety of women's experiences in the labour market, it becomes clear that some women in all wage categories will decide to stay home with young children. For a high-waged woman, the deciding factor is likely to be the nature of the job, which will determine the personal consequences of her time away from work. If the personal costs are high and the job flexible, as in the case of a professor, she is not likely to take time off work. If the personal costs are high but the job inflexible, like the lawyer, she might decide that a work gap is worth the risk. If the personal costs are low, she might or might not take time off work depending on the nature of the job and the availability of daycare. For low-income women, the stakes and the consequences are different. It is, however, abundantly clear that each of these women is quite capable of making the decision that works best for her and her family. They do not need to be coerced or "incentivized." A basic income offers some women more opportunity to make decisions that they could not afford to make without a basic income. Choice is valuable.

## Gender, Unpaid Work and the Power Gap

Gender equality is about more than earnings capacity. It is about the ability of women to make their needs known in the halls of power and to assert their authority and wisdom in business and government. It is also about sharing equitably the unpaid care work that helps society to function. Many have speculated about how a basic income might affect the gender norms that govern society.[12] The division of labour, both paid and unpaid, between men and women is governed by a variety of factors including simple biology, the complex set of social norms that have evolved over centuries and the specific policy context in which decisions are made. It would be unreasonable to expect any single policy, including basic income, to bring about profound changes in gender relations on its own. However, gender norms do change, and they sometimes change very rapidly.

Some tasks will always fall to women as long as women continue to give birth. The actual physical labour of birth itself will always interrupt women's careers. This, however, is much less significant than decisions made within the family and within society about how to care for infants. The assumption that a mother's care is necessary in the early months and years of life is based not only on gender norms, but also on whether society organizes itself to make available appropriate parental leave and child care at reasonable prices to share the task of raising infants with new mothers. Among couples who choose to have one parent stay at home, there are economic benefits for the highest earner to continue working for pay. While the proportion of wives who out-earn their husbands is growing rapidly, most male parents still earn more than female parents.[13] Among single parents, the decision about whether to work depends less on power dynamics and social norms than it does on the range of social policies available, including affordable daycare and income replacement.

A basic income alone will not change the world. However, there are ways to deliver a basic income that help to equalize power relationships in society and within the family. Even if a basic income is calculated on the basis of total family income, the lower-earning spouse might be the one who receives the money. This is a common decision in Canadian social policy that began with federal family allowances in the post-war period and continued through various forms of child benefits. The extent to which basic income can actually offset complex power differentials is debatable, but the knowledge that for at least one day a month, there will be income available to a person with no other dependable source of income is profound.

Gender roles evolve over a lifetime. Much attention has been paid to mothers of young children, particularly single mothers, and rightly so because the poverty rate among this group of Canadians is substantial. In 2018, 26.2 per cent of children under eighteen living with a single parent lived in poverty.[14] The Canada Child Benefit has been responsible for a significant decline in child poverty, but the reality is that income assistance rates are simply too low to allow single mothers to raise their children. By contrast, children living with both parents do much better. Only 5.8 per cent of children under eighteen living with two adults lived in poverty. Clearly a basic income would help parents, especially single parents, with young children.

However, children eventually grow up, and most of the mothers who do not work when their children are preschoolers do enter the labour force and become wage-earners and taxpayers. But there are many reasons a woman might leave the labour force again, even after her children are grown. She might be called upon to provide care for an infirm spouse or parent, or a grown child or grandchild with health issues might need assistance beyond that available through public programs. Women's careers have been marked by more and longer periods out of the labour force than have men's careers, and only some of these gaps relate to childbirth.[15]

Many adults are dependent on the earnings of a partner to share the cost of living. An adult who lives alone faces a substantial risk of poverty; 31.5 per cent of adults under sixty-five who lived alone in 2019 lived in poverty. Among seniors, the poverty rate was 7.9 per cent for singles, but seniors living with a partner faced the lowest poverty rate of any family type — 1.7 per cent — thanks to the Old

Age Security pension and the Guaranteed Income Supplement.[16] The decision to adjust the Guaranteed Income Supplement and tie it to the cost of living has reduced the poverty rate among single adults over age sixty-five and reinforced the benefits of an adequate, dependable source of income.

## A Basic Income Is a Source of Autonomy and Respect

Money plays many roles in society, but one of its most important features is that it is a source of autonomy and power. The autonomy is obvious: an individual with money can buy exactly what she wants, when she wants it and from whomever she likes. She can go to Whole Foods or the local farmers' market, or she can shop at Price Chopper or the local corner store. She can buy organic carrots, milk, candy or even cigarettes. She may decide to divert a little of the budget to buy nail polish for three dollars at Dollarama. An independent woman can spend her money exactly as she likes. It is a matter of autonomy not to be told, implicitly or explicitly, that she does not have enough sense to know when she can afford to buy her son hot chocolate at Tim Hortons, or whether a new pair of tights for a job interview might be more important. It is her money, and her decision.

The power associated with a basic income might be a bit less obvious. An individual with an adequate, secure and predictable income can make decisions that someone without such an income might find difficult. Several years ago, when I first began working with low-income women, I was astonished at how quickly any conversation about provincial income assistance turned to the fear of having their children taken into care. I think many of us imagine that the reasons for child apprehension — abuse and neglect — are somehow independent of our income, and we can all remember or point to wonderful parents who raised successful children on very limited means. However, if you followed for a day a single mother of young children who receives income assistance and asked her to describe the decisions she is making, the connection between poverty and powerlessness would become much clearer.

One example of the poor parental decision making that can draw the attention of authorities is leaving children unsupervised. How could a mother leave preschoolers at home alone? Suppose you have two children in diapers, and the laundromat is on the corner. If they were napping, would you leave for ten minutes to take a load out of the washing machine and put it in the dryer? Or would you wait for them to wake up, put on their snowsuits and walk them down the street, trying to keep them safe and supervised while dealing with the laundry? For parents with a partner, an apartment with a washing machine or the money to pay a babysitter, the issue would never arise. How old is old enough to babysit? Would you leave them for twenty minutes with an older child? A ten-year-old? How about a seven-year-old, when you know that seven-year-old regularly walks to and from school alone, crossing busy streets and negotiating a challenging neighbourhood? (And if you are the mother of that seven-year-old, you may be in trouble on that account, as well.)

It is not always bad decisions that draw attention to the well-being of children. Your children, like my children, do silly things. They fall down and bruise themselves; they get into fights with one another. They fall off bikes and end up with bandages. Most teachers and principals know that children get banged up and never think to question the reported source of the injury. If your children also go to school when they have colds, runny noses and earaches because you have to work, it will be remembered. If you do not attend parent-teacher meetings because you are working odd hours, or perhaps because you are uncomfortable with the authority structures in schools, that too will be remembered. All of these things, and a hundred others, can tip the balance and induce a well-meaning school employee to call the child welfare system. Or perhaps it is your mother or a neighbour who calls the authorities after an argument.

You might be investigated, and the case closed, but you now have a file. Perhaps they want to help you. They recommend parenting classes, but you miss a few because of your shifts or because you could not find an adult friend to stay with your kids. Or you live in a neighbourhood with poor public transportation. Or you do not like the facilitator who seems to know little about the world in which you live, or you bring a bit of attitude because you believe yourself to be a good mother, or you are just too tired to go. That doesn't look good.

Or perhaps you do neglect or abuse your child. Most of us cringe when we remember some of the things we have or have not done while raising our children, and we hope they forgive us. For most of us, their forgiveness is all that is required, but for a mother on income assistance who has come to the attention of the authorities, many more questions are asked. Do you smoke when your children are at home? Do you use drugs? Drink? Where do you get the money for cigarettes and alcohol? Is there food in the fridge? Are you feeding your kids properly? Are you reporting your income accurately to the authorities each month? How many nights a week does your romantic partner stay at your apartment? At this point, two systems might come into play. You will be asked to provide additional information to the welfare authorities and, if you ignore or postpone responses, your already inadequate income might be reduced or delayed.

Suppose the worst happens, and your children are taken into care. The authorities are committed to reuniting families, so they will give you a series of tasks to perform to improve your parenting skills and demonstrate your capacity to care for your kids. Your children might visit you if there are volunteers to provide rides. If not, visits might be cancelled with no notice even though you may have re-scheduled shifts to be available. Or you can visit your children — if you can arrange time off work and a ride. If your children are confused by the situation and cry, you might feel bad and decide not to visit the following week. That is a mistake; it shows inadequate commitment on your part. And your attitude is important; if you have the wrong attitude people will draw conclusions about your parenting skills. Then there are other implications. When your children are in care, your income assistance is reduced, and your Canada Child Benefit stops. Of course, this is only reasonable because foster parents are taking on the financial burden of raising your children. Except that when your income falls, you can no longer afford your apartment, which makes it more difficult to demonstrate that you could care adequately for your children if they were returned. The income assistance provided to single adults is pitifully inadequate. A temporary care order can quickly escalate.

Mothers who rely on income assistance do not have the luxury of being bad parents or even having a really bad week. There are bad parents in all income classes, and every parent has been a bad parent at some point, but most of us are insulated from relentless supervision because we have a secure, adequate and predictable income. Money is power, and not just for the plutocrats who run the world. An adequate, secure income is an almost inconceivable source of power for a poor mother.

## Violence And Women[17]

*The Final Report of the National Inquiry into Missing and Murdered Indigenous Women and Girls* recommended a guaranteed livable income. This is a hard report to read, and even harder for those of us who are not Indigenous to really understand, but it is essential that we try to do so. From my limited perspective, it seems that the stories shared with the commissioners all revolve around poverty. Women were working in unsafe jobs and living in unsafe housing because they didn't have the resources to do otherwise. Women took rides from strangers along notoriously dangerous highways because there was no public transportation. Toxic relationships were sometimes tolerated for far too long because women lacked the financial ability to leave, or because abuse and disrespect were so routine in their lives that it had become normalized. Poverty was the handmaiden of violence.

However, the narratives of the witnesses made it clear that violence is not just a random act perpetrated on a physically vulnerable person by someone stronger. The very systems that we put in place to help people can sometimes be a source of systemic violence. There are, for example, many ways to address poverty besides a basic income. Governments could provide public transportation and fund shelters more generously for victims of intimate partner violence. They could subsidize job training programs and offer guaranteed services rather than a guaranteed income to women who need support. They could simply increase income assistance rates under existing programs. Why did the commissioners call for a guaranteed livable income? We can use the example of Canadian health care, a program of which Canadians are justifiably proud, and recognize that the best of intentions don't always lead to equitable outcomes. Indigenous health lags far behind that of non-Indigenous Canadians, at least in part because the delivery of the service has been designed by non-Indigenous people according to the values of the dominant culture. As a consequence, Indigenous people sometimes feel unwelcome and do not benefit as much as they might from the service. Our own research with Indigenous health researchers in Manitoba demonstrates that health improves in First Nations communities when local communities have greater control.[18]

Similar issues have emerged when Indigenous women or newcomers are offered "job-readiness" classes or parenting classes designed according to the norms of the dominant culture. These classes can be perceived as judgments about how people choose to live their lives; they can be stigmatizing. This, too, is a form of cultural violence. Offering poverty relief only in the form of services rather than income sometimes requires people to give up important parts of themselves and their culture to access help. Services that can be accessed on a voluntary basis by people who want them are important, but income that people can spend as they like is at least as important.

A guaranteed livable income — a basic income — would give all women the freedom to make their own decisions. These decisions and the values that shape them might not be consistent with those of the mainstream culture. Money is not judgmental. It is freedom.

## Basic Income and the Multiplicity of Female Experiences

Basic income would not change gender norms overnight. It would not eliminate intimate partner violence (although it might provide the means for someone to leave an unhappy relationship). It would not even, in itself, encourage more men to take on unpaid caregiving tasks, at least not as long as enough women are still prepared to do them. Some women still fare badly enough in the labour market that taking an unpaid sabbatical to do something else seems a reasonable option. On the other hand, basic income would also not cause mass female flight from the paid job market. It would, however, provide many Canadian women with a secure, adequate and predictable income that is not subject to the discretion of caseworkers. This simple change would empower women (and men) in ways that are almost unimaginable to people who have always had adequate resources.

Not all women are white, highly paid professionals for whom the price of housing in Toronto or Vancouver and the cost of daycare are the most pressing concerns they face. For these privileged women, any gap in work history will have lifelong consequences in terms of earnings, pensions and career advancement. There is no question that these women work hard, struggle with work-life balance and probably daydream about not having to work. They are certain that daycare subsidies are a more important expenditure than basic income, because they can see how it would improve their lives. They imagine that a basic income would create an incentive for similar women to leave the workforce, and they worry about losing the progress that women have made. However, the reality is that basic income would be irrelevant to such women. If they are single, they would not leave behind a high salary to live on the amount of money provided by any feasible basic income; if they have a partner, it is almost certain that their family income would be too high for them to qualify anyway.

The only women for whom basic income may create an incentive to leave the labour market are low-wage workers. Some would be better off financially not working than they would be working, especially when they take child care into consideration. How is the world better off if a woman pays someone else to care for her children while she struggles at a low-paid job? Staying home for a few years with young children would not have an appreciable impact on the lifetime earnings, pensions or career progress of low-wage women. Insecure low-wage work will always exist, and when unskilled women re-enter the workforce after their children grow up, they would not be worse off than if they had continued to work. A few years more or less experience will not change the probability of significant career progress. However, a basic income would give her the capacity to train for better work that enhances her opportunities.

A basic income is particularly important for women dealing with the consequences of trauma, perhaps intergenerational trauma, and racism. Job-readiness or parental skills classes, designed by well-meaning people to help women who need assistance, are wonderful opportunities as long as the decision to use such services is voluntary. When, however, financial support is tied to such services and a woman must show "progress" according to a set of norms that have little to do with her life or cultural background, it is just another source of violence in the lives of women who have seen too much violence already.

A basic income would not undermine women or reverse the gains that we have made in recent years. However, women who have not shared the labour market gains some celebrate would gain a great deal. A basic income is good for women.

# Chapter 7

# How Basic Income Affects Different People

The pandemic didn't play fair. People who were already struggling before the economic shutdown bore the brunt of the shock. While some people self-isolated at their cottages or worked from home, others continued to work at jobs providing essential services. Some bought games and music to entertain their kids at home, while others shared a work laptop in a crowded apartment with kids trying to connect to classrooms online. People with disabilities, people living on the streets and people who relied on provincial income assistance received no emergency support from the federal government during the lockdown, even though the food pantries, shelters and other agencies they relied on struggled to stay open with fewer volunteers. The first jobs to disappear were the last to call back workers when the economy began to reopen, and some of the jobs never came back. COVID-19 cast income inequality into stark relief, and it also forced us to recognize how race, gender, class and age affect the different ways in which we all experience the world.

Government programs affect different people in different ways. While all of us would benefit from the existence of a basic income that reduces the risk of income insecurity, there are particular issues that are important to some groups of people. Some people face higher-than-usual risks of low income: people with disabilities, women, Indigenous people, single mothers, youth aging out of foster care, people aged forty-five through sixty-four who live alone, young people, queer people and recent immigrants. As a consequence, these groups of people would benefit from any program that effectively reduces poverty. Basic income, however, may have additional effects for some of these groups that should be carefully considered.

Basic income redistributes income. It can offset, at least in part, the financial consequences of social inequality, but it cannot address, on its own, the deep divisions that persist in our society. Basic income will not eliminate systemic injustices like racism or sexism, nor is it reasonable to expect it to. It will not reverse a legacy of colonialism experienced by Indigenous people. Basic income does not prevent or excuse anyone from working towards greater equity. It does, however, make the lives of those living with the consequences of systemic inequities more bearable and give them breathing room to address the underlying issues.

It goes without saying that no one is just a person with a disability, or just a newcomer to Canada, or just a woman. Every one of us wears many labels, some more apparent than others. Racialized women face different stresses and opportunities than do white women; and Indigenous men with mobility challenges who live in remote communities face different challenges than do newcomers to Canada with invisible disabilities. Gender-nonconforming youth aging out of foster care will have different lives than undergraduates living with their parents in middle-class suburbs. Basic income will benefit every one of us in different ways. For some of us, its advantages will be much more immediate; for others, it represents a sense of safety that lives at the back of our mind and gives us the courage to take a risk. For all of us, basic income raises particular issues that we need to think about before the policy rolls out system wide.

## Indigenous People

Almost 5 per cent of the Canadian population identify as Indigenous — Métis, First Nations, non-Status or Inuit. Canada does not routinely collect detailed data on income by race, but the Census, conducted once every five years, does allow us to compare outcomes. According to the 2016 Census, Indigenous people in Canada had a low-income rate of 23.6 per cent, compared to 13.8 per cent for non-Indigenous people.[1] The poverty rate for Indigenous children was twice as high as for non-Indigenous children. The average total income of an Indigenous person in Canada was 75 per cent that of a non-Indigenous person. The average total income for a First Nations person was $31,519 — 66 per cent of that received by a non-Indigenous person.[2] On the basis of the numbers alone, Indigenous people and especially First Nations people would, on average, gain from a basic income because they are more likely to be living with low incomes.

For Indigenous people living off reserve, the consequences of a basic income will be much the same as they are for other Canadians. Basic income provides insurance against income insecurity, as well as a few extra dollars for those living on low incomes. It provides a cushion to allow people to think about training for new jobs or to start new businesses. When we consider people living in Indigenous communities, however, there are two issues that require special consideration. First, Indigenous people have the right to be involved in the creation of policies that will affect their communities. Second, many Indigenous communities are in rural and remote locations, which affects the impact of basic income.

In the wake of the Truth and Reconciliation Commission, any policy affecting Indigenous people must be developed in collaboration with First Nations, Inuit and Métis leaders. Indigenous people have their own sovereign authorities. Consultation with these authorities would be no less, and no more, complex than negotiations between provinces and the federal government, or negotiations required for any other national policy. Basic income offers an opportunity to test our commitment to the hard work of real reconciliation, which, in this case, should leave open the possibility for Indigenous leaders to decide that a basic income is not appropriate for their communities or that basic income, on reserve, should work in different ways than it does elsewhere. We consider these issues further in Chapter 10.

One issue that might be relevant to the negotiation is the philosophical justification for a basic income. I have treated basic income as a simple income redistribution policy and made no attempt to justify it beyond the desire to reduce income insecurity. However, basic income can be thought of as a dividend payable to residents for the use of the original resources of the land. These resources have resulted in economic growth that has benefited some people more than others. Alaska's Permanent Fund, for example, pays all residents an annual dividend funded by the revenue from oil sales.[3] This is an interesting model with obvious relevance for Indigenous people; it seems to embody the original intention behind Treaty Payments, which are now mostly ceremonial.

Whatever the outcome of the deliberations, a basic income is not a substitute for other programs designed to deliver needed housing, health care, education and food security to Indigenous communities, many of which are in isolated locations. One of the consequences of isolation is that necessary goods, like food, are often only available at great expense because of shipping costs. Heating and household maintenance are very expensive due to the extreme weather of many locations. Transportation, particularly transportation to major urban centres, is often simply unavailable. Rural bus service is extremely limited in most parts of the country and roads might not exist or exist only in some seasons. Northern airfares on scheduled routes cost much more than urban Canadians pay to travel to Asia or Australia, and airports are often far from where people live, which adds to the cost of a trip to the city.

The cost of living in isolated parts of Canada makes clear one characteristic of a basic income program: basic income alone cannot solve all issues related to poverty. Basic income relies on the premise that individuals can buy the goods and services they want to buy, but a cheque from the government will not help a great deal when markets do not exist or do not work well. Food security will not be enhanced by giving northern residents the same basic income that someone in Scarborough receives then directing them to a market that charges twenty-five dollars for four litres of milk — if it is available at all. Housing security will not exist when there is no rental market for housing. This is an issue confronting all universal programs in Canada. It would be extremely complex and not particularly effective to adjust national programs like the Old Age Security pension and the Canada Child Benefit to take account of regional costs of living. Nor should we adjust the basic income. More reasonably, we could recognize that people (both Indigenous and non-Indigenous) living in remote conditions require additional support along with a basic income.

Many Indigenous communities lack the infrastructure that we take for granted in high-income industrialized nations. A basic income cannot substitute for access to clean water and decent wastewater arrangements. A basic income will do little to ensure access to education if the local school is closed because of structural issues or black mould. Access to health care will be limited, even in non-remote locations, if public transportation to larger cities is inadequate, and residents must rely on medical referrals with restricted access. A basic income will only work if it is built on the good public infrastructure that we should be able to provide universally in a high-income country: the existence of clean water, access to health care, public transportation, and functioning markets with access to affordable housing and good-quality food at prices comparable to those paid elsewhere in the country. A basic income provided to people living on reserve is no substitute for basic infrastructure. The two would work in tandem, supporting a decent quality of life comparable to that enjoyed by people living elsewhere in the country.

## Racialized People

People who identify as non-white in Canada have, on average, lower incomes than do white Canadians, and this population is growing. According to the 2016 Census, non-white Canadians made up 22.7 per cent of the population and received, on average, incomes that were 74 per cent of those received by white Canadians, a number that has remained virtually unchanged over the past decade. The low-income rate among non-white Canadians was 20.8 per cent, compared with 12.2 per cent for white Canadians.[4] It is easy to be unaware of the ways that people of different races or ethnicities experience life in Canada because so few of our systems are set up to record race. Just as our income data does not routinely record race, except in the Census, the data compiled by our health administration systems does not include data on race. This has led some of us to complacency — a belief that if we think race doesn't matter, then it doesn't. With the exception of new immigrants, who might face a period of hardship as they settle in, or perhaps Indigenous people who have faced generations of bad policy, we like to think that all other Canadians have equal access to the opportunities they need to succeed.

Race, like gender, remains an important barrier to economic well-being. Because Canadians of colour are, on average, more likely to earn low incomes, face job precarity and suffer from poverty, they would also benefit disproportionately from a basic income. Basic income cannot address the fundamental challenges posed by race and ethnicity in Canada, but it can offset some of the economic consequences and provide a platform that helps people to seize opportunities that may have been out of reach.

## Young People at the Beginning of Their Working Lives

Many young people remain financially and emotionally dependent on their parents well into their twenties. Decisions to stay in school longer and delay marriage and parenthood have changed popular perceptions of when adolescence ends, and adulthood begins. Some experts in pediatric medicine and child development have argued that changing the definition of adolescence to include those up to twenty-four years of age might lead to more "developmentally appropriate" framing of laws, social policies and systems.[5]

Like every other group of people, youth aged eighteen through twenty-four are not homogeneous. Some are fully independent, supporting themselves in the workplace. Others are on their own and not faring nearly so well. Youth experiencing poverty have different developmental needs than adults. They are learning to be independent and often take more risks than adults. They are less likely to make use of formal services, and often rely instead on the informal help of friends and acquaintances. They are vulnerable to exploitation and often have significant government involvement in their lives. The 2018 Winnipeg Street Census, for example, reported that of those experiencing homelessness in Winnipeg, half had had some involvement in the child welfare system. Moreover, the majority, 63 per cent, first experienced homelessness at eighteen years old. Gender diverse youth were particularly vulnerable.[6]

Young people who turn eighteen with few skills, no resources and no parents to fall back on do require a program to alleviate poverty and help ease their transition into adulthood. It is not clear whether an unconditional program such as a basic income or a program with some constraints and conditions would better meet the needs of these young people. Basic income rests on the premise that adults have the right to make their own decisions, and to bear the consequences of those decisions. We wouldn't offer a five-year-old basic income for obvious reasons and all societies have the equivalent of a public trustee to oversee decisions made on behalf of adults who are not competent to care for themselves. It is reasonable to ask at what age an acceptable proportion of the population has the foresight to understand the consequences of their decisions.

Youth just entering the labour market have little work experience and do not generally command high wages. This is, for most people, a temporary situation. Thoughtful and mature young people might choose to use a basic income to supplement earned income while working to gain experience, becoming involved in education or even travelling to learn something about the world and about themselves. Basic income would also give a young person the opportunity to choose among employment opportunities to ensure that the work they take on will actually contribute to their skills and pay off over time. In a sense, what a basic income can do for young people is to level the playing field; many people from middle- and high-income families have always had the opportunity to work part-time or in low-paid jobs or to take on volunteer tasks to build their résumés while relying on their parents to subsidize them. Some choose to combine work with education or travel. Most parents who subsidize these activities for their own children believe they will pay off in the longer run, and it is reasonable to assume that other young people could also benefit from similar opportunities.

However, as many parents and most teachers will attest, not all young people are mature enough to make good decisions. Gaining self-knowledge and experience, through work or travel or volunteer activities, can pay off in terms of better employability and higher wages later in life, but long periods of time without useful engagement can have negative consequences. This is known as labour scarring. Young people without work quickly forget the specific skills they might have learned with previous employers as well as general skills associated with working for a living, and the effects can persist far into adulthood. This deterioration of skills is associated with lower employability and lower wages over the long run. The negative effects are compounded if future employers perceive periods of unemployment at a young age to be indicators of lower productivity or poor work habits, or if the psychological effects of youth unemployment affect confidence and people skills. Unemployment in youth that is not offset with training or other educational activities is associated with lower wages and bouts of unemployment in adulthood.[7]

Some people of all ages can make very poor decisions if they are given the freedom to do so. Adults who harm no one but themselves should be free to make their own decisions without the oversight of a committee of experts who believe they know better. This is the fundamental advantage of a basic income over existing income-assistance programs in which caseworkers can intervene to "help" adults who do not want to be helped. The freedom to make bad decisions, however, is usually limited to adults.

We do have some evidence that people aged eighteen through twenty-four might benefit from programs that have explicit work, education or engagement requirements. While such programs really haven't shown positive effects for the population at large, and in fact seemed counterproductive in the basic income experiments conducted in Finland and Utrecht, we have a recent Canadian pilot that suggests that young people might benefit.[8] In 2018, an evaluation was published of the income assistance programs delivered on reserve in Canada.[9] One of the initiatives that was lauded as a great success was a specific pilot program aimed at on-reserve youth aged eighteen through twenty-four, which made income assistance conditional on meeting a clear set of expectations with respect to school or job training, job search or other community engagement, and also offered supports such as wage subsidies, child care and active case management. The pilot included one hundred communities, and 11,000 youth. In the year before the program was introduced, only 7 per cent of youth became independent of income assistance, while 29 per cent became independent in the year after funding was introduced. This suggests that youth, at least, can benefit from labour market activation programs that have not uniformly been shown to be effective for older adults.[10]

Determining the age at which a reasonable majority of people show the capacity to make rational decisions is also something that a well-designed experiment could help us do. For this particular group, support may well require conditions such as job search, or hours contributed to education, training or approved volunteer activity.

## Newcomers to Canada

In the 2016 Census, there were 1.2 million immigrants (3.5 per cent of the total Canadian population) who had arrived within the previous five years. Their low-income rate was 31.4 per cent, and the average total income of a recent immigrant was 63 per cent that of a non-immigrant.[11] For most immigrants, this is a temporary situation and their incomes increase as they settle in and gain Canadian experience. Some groups, particularly refugees, take longer to adjust than others. Should newcomers to Canada be eligible to receive a basic income?

Accidents of history and geography allow Canada to have reasonably good control over its borders. Recent increases in refugee claimants who arrived through non-traditional channels have attracted a lot of attention, but the numbers are small enough that we can easily absorb these newcomers along with regular immigrants and refugees and, as our history has shown us, benefit from the energy and productivity they bring to Canada over the long run. Few Canadians see newcomers as a threat to the feasibility of basic income. Offering newcomers enough to live on while they establish themselves is a good investment.

## People with Disabilities

Many people live with physical or mental impairments, but not all impairments are disabilities. Impairment only becomes a disability when a person's social and physical environment does not meet their needs, making it more difficult for them to perform daily activities. Past studies have consistently shown that people with disabilities are less likely to be employed or to have a university education; they have lower median incomes overall and are more likely to live in low income.[12] Fewer than half of Canadians with disabilities are employed at all. A Statistics Canada study found that approximately 20 per cent of the population aged twenty-five through sixty-four lived with a disability in 2014, and of these, 23 per cent were in low income, compared with 9 per cent of those without a disability. The low-income rate varied by disability type, with those suffering both mental-cognitive and physical impairments most likely to be affected. People with a disability aged forty-five to sixty-four who lived alone and single parents with a disability accounted for nearly a quarter of the total low-income population in 2014.[13] In 2010, a study by the Caledon Institute of Social Policy called for a basic income plan for Canadians with severe disabilities.[14] While many disability rights activists support basic income, others worry that a basic income might be used as a substitute for services designed specifically to meet the personal and unique needs of people with disabilities. The threat of losing direct services is actually greater under existing arrangements than it would be with a basic income.

Some people with disabilities face additional costs associated with their disability.[15] These costs fall into two categories: specific costs and general costs. Specific additional costs are for pharmaceuticals and adaptive devices such as wheelchairs and hearing aids. Arrangements differ by province, but these are normally paid for by provincial insurance for those people who receive provincial disability support. General costs are not covered by any insurance plan and vary dramatically between individuals. Such costs might include, for example, higher rent for an apartment with an elevator or located close to shops and services.

Under existing arrangements, most provinces tie support for specific needs associated with disabilities to provincial disability support programs. As a consequence, someone with a disability who does not work and receives provincial disability support has access to additional services and funding to meet the extra costs for such devices as hearing aids or wheelchairs, as well as pharmaceutical and dental coverage. Someone with a disability who is in the workforce might live on an income no higher than someone receiving provincial assistance, but not be eligible for these services because they are tied to income support programs. This is a particularly inefficient and unfair arrangement that makes it difficult for people with disabilities to participate in the workforce because they fear losing the benefits they need. The design of current programs impedes the opportunity for people with disabilities to participate more fully in the workforce or even to become self-employed. There is always a fear that, should they be too successful, they will lose all the direct support they need.

There is a very simple way to fix this problem, modelled on the way that Manitoba and Saskatchewan offer pharmaceutical coverage to their residents. Programs to cover specific costs associated with a disability might be opened to everyone on the basis of the level of their income, so that working people earning exactly the same annual income as someone receiving provincial disability support would receive exactly the same support for their additional costs. Co-payments would increase as income increases. This change would eliminate the welfare wall that currently exists for those who receive provincial disability support. A well-designed basic income would adopt this approach of separating the provision of direct services from the receipt of income support. They are two entirely different needs and should be addressed by two entirely different programs.

> I would like to say that the program is called "Ontario Disability SUPPORT Program." What support do I receive? The best thing I can say about it is that it pays for most of my drugs. Without that support, my family would be beyond broke. — Amanda

General disability-related costs are more difficult to assess. For many people, there are none. For a very few, the costs are prohibitive. For this very small proportion of the population with heavy disability-related needs, there must be some provincial capacity to assess needs and to devise personalized support. It is futile to try to attach an additional "disability payment" to a basic income in hope that it will meet all needs.

A basic income would, however, meet the needs of most people with disabilities. If the basic income program made no distinction between people with disabilities and those without, there would be an additional benefit. No one would have to qualify for support beyond demonstrating financial need. The qualification process is a source of frustration and despair for many.

> I am 34 years old and I have epilepsy. Kira is my seizure response dog. I was finally approved for ODSP [the Ontario Disability Support Program]. How low do you want a person to feel? It is a system that needs to change. They dig really deep into your personal life to see if you qualify, and then review it as if your disability is going to go away. I receive $928 a month, which includes an allowance of $78 for my service dog. — Amanda

The documentation of disability is not simple. Impairments exist along a spectrum, but under existing programs, a decision must be made about when an impairment becomes a disability and therefore eligible for support. An individual applying for support must present documentation from a medical practitioner who is asked to provide medical data and to document the extent to which the impairment interferes with the activities of daily living and the applicant's ability to work or attend school. Often, the outcome depends as much on the skill of the clinician completing the forms as on any objective assessment of disability. It is not unusual to apply several times before succeeding. This process creates two sets of casualties. Those who are ultimately successful, like Amanda, read the clinical assessment and walk away convinced that their future will be bleak.

Those who are not successful often find themselves ineligible for support and yet unable to find and hold a job. People suffering from mental health and invisible disabilities are particularly vulnerable to disqualification.

Some advocates insist that case management is essential for people with disabilities, imagining a situation of malfunctioning wheelchairs and other unmet needs with no bureaucrat assigned to ensure that an individual's needs are met. One of the most debilitating fictions about income assistance and disability support is that recipients are incapable of planning, incapable of making good decisions and incapable of caring for themselves without the assistance of caseworkers. In some instances, the most important benefit of a caseworker is to work through a maze of confusing regulations and bureaucratic dysfunction that ought not to exist in the first place. That is, the poor design of the income assistance or disability support program itself generates the need for a caseworker.

I have had issues with ODSP in different ways.

First off I have had about three or four caseworkers and this was not by choice, they just bumped me to someone else without telling me.

I bring in my forms, appointment cards, cover letter, list of transportation and my form they give me to fill out and get them date stamped. Excuse my language but I can't tell you the number of times because it was happening so frequently the shitload of letters I got saying they didn't receive my forms! I started calling with copies of the info I have and stated back to them "well I have a copy date stamped from the office saying that the papers were delivered on — and I personally handed them in so I know they were delivered."

I have also been on the Rent-Geared-to-Income Housing list for twelve years. I understand that everyone needs a place to live and right now I have that with my parents. However, not being able to live on my own does in a way deprive me of a chance at independence.

ODSP does cover medical things. However, they don't tell you everything that is covered so unless you set up a meeting with your caseworker you might not know that orthotics are covered. We only found that out by overhearing someone at the desk and somewhere on the form it asks if you are on ODSP.

I think having a caseworker may be a good thing in the long run, I just wish it was consistent and that they gave you a solid list of medical benefits and coverage in a hard copy so that you aren't searching for hours to find an answer. You can only search so far on their website. Mom only knows some stuff by being part of an online ODSP support group. — Amanda

Would a basic income that offered clearer entitlements and fewer opportunities for discretionary decision making still require caseworkers to provide "wraparound care" for everyone — whether they wanted it or not? One of the best reasons for a basic income is that it respects the decision-making capacity of ordinary people.

People with disabilities would benefit from a basic income, as long as a system is in place to assess the special needs of the very small group of people who face prohibitive costs associated with their disability. All provinces have public trustees to assist people deemed not competent to make their own decisions. Most programs can manage special cases and catastrophic costs. It is unreasonable to imagine that a basic income program could not.

## People Who Use Substances

Most people who would receive a basic income in Canada are people who just need a bit more money to feed their kids and pay their rent. The "root cause" of their poverty is that their incomes are too low to meet their needs. People who use drugs are not the representative recipient of basic income. Nevertheless, addiction is a real issue for many people, and the relationship between poverty and substance use is complex. Would a basic income encourage substance use, or would it provide the means of escaping addictions?

The Canada Emergency Response Benefit (CERB) was not a basic income, but it did provide money to some people who use drugs or alcohol. Low-barrier shelters that admitted people who may not be sober were the first to sound the alarm: when the CERB cheques began to arrive, workers noticed an increase in drug use. Opioid-related deaths spiked in Vancouver, and the media amplified the voices of those who claimed more drugs were circulating in tent cities across the country. These events touched a nerve for some members of the public. The critical public response took two forms. Some worried about the increase in deaths and argued that we should stop the money to protect vulnerable people from harming themselves. Others were more focused on morality: why should the public give money to people who will only waste it on drugs?

There are many issues related to drug use in Canadian society, and it is too simple to argue that CERB caused an increase in opioid deaths without examining the roles played by disruptions in the supply chain and closures or restrictions on the availability of safe consumption sites and other services. But the fear remained: would a basic income simply feed addictions?

People begin to use opioids for a variety of reasons, but one of the major risks for addiction is a job-related injury that results in a prescription for opioids from the Workers' Compensation Board. The WCB is an insurance program required to cover its costs, and workers off the job for extended periods of time increase those costs. Witness after witness told a *Globe and Mail* investigation published in June 2020 that they received a prescription for four weeks worth of painkillers with few questions asked from medical practitioners hired by the WCB.[16] Pressured to return to work before they had fully healed, they had no option but to use opioids in order to function on the job. When the prescription ran out, they turned to other suppliers because they needed a paycheque in order to survive. A basic income would allow workers, rather than employers or the WCB, to determine when they were healthy enough to return to the job.

Not everyone who uses substances is coerced by inadequate social programs. In a series of interviews with people who use substances, frontline service providers, clinicians and public advocates, we gathered a wide variety of opinions and policy recommendations, but everyone agreed on some things.[17] Everyone acknowledged that, despite the attention drawn by the opioid epidemic, alcohol remains the substance that causes the greatest personal and social costs. People who use drugs or alcohol come from all social classes and backgrounds, but the more money someone has, the more opportunity they have both to hide their addiction from others, and to access the resources they need to overcome it. All our informants acknowledged that someone with an active addiction will find the money, somehow, to feed that addiction. If they receive provincial welfare, they will spend at least some of that money on their drug of choice. If they received a basic income, they would spend some of that money on their drug of choice. If they receive food vouchers or bus tickets from well-meaning bureaucrats who hope to ensure they at least have food on the table, they will sell those vouchers at a discount in order to buy drugs or alcohol. If government systems withhold money in the hope of reducing substance use, users will find other ways to get the money they need — ways that often cause even greater harm to themselves and others. Some engage in sex work, while others turn to poverty related crimes. Users, we were told, will use until they decide, for themselves, to make changes in their lives. Most (but not all) of our informants recommended legalization so that people are not criminalized for holding drugs for personal use. Criminalization reinforces addictions and makes recovery more difficult. Most, but not all, also recognized the importance of safe consumption sites and other harm reduction strategies.

When people who use substances do decide to make changes in their lives, they need access to money so that they can rent an apartment and move out of the circumstances of their former lives. Some would need to leave dysfunctional relationships. Many would be dealing with layers of trauma in their lives, sometimes intergenerational, and be in no position to immediately get and hold a job that will pay enough to live on. Many would relapse and need second or third or fourth chances to get sober. Recovery is not linear.

Basic income will not magically cure already existing issues in people's lives, including addictions. On the other hand, it is unlikely to make life worse for people who are already actively using substances. Basic income might reduce the need to engage in even riskier ways to get money, but some of the money received by people who use substances would certainly help fund addictions. On the other hand, basic income becomes absolutely essential when people have decided to change their lives and work to become sober. They would need a basic income — money that is provided to them without judgment — so that they can rent an apartment, buy food and meet their other needs. They don't need a caseworker to force them to attend a job readiness program that they may not yet be in a position to benefit from, and they certainly don't need to be punished for relapses.

For people who use substances, basic income is controversial just as safe injection sites are controversial. Both can be characterized by the unsympathetic as fuelling addictions and rewarding undesirable behaviour. However, harm reduction strategies do work — they reduce deaths and provide resources for people who want to make changes in their lives.

Most importantly, and this bears repeating, the vast majority of people who would receive a basic income are no more likely to use substances than anyone else.

## Race, Age, Ability and Basic Income

A basic income respects individual differences. People could use their basic income to meet their own needs and those of their families as they see fit; they need not rely on government bureaucrats to discern and address their particular needs. As different as each individual and family is, however, there are some experiences that affect those of particular races, genders or ages in unique ways.

When we examine the data by race, age and ability, we see both why we need a basic income in Canada and how basic income needs to be developed in the context of other social policies. Basic income will not eliminate racism, systemic or otherwise, nor will it reverse the gains made in recent decades through changing social attitudes and the policies that reflect these changes. Basic income cannot offset the astronomical food prices, broken water delivery systems and substandard housing on First Nations reserves, nor will it bring roads to isolated northern communities. Basic income will not ensure that foreign experience and credentials are fairly considered by the Canadian labour market, nor will it guarantee equal opportunities for racialized Canadians. In all these cases, however, it would make the lives of recipients of all races and genders a little easier, reduce the poverty rate and ease the fears of those living with insecure incomes. It would facilitate individual choice and offer dignity to many people who have been scrambling from crisis to crisis. Basic income is not an invitation to ignore the profound rifts in our society, but it is an opportunity to improve the well-being of many.

# Chapter 8
# Mythbusting

Any significant change in social policy raises concerns among the people who would be directly affected by it, among those who expect their taxes to pay for it and among those who have an interest in existing programs that might be affected or even eliminated by the change. All of these disparate interests and competing groups share one fundamental characteristic: they believe that any potential gain from change is not worth even the smallest risk of loss. These fears underlie several myths about basic income.

## MYTH #1
**A basic income is just a covert attack on the social welfare system.**
Like any other social program, basic income can be adequately designed and funded, or it can be badly designed and underfunded. Canadian advocates for a guaranteed livable income define basic income as one component of a robust, responsive and comprehensive economic, health and social safety net that includes housing, child care, education, pharmacare, dental, physical and mental health strategies. Those who distrust basic income point out that

among its advocates have been people like Milton Friedman, who argued that a basic income could be substituted for all other social supports.[1] More recently, the Fraser Institute has taken a similar direction.[2]

Canadian advocates do not propose a stripped down and underfunded basic income, but rather a basic income that ensures no one is forced to live in poverty and no one is deprived of necessary public services. Public education and health insurance are not under attack, and labour legislation and minimum wage laws would not be abandoned.

Some services, such as extended health care, can be shown to be more efficient and effective if delivered publicly. Public services are especially important when demand is high and need is not uniform across the population. In health care, for example, a small number of people use a very large portion of the benefits because they have complex health conditions. Delivering such programs publicly means that services can be allocated to the people who need them, and low-cost individuals can subsidize high-cost individuals.

**Reality Check: Basic income in Canada is one policy among many, rather than a replacement for all existing social programs.**

## MYTH #2

**Eventually, governments will want to cut back on expenditure. It is better to keep an inefficient, complex, uncoordinated and bureaucratic system in place because it will be harder for a government to control.**

If income assistance and disability support payments were replaced by a basic income, there is no guarantee that a future government would not reduce the basic income. Unfortunately, that is true of all social programs, including the existing ones. Over the past thirty years, cash entitlements to income assistance have declined in real terms, and individuals have increasingly been forced to use food banks, school breakfast and lunch programs and other directed, usually stigmatized, benefits to meet their basic needs. In Ontario, for example, the value of income assistance for a single person in 1992 (in 2013 dollars) was $12,273 while it was only $8,224 in 2013.[3] Basic income is an opportunity to reverse that trend and to return dignity to families.

**Reality Check: The complexity of the current system has not prevented cutbacks. Badly designed and bureaucratic systems waste money that could be redirected to recipients. Elected representatives are accountable to the public that elects them, and Canadians need to hold them to account.**

## MYTH #3

**A basic income requires less bureaucracy, which means that a lot of good administrative jobs will disappear. In some small communities, these are the only good jobs.**

If provincial income assistance were replaced by a basic income, fewer people would be required to enforce the complex set of regulations associated with income assistance. However, there would still be a requirement for some administration. A basic income is not entirely mechanical; it must be able to respond to emergency situations and to answer questions from applicants, and this requires administrators. If, however, some people are no longer required to enforce existing regulations, there is an opportunity to redeploy highly educated and highly engaged labour into useful tasks that could actually benefit clients. People become caseworkers and social workers because they want to be useful. The current system wastes their time and the time of their clients because of the need to interpret confusing regulations in order to meet the needs of clients. Few workers are happy with a system that expects them to ensure their clients comply with all the complex regulations instead of allowing them the freedom to develop supportive relationships and help their clients build better lives. Both clients and caseworkers would benefit if they could partner to meet the real needs of their clients.

**Reality Check: It is always better to employ labour in useful tasks than to waste it.**

## MYTH #4

**A basic income is just a wage subsidy. It will benefit employers because they will be able to pay workers who receive a basic income less, and workers will be no better off.**

In Canada, we have a wage subsidy program called the Canada Workers Benefit (formerly the Working Income Tax Benefit), which is modelled on a similar program in the United States called the Earned Income Tax Credit. These are forms of workfare: to receive benefits under these programs, an individual must work and receive a wage. The wage is then subsidized by the program. Up to a certain income level, every dollar earned results in an increase in benefits. Someone who does not work receives nothing. This kind of a program puts all the power in the hands of the employer, and workers have no choice but to accept almost any work, at whatever wage is offered, to meet their most basic needs. This happens only in cases where workers must work in order to receive the benefit.

A basic income works differently. It is not a wage subsidy; it is not tied to the hourly wage rate and workers do not have to work in order to receive it. No one would be desperate to take any job offered at any wage because they are not required to work in order to receive a basic income. If the position is degrading or the wage insufficient, they can refuse a job offer. This puts power in the hands of workers; a potential employee has the power to walk away.

Mincome offers some evidence to support the claim that, if anything, a basic income would raise wages. David Calnitsky digitized employer surveys that were completed by Dauphin business owners during the Mincome project and by business owners in some nearby towns in which workers were not eligible for a basic income. The Dauphin business owners claimed that they were forced to raise wages in Dauphin after the introduction of Mincome because (in the words of one disgruntled respondent): "[Mincome is] just spoiling people rotten and upsetting the workforce something unreal. The hours people have to work, the wages they get, and the output they give (which isn't much) just make it impossible for the average employer to even stand a chance at hiring help."[4] Mincome, at least in the view of some local employers, gave workers far too much power because it allowed them to reject low-paid or poor-quality jobs and to demand higher wages.[5]

The Canada Emergency Response Benefit, even though it was not a basic income, attracted similar complaints from some small business owners who complained that workers they had laid off in the first weeks of the pandemic were reluctant to return to work when they were called back, without taking into account the child care responsibilities that accompanied school closures or the inability of the employer to ensure worker safety or to guarantee a minimum number of hours.

The argument that any improvement to social security acts as a drag on wages is an old one, but there is little evidence to support it. For example, a proposal that Canadian families should have access to a family allowance paid to mothers was debated in Parliament as early as 1929.[6] This proposal was opposed on the right by groups such as the Social Services Council that argued family allowance undermined the principles of marriage because it would be paid to mothers rather than fathers. On the left, it attracted the opposition of the Canadian Trades and Labour Congress, forerunner of the Canadian Labour Congress, which argued Family Allowance would act as a wage subsidy and suppress wages. Family Allowance was not introduced in 1929, and as a consequence, Canadian families had no access to this financial support through the lean years of the 1930s — the longest stretch of real wage decline in Canadian history. Family Allowance was again debated after World War II. It was supported by the Co-operative Commonwealth Federation, forerunner of the NDP, in 1942, and opposed again by the Canadian Trades and Labour Congress on the grounds that it would be an alternative to a general increase in wages. The Canadian Trades and Labour Congress argument convinced the Department of Finance, which was already worried about wage inflation after the war. The Department of Finance supported the introduction of Family Allowance hoping that it would indeed limit wages just as the unions predicted. The policy was consequently adopted in Canada just as the most sustained period of real wage growth in history began. Far from suppressing wages, it accompanied a real wage increase. The *Family Allowance Act* was the keynote of the 1944–45 parliamentary session and was described by one advocate as "the most radical, expensive, unlikely and popular legislation of the 1944 postwar program."[7]

Anyone who, despite the evidence, remains convinced that basic income will suppress wages can take solace from the fact that we still have labour legislation and minimum wage laws in Canada. A basic income does not do away with the need for regulation.

**Reality Check: Basic income is not a wage subsidy, and it will neither reduce wages nor slow wage increases. It would reduce coercion of low-wage workers, because workers would have the opportunity to walk away from poor job offers. If anything, basic income might put pressure on low-wage employers to improve the terms and conditions of work.**

## MYTH #5

**A basic income will reduce the number of people working low-wage jobs, and we need someone to do that work.**

A basic income would give workers the ability to walk away from jobs they consider poorly paid or demeaning. Employers might raise wages (which also entails raising prices) to attract workers. If consumers are not prepared to pay higher prices, either the firm will go out of business, it will produce abroad with lower-priced labour, or it will automate. Automation is a growing possibility in many industries, but the trend towards automation has been underway for a long time. In 1964, most tomatoes in California were picked by low-wage migrant workers. President Lyndon Johnson was concerned that competition from these workers was driving down wages for Americans and responded by making it more difficult to hire migrant workers. By 1966, 94 per cent of the tomatoes in California were harvested mechanically.[8]

Many low-wage jobs are in the service sector and, specifically, in the restaurant industry. Franchise owners complain that they cannot pay higher wages because consumers will not pay more for the food they serve. These jobs cannot be done abroad, but some of them can be automated. If the jobs cannot be automated, and consumers are unwilling to pay enough to staff the restaurant, then we will have to do without the cheap food such places serve. This is the same issue that faces low-wage employers when the minimum wage increases.

Some people take this argument one step further. They note that some of the biggest consumers of fast food are low-income people. Therefore, they argue, raising minimum wages or introducing a basic income hurts low-income people the most. We should, however, recognize that low incomes and low prices are connected. We can continue to operate the low-price, low-wage, low-income economy we have been chasing in recent years, or we can recognize that it is possible to extract ourselves from this vicious cycle and pay decent wages even in the restaurant industry, as do many European countries. Higher prices allow the payment of higher wages. Higher wages allow even low-income people to eat out; this would increase demand for restaurant food and support the higher prices. It is unfair to force low-wage workers to bear the additional burden of widespread poverty.

**Reality Check: Some low-wage jobs might be lost because workers have the freedom to reject jobs with low wages or poor working conditions. If employers will not, or cannot, increase wages or improve working conditions, they will shift production abroad,**

**automate or shut down. A basic income will help displaced labour adjust to new job opportunities.**

## MYTH #6
**A basic income will just shift bad jobs abroad, and we should do our own dirty work.**

Some might argue that a basic income in Canada will have the effect of shifting the lowest-paying and least pleasant jobs abroad. Indeed, one of the consequences of higher-priced labour in Canada is that some employers will look for alternatives, either in the form of automation or by shifting production to a lower-wage region. This trend has characterized production in high-wage countries for almost fifty years. When local labour becomes "too expensive," producers shift production to places where wages are lower. Many people look at the conditions associated with textile production in Bangladesh, for example, or electronics factories in China, and question the morality of sending our most indecent work abroad for others to do. This is not the fault of Canadian labour legislation or "privileged" workers in high-income countries or basic income, but rather the result of consumers in high-income countries who choose to purchase products produced by exploited labour. Nevertheless, there are two quite disparate views about the extent to which workers in low-income countries suffer because high-income countries shift their least pleasant and lowest-paying work abroad.

The standard economic argument claims that everyone benefits from trade. Workers in low-income countries benefit from the additional work created by our demand for the low-priced products created in conditions that we would not impose on workers in our own country. As long as foreign workers are not coerced to work under exploitative conditions, as slaves or children might be for example, the assumption is that they have freely consented and presumably benefit or they would not take the job. The freedom to leave such work acts as insurance; the alternative opportunities available to these workers must be less pleasant than the jobs they accept. Therefore, as bad as the conditions may be, foreign workers benefit in the sense that they are better off than they would be without this additional opportunity. And, in fact, there is some evidence to support that perspective. In recent years, Chinese workers have become "too expensive" for much of the work that we used to export to China, and the work is instead sent on to even lower-wage South Asian countries. The increased demand for Chinese workers to produce products for the North American market put upward pressure on Chinese wages and improved their working conditions.

While these workers are worse off than workers in high-income countries, they are better off than they used to be. In turn, it is claimed, South Asian workers will soon benefit from production for the North American and European markets, and their wages and working conditions will improve. However, it is hard to accept this argument when we read of textile factories that lock their workers inside and hide child employees when foreign inspectors arrive.

An alternative view asks whether lack of coercion is sufficient to ensure that labour is free to consent. Workers are not free to consent to work at indecent jobs when the only other opportunities open to them will not feed their families or allow them to live with a modest degree of self-respect. If they do not have the capacity to live decent lives without working under exploitative and degrading conditions, we cannot claim that they are benefiting from the work we send abroad. However, the solution is not to force Canadian workers to accept lower wages or inappropriate working conditions so that Canadian consumers still benefit from low-priced consumption goods. The solution is to work for improved labour conditions abroad, to put binding restrictions on the use of temporary foreign workers in Canada and to advocate among Canadian consumers to ensure that our consumption dollars do not support labour exploitation either abroad or at home. If Canadian consumers continue to buy cheap goods produced abroad, then they are encouraging such conditions by default and have effectively decided that the working conditions of foreign labour are not their concern. In any case, it is both unfair and ineffective to try to improve the conditions of foreign workers by forcing low-wage Canadian workers to work at these jobs by depriving them of a basic income.

**Reality Check: A Canadian basic income might result in some of the lowest-paid and least-pleasant Canadian jobs moving abroad. If we are concerned about the conditions of labour in other countries, the solution is to advocate among Canadian consumers to ensure that our consumption dollars do not support exploitation rather than to deprive Canadian workers of a basic income.**

## MYTH #7
### A basic income will just raise prices.

From the perspective of Toronto or Vancouver, it might seem obvious that housing is the greatest need, and that families will try to spend any additional income on better housing. As a consequence, all families will try to rent better apartments but, since there is no increase in housing supply, landlords will take advantage of the increased demand and raise rents. Families might receive a basic income but would pay all of it to landlords and, in the end, be no better off. However, there is very little empirical evidence to support this claim and what we do know suggests otherwise.

Rent has been increasing as a proportion of the budget of low-income families for many years, particularly in large cities. If higher rents were caused by increases in the spending power of low-income families, then we would expect to see a direct relationship between income and rent. However, income assistance rates and minimum wages have lagged far behind rent increases over the past two decades.

In 2016, the Canada Child Benefit was made much more generous. This raised the real incomes of families with children, especially single mothers, suddenly and dramatically. This is a sort of natural experiment. There is, however, no evidence of a sudden and dramatic increase in rents for the kind of housing rented by families with young children. Moreover, there is ample evidence that families who received the Canada Child Benefit had extra money to spend on better nutrition, children's activities, transportation, and so on. The money did not entirely disappear into higher rents.

The province of Manitoba also provides some direct evidence that a basic income will not raise rents proportionately. Manitoba introduced a program called Rent Assist in 2014. Rent Assist offers a monthly payment to Manitobans, working or not, based on their incomes, the number of people in their families, and the median rent where they live. There are some exclusions; people living in subsidized or student housing, in institutions or on reserves are not eligible. Those receiving provincial income assistance automatically get the full amount of Rent Assist. Those who work receive an amount that declines gradually as their income increases. The payment is designed to help individuals afford rent equal to 75 per cent of median market rents, but it is not based on how much an individual actually pays for rent. No one is required to present receipts to demonstrate that they have spent the money on housing; once they receive it, they can spend it as they like. There is strong evidence that Rent Assist has improved the living standards of low-income Manitobans. In a study for the Canadian Centre for Policy Alternatives, Sarah Cooper, Jesse Hajer and Shayna Plaut said:

> Rent Assist . . . makes a significant difference in tenants' sense of housing security and well-being. Over three-quarters of the people interviewed stated, unprompted, 'I can breathe. I know that I have a roof over my head and food on the table' or a statement of similar effect. They noted that this is a significant and positive change, enabling them to focus on other aspects of their life such as furthering their education, raising and/or gaining custody of their children and rebuilding their mental and physical health.[9]

Rent Assist has allowed tens of thousands of Manitobans to find housing that better meets their needs, while improving the quality of their lives overall.

Even in Toronto and Vancouver, families are not identical. Low-wage working people who receive basic income might decide that better daycare is their primary need and allocate their money accordingly. Others will be satisfied with the housing they have and decide to spend a bit more on a better diet, or to buy new clothing or bicycles for their children. Others live outside high-rent jurisdictions; rents are much lower in Thunder Bay and Lindsay than they are in Hamilton or Toronto, and any attempt on the part of a single landlord to raise rent in response to an increase in basic income is likely to fail in smaller cities because there are other landlords and other apartments for low-income individuals. Landlords are also limited in their ability to raise rents if rent controls exist.

Basic income is not like income assistance because people who receive a basic income have control over their own expenditures. Many of us have seen low-rent housing become more expensive when shelter rates associated with income assistance increase. This is particularly the case when landlords are paid directly by the province on behalf of clients. Many landlords, particularly those offering the lowest quality and cheapest rooms, prefer this arrangement and will agree to rent to income assistance recipients only when they are paid directly by the government. The rents are calibrated directly to what the province will pay; when the shelter allowance is increased, landlords raise their rents accordingly. The result is that the government pays more but only landlords benefit. Moreover, when landlords are paid directly, tenants lose what little power they had to demand that landlords undertake necessary repairs or ensure the property is pest-free. Income assistance, and particularly rents paid directly to landlords on behalf of "vulnerable" clients, is largely responsible for the deplorable conditions of low-quality housing in our cities.

We can see the difference between income assistance and basic income if we examine the experiences of low-income people when they turn sixty-five. When someone who receives provincial income assistance turns sixty-five, they are required by the province to apply for Old Age Security and Guaranteed Income Supplement. One of the biggest impacts of this birthday is an immediate improvement in housing, and not just because they receive more money. They also gain control over their money. David Northcott, the former director of Winnipeg Harvest Food Bank, loves to tell the story of "Big Bill" Adamson. Big Bill sorted potatoes at Winnipeg Harvest and, like many of the volunteers at the food bank, he was also a client. He lived in a tiny residential hotel room in downtown Winnipeg. He received provincial income assistance, but more than half of it was paid directly to his landlord because he was deemed at risk of homelessness. As he grew older, he was increasingly unhappy with his housing. He didn't feel safe. Bill wore all his clothes all the time, so no one would steal them. He often struggled with hygiene because the shared shower was broken or otherwise unusable. When he wanted to eat, he lined up at the mission across the street or relied on packaged food because he had no access to cooking facilities. Bill had his demons and sometimes disappeared for a few days or a few weeks. One day, he came back to work at Harvest after a few weeks' absence, looking remarkably different. He'd had a haircut and wasn't wearing all his clothes. The transformation was dramatic enough that it elicited a bit of curiosity among the other volunteers and staff. Eventually someone ventured to ask, "So Bill. What's new with you?" Bill laughed and said, "I'm a new man. Well, actually, I'm exactly the same man I was last month, but I've had a birthday and now they've decided I'm a fine gentleman." The day Bill turned sixty-five he was eligible for Old Age Security and the Guaranteed Income Supplement for seniors and no longer dependent on provincial income assistance. Overnight, his income doubled and, more importantly, it was paid to him rather than to his landlord. He rented a modest apartment with its own bathroom, and he had access to cooking facilities for the first time. Instead of lining up for hours to eat dinner at a downtown charity, or buying ready-made food to eat from the package, he could go to a grocery store and buy several cans of beans or chili at a time and prepare his own dinner in his own apartment. He could eat what he wanted to eat, when he wanted to eat it. These small luxuries were only available when he escaped from provincial income assistance.

There are other examples where particular commodities might increase in price because of basic income. One of the consequences of COVID-19 was that we became very aware of the low wages of agricultural workers, as well as workers in slaughterhouses and fish plants. These jobs already had trouble attracting labour before COVID-19 and relied heavily on temporary foreign workers. During the pandemic, workers stayed away from these jobs largely because the employer couldn't guarantee a safe environment. The firms were forced to implement safety measures and offer bonuses. Food prices went up as a consequence. If basic income gives workers the capacity to demand higher wages and better conditions in such jobs, consumers will pay higher prices. It is also possible to imagine that there might be particular instances where prices increase — at a local restaurant in a low-income neighbourhood, for example. If customers suddenly have more money to spend on modest luxuries, the restaurant might raise prices. There will, however, be no general increase in all prices when a basic income is introduced.

**Reality Check: There will be no general increase in the price level associated with a basic income although some prices for particular items might rise when low-income people suddenly have more money to spend or when the wage of labour in particular industries increases.**

# MYTH #8

**A basic income is not a good way to reduce poverty. We need programs directed to the root causes of poverty that address the complex needs of homeless people with mental health and substance abuse issues.**

The root cause of poverty for most people who would receive a basic income is a lack of money. More than half the people who would benefit from a basic income are working but not earning enough money to raise themselves and their families out of poverty. Most of the rest are single parents of young children. Even among poor adults living alone, most are not homeless or mentally ill. A very small proportion of people who would be eligible for basic income support are homeless people with complex mental health and substance abuse issues. Just to put the numbers in perspective, it has been estimated that approximately 235,000 people in Canada experience some form of homelessness each year, but only a very small proportion of these represent the core homeless with complex needs who are targeted by such programs as Housing First, a program that offers very significant supports to clients, providing them with permanent and stable housing, supportive services and connections to the community-based supports people need to keep their housing and avoid returning to homelessness.[10] By contrast, the Parliamentary Budget Office estimated that more than 7.5 million people across Canada would benefit from a basic income if the Ontario plan were rolled out nationally.[11] The vast majority of people who would receive support from a basic income do not require intensive support services. They simply require enough money to meet their needs.

There is, however, a need to think more clearly about homeless people with complex needs. Housing First, which is an excellent model for addressing these needs, comes into people's lives after they have spiralled out of control. Its purpose is to reduce use of services such as emergency department care in hospitals, police interventions and similar services that are very heavily used by a very small number of people with significant issues. People, however, are not born homeless, addicted and mentally ill. When people end up on the streets, it is usually because of a series of bad breaks, often coupled with poor decisions. Marriages end, businesses collapse, young people leave unhappy homes and people overuse alcohol and drugs to avoid the reality in which they find themselves. Substance abuse leads to evictions, and a lack of money makes it difficult to find new housing. Homelessness is a barrier to even menial jobs, and unemployment exacerbates poverty and deprivation. Homelessness makes any existing mental illness or substance abuse issue harder to deal with. Social isolation makes all these problems worse. Housing First intervenes at this point to try to help people recover. What if everyone had access to enough money to support their basic needs before their lives became so desperate?

Most basic income recipients are not homeless people with substance abuse and mental health issues. However, even people vulnerable to substance abuse and mental illness might avoid worse outcomes if they had access to an adequate basic income before they became homeless. Having enough to eat and a roof over your head makes it easier to access the other services you require. Basic income doesn't replace all these other services; it makes it possible for people to benefit from them. That is, after all, the philosophy behind Housing First.

**Reality Check: Most people who would receive a basic income are not homeless people with substance abuse and mental health issues. The vast majority are currently living as well as they can with the resources available to them. Basic income will simply make their lives a bit easier and reduce the financial risks that might lead to homelessness. The very visible, but nonetheless small, proportion of people who are homeless and have complex mental health needs require additional supports. A basic income makes it possible to take advantage of the other services on offer.**

## MYTH #9

**We can get better results with less risk by building on the programs we already have in place.**

Many of the benefits of a basic income occur because a family has a more adequate, predictable and secure income than they had previously. Consequently, health improves, and children do better at school. Families feel less stigmatized and are more able to fully participate in the community. If we put the same amount of money required for a basic income into existing programs, however, we would not see the same effects.

If we were to expand income assistance and disability support instead of introducing a basic income, families that receive income assistance would welcome higher incomes. However, an expansion of income assistance does nothing for working Canadians whose incomes are too low to allow them to escape poverty. Therefore, the health and educational benefits to be expected from a basic income will not be realized if the financing is directed instead to income assistance.

Moreover, the bureaucracy and administrative inefficiency of provincial income assistance exists because the programs are governed by too many rules. The rules were put in place to ensure that those who can work look for jobs and that only those who have no other resources available to them receive support. Paradoxically, these difficulties are even more onerous for people with disabilities. People with disabilities receive higher income support under existing programs than do people who receive income assistance, but qualifying for disability support is challenging and the outcome is unpredictable. Additional supports may or may not be available, depending on the discretion of caseworkers. As is the case with general income assistance, caseworkers are charged with simultaneously advocating for their clients and policing recipients to ensure that no fraud occurs. The bottom line is that expanding a broken system by investing more money in it will not fix its structural problems.

While basic income has been seen in Canada as a replacement for income assistance, there are other programs that could be expanded instead, but these will also not achieve the results of basic income. One possibility would be to enhance, for example, the Canada Workers Benefit. This has the advantage of addressing the needs of low-wage workers and it simultaneously satisfies those taxpayers who fear that a basic income will encourage people to work less. This is a form of workfare.

This policy has been implemented across most high-income countries to a greater or lesser extent. The United States has, for many years, been eliminating cash entitlement programs and replacing them with various forms of earned income tax credits and other forms of workfare. The Organisation for Economic Co-operation and Development has, for decades, supported these "active labour market policies."[12] These programs focus on shifting government spending away from income assistance that has no work requirement to programs with work and training requirements, and reforming tax and benefit systems to remove work disincentive effects and make work pay.[13] One significant limitation became clear during the recession of 2008: these policies do little to help people when there are no jobs to be had. The economic theory behind creating work incentives is very clear and convincing, but there does not seem to be strong evidence that they actually work very well.[14] As a consequence, many countries are turning away from heavy-handed workfare programs.

In the United States, the trend in many states has been to ask for more in exchange for aid. Time limits, asset tests and work, training or volunteer requirements have been added to the Supplemental Nutrition Assistance Program (food stamps), as was done in the 1990s with Temporary Aid to Needy Families — a program that is still frozen at the same level of funding. The results are ambiguous at best. Work requirements in the United States largely coincided with a period of economic growth, so many people did move off welfare rolls and the poverty rate did decline. However, these individuals would have done so anyway — without the work requirement. And while the individuals and families that have succeeded are doing better financially, those who are left behind are the most vulnerable, and they are subsisting on less and less support. People with disabilities, particularly those with invisible disabilities who cannot qualify for disability support, people with addictions or criminal records and those who live in areas with limited job opportunities and no public transportation find the requirements difficult to meet.[15]

Without doubt, an expanded Canada Workers Benefit is better for low-wage workers than no program at all.[16] It remains an open question whether it actually encourages more people to work. In the same way that a basic income probably encourages a small number of people to work less, an expanded workers benefit will probably encourage a small number of people to work more. However, a wage subsidy cannot meet the needs of the most vulnerable: people with barriers that prevent them from working need unconditional income assistance best met through a basic income.

Instead of enhancing income replacement programs, some people argue that we should instead raise minimum wages and enhance labour legislation. In fact, strong labour legislation and minimum wages complement basic income. Everyone, especially the low waged, benefits from strong labour legislation. However, it cannot be a substitute for basic income for the simplest of reasons: most poor families have no one working at minimum-wage (or near-minimum-wage) jobs, and many of those working minimum-wage jobs do not live in poor families.

Workers aged nineteen or younger are much more likely to work for minimum wage than anyone else, with the next highest incidence of minimum wage among those aged twenty through twenty-four.

In 2016, almost half of fifteen- to nineteen-year-olds worked for minimum wage as did 15 per cent of those twenty through twenty-four. While the growth rates of older workers working at minimum wage are dramatic, it is still the case that only 3 per cent of prime-age workers and 4.3 per cent of those over fifty-five are working for minimum wage. Many others, of course, will be working at wages just slightly higher than minimum wage. Without denying the real hardship of low-wage work, one of the reasons the incidence of minimum-wage work has increased in recent years is because legislated minimum wages have been increasing more quickly than the general wage rate. This has led to a compression of wages at the low end. People who used to earn just slightly more than minimum wage did not receive wage increases when the legislation changed.

A minimum-wage increase, then, would increase the incomes of some adults and some low-income families. However, using increases in the minimum-wage rate as a lever to reduce the incidence of poverty is, at best, extremely inefficient. An increase in the minimum wage will increase the disposable incomes of many people who do not live in low-income families. Two adolescents will benefit for every adult woman who gains from a wage increase, and four young people aged fifteen through nineteen will take home larger salaries for every adult male who benefits. While higher incomes are, no doubt, appreciated by teenagers, and while some teenagers live in low-income families and contribute to total family income, it is much more efficient to target assistance directly towards low-income families than to increase the wages of all low-income workers and hope that some of that largesse will increase total income in low-income families.

Table 8.1 Share of Employees Working at Minimum Wage (or Less) By Age, Canada and Provinces, 2006 and 2016

| | Total, 15 years and over (%) | | 15–24 years (%) | | 15–19 years (%) | |
| | 2006 | 2016 | 2006 | 2016 | 2006 | 2016 |
|---|---|---|---|---|---|---|
| Canada | 4.4 | 6.9 | 16.1 | 26.5 | 31.3 | 49.1 |
| Newfoundland | 7.6 | 5.9 | 26.2 | 19.7 | 38.5 | 35.3 |
| Prince Edward Island | 4.6 | 8.2 | 1.8 | 3.1 | 1.4 | 1.9 |
| Nova Scotia | 5.9 | 6.6 | 21.6 | 23.7 | 37.2 | 44.1 |
| New Brunswick | 4.2 | 6.6 | 14.7 | 26.2 | 29.9 | 50.9 |
| Quebec | 4.2 | 6.1 | 15.7 | 24.9 | 31.0 | 44.7 |
| Ontario | 4.8 | 9.2 | 20.1 | 26.7 | 41.1 | 69.9 |
| Manitoba | 4.8 | 6.8 | 16.3 | 22.7 | 29.5 | 35.6 |
| Saskatchewan | 5.5 | 3.5 | 17.9 | 12.3 | 31.9 | 24.1 |
| Alberta | 1.7 | 4.5 | 5.1 | 15.5 | 9.4 | 27.6 |
| British Columbia | 4.7 | 4.8 | 14.4 | 15.7 | 26.0 | 30.5 |

Source: Armine Yalnizyan, "Why a $15 Minimum Wage Is Good for Business," *Macleans*, June 2, 2017.

Reality Check: A basic income will allow Canadian families to live with dignity as the economy and the jobs it produces evolve. It will reduce the depth and breadth of poverty while simultaneously addressing the design flaws of existing programs that do not reach everyone. Neither putting more money into existing programs, nor redesigning these programs by tinkering at the edges nor wishing to turn back the clock on economic change will yield better results.

## MYTH #10
### Isn't it better to offer a jobs guarantee?

The idea behind a jobs guarantee is that the government should either subsidize business or act as an employer of last resort, to ensure that the economy operates at full employment and that everyone who wants to work has the opportunity to do so. Everyone would therefore contribute to society as a worker and would gain the self-respect and positive benefits associated with independence and hard work.

While this proposal sounds good and has attracted a lot of attention, governments have not generally proven themselves capable of creating decent jobs for everyone. In practice, a jobs guarantee means that the

| 20–24 years (%) | | 25–54 years (%) | | 55 years and over (%) | |
|---|---|---|---|---|---|
| 2006 | 2016 | 2000 | 2016 | 2000 | 2016 |
| 6.7 | 15.1 | 1.7 | 3.1 | 2.5 | 4.3 |
| 19.2 | 11.7 | 4.4 | 3.3 | 5.3 | 5.0 |
| 7.6 | 19.0 | 1.6 | 3.7 | 2.6 | 4.7 |
| 12.1 | 13.8 | 2.6 | 3.4 | 3.1 | 4.4 |
| 5.1 | 10.9 | 1.8 | 3.0 | 3.3 | 5.0 |
| 6.9 | 15.5 | 1.8 | 2.5 | 2.9 | 4.0 |
| 7.1 | 20.3 | 1.6 | 4.0 | 2.0 | 5.0 |
| 6.6 | 15.6 | 1.8 | 3.7 | 3.3 | 3.3 |
| 7.2 | 5.9 | 1.9 | 1.5 | 4.0 | 2.6 |
| 2.2 | 9.2 | 0.8 | 2.3 | 1.0 | 3.1 |
| 7.5 | 8.3 | 2.2 | 2.4 | 3.7 | 3.5 |

government will subsidize private-sector employers to create more minimum wage jobs for low-skilled workers who are generally the most vulnerable to involuntary unemployment. Low-skilled workers who earned near minimum wage before the jobs guarantee would soon find themselves competing with subsidized workers to keep their jobs. This has the effect of shifting much of the cost of low-wage labour from private firms to the government. While wages cannot fall below minimum wage, the increased competition from new workers at the bottom of the wage scale will not encourage firms to raise wages, even for those workers earning slightly more than minimum wage.

A jobs guarantee creates monitoring costs in addition to the direct subsidy. If assistance depends on work, administrators are required to ensure that individuals are linked with available jobs, appear at job interviews, accept job offers and perform the jobs for which they are hired. Others must monitor the various labour markets to ensure that subsidies are sufficient to ensure full employment. Still others are required to ensure that those firms receiving subsidies actually create the new jobs they promise to create. This is an expensive proposition, and its administrative costs would far exceed traditional income assistance programs.

There is, however, a further problem. Whenever traditional income assistance programs are reduced, or time limits are placed on assistance, the disability lists in the same jurisdictions swell. A jobs guarantee would not apply to people "incapable" of working; there would be exceptions for the "genuinely" disabled. The difficulty is that there is no clear distinction between people with disabilities and those without. There is always a grey zone in which milder barriers to work exist. Whether an individual with such disabilities is designated disabled depends on whether that individual seeks disability status, and whether they can convince a practitioner to support the designation. In a jurisdiction in which being disabled is a condition of receiving support, it is only reasonable to expect that more people would seek disability status, and more practitioners would support disability designations for people with milder barriers to work. Guaranteed jobs will have the perverse effects of increasing monitoring costs, acting as a drag on market wages and reducing the size of the labour force by causing disability rosters to soar.

**Reality Check: If the "jobs guarantee" works by subsidizing private employers, it creates incentives for firms to replace unsubsidized labour with subsidized labour, and thereby shifts costs from the private to the public sector. A jobs guarantee alone is not sufficient to provide support for working-age adults. Providing potential workers with job opportunities and information on a voluntary basis might enhance their well-being, but everyone needs access to an unconditional basic income.**

## MYTH #11

**We should offer guaranteed services rather than guaranteed incomes. That way, people will still have a roof over their heads and food on the table, even after the money is gone.**

During the debate leading up to the introduction of Family Allowances in 1945, critics argued that the money should be distributed by way of services rather than cheque, while advocates argued that services alone were paternalistic.[17] The same debate recurs every time income supports are proposed, and basic income is no exception.

We all rely on government services and a basic income doesn't eliminate the need for high-quality services funded by the government. But public services alone can never meet all our needs. Not many Canadians would rally behind a call for "food banks for everyone!" We recognize that receiving direct food aid can be, and often is, demeaning and stigmatizing. Few people line up at a mission for their supper, even though it's free, unless they are desperate. We all want the ability to make choices about how we live our lives.

Catherine lives with severe physical disabilities. She is thirty-five years old and lives in a nursing home with others four decades her senior, many of whom have cognitive impairments. She is a social justice advocate and often attends meetings at the public library and elsewhere in the community, but the logistics are not easy. She must arrange for transportation, which is available for those with physical disabilities in the large city where she lives, but access to appropriate transportation is not guaranteed. Like any public service, it is prioritized and those with the most pressing business get available seats. People with similar disabilities living in smaller towns have no transportation at all. If the meeting Catherine attends is scheduled during meals at her nursing home, there is no food available for her when she returns. Her physical needs are met by the nursing home where she lives, but how much better would her life be if she had access to the money necessary to arrange her own additional supports? If Catherine had a basic income, she would have the capacity to arrange accessible transportation when denied access to public services. She could hire someone to help her access public events more fully, including the ability to share meals outside her institution and to live life according to her own schedule. Money that she controls would allow her to supplement the services she receives based on her own priorities.

Health care, pharmacare, public education and many more services are essential. We all have a stake in making sure these public services function well because we all rely upon them. It is, however, undeniable that universal services work much better for some people than for others. Those who are not part of the dominant culture — newcomers to Canada and Indigenous people, for example — sometimes find public services delivered in ways that don't meet their particular needs very well. The health care system may or may not have translators available. Public schools may or may not have the capacity to deal with traumatized refugee children. Troubling interactions between police services and racialized people have been documented across Canada.[18] All of these services are essential, but racialized people who are also living in poverty are in particular jeopardy. They are both more likely to come into contact with public services, and less likely to have their needs met by those services. No public service has an unlimited budget and therefore decisions must be made about how to prioritize needs. A basic income that allows a parent to hire a tutor, a translator, an advocate or a mental health worker would make public services more accessible and effective for marginalized people. The ability to pay privately for mental health services would supplement an overburdened public system focused on more pressing cases.

When a basic income is implemented, people with disabilities must have access to the supports and services they need. The long-standing practice of linking such services to income replacement in provincial disability programs is both unfair and inefficient. It discourages people with disabilities from working because they fear losing access to supports and services they might require. Low-income working people are sometimes forced to leave a job they enjoy in order to qualify for medical devices or services required for their disability. This is not a system that should be maintained. Instead, disability supports should be available to everyone who needs them, either without charge through the healthcare system or, depending on the particular service, based on the amount of income they have whether it comes from working or from disability payments. This change would ensure that people with the same needs and resources will have access to the same services and medical devices whether they are working or receiving provincial income assistance.

Services are sometimes a more efficient and effective way of meeting the needs of the population and it is essential to advocate for adequate budgets. However, a basic income provides autonomy and choice and allows people to define and address their own needs. Both are essential. **Reality Check: Basic income does not replace public services. However, services alone are not sufficient. A basic income allows people to make their own decisions about how best to meet their own needs.**

## MYTH #12
**Low-income Canadians lack the financial skills to manage their money. They need caseworkers to make sure that the money lasts — that there is food in the refrigerator and the rent is paid.**

During the Ontario Basic Income Guarantee Experiment, recipients spent the money they received on food, housing, clothing, kid's activities and education.[19] In cash transfer experiments in low-income countries, people spent the money on food, health care, education, housing and business investments.[20] No doubt some of the money was also spent on alcohol, cigarettes and other "vices," just as most people spend some of their wages on their habits, good or bad. However, offering financial planning assistance, which anyone can then decide to make use of or not, is a far cry from imposing help on people who don't want to be helped.

Many of us could use some basic knowledge about how to manage our finances and even more of us lack the confidence to make good financial decisions. Most low-income families, however, already have a wealth of knowledge about how to manage their money. Their income is simply too low to live on. No amount of management will help, and it is more than a little patronizing to suggest that they just need greater money management skills.

Holly Keilty is a financial counsellor at Community Financial Counselling in Winnipeg. She works with many people who receive support through provincial income assistance:

> One of the biggest challenges I face as a financial counsellor is not being able to help. How do you help a client who doesn't have enough income to budget? We go over rent, food, a few more categories and that's it. There's nothing left to budget with the cost of living being so high and benefits and wages being so low. How do you help someone when there's no money to budget? It's insulting to low-income clients to be told to seek budgeting help, when most of my low-income clients are actually quite good at budgeting, they just need more income. Most people with low incomes know exactly what they would do with more income if they had it, and they would use it extremely efficiently.

There are, however, people who do face money management challenges. For example, there are particular issues facing criminalized women. Many have trauma related to sex work or having been trafficked in the past. Some use alcohol or drugs. Institutionalization, either as children in group homes or as adults in the prison system, doesn't give anyone the opportunity to learn how to manage their finances. As a result, criminalized women sometimes lack knowledge and confidence related to finances and are often victimized. Similarly, young people aging out of the foster care system have had few opportunities to learn how to manage money. Community credit counselling, available to anyone who wants it, would be a useful service to provide. However, depriving low-income Canadians of a livable basic income out of concern that they will not manage their resources well, or depriving recipients of the right to make their own decisions, is patronizing.

Holly believes her clients are disadvantaged by the current provincial income assistance program: they receive too little money and have too little control over their finances to make effective changes in their lives. Holly says, "It's the hopelessness that gets to me. Clients lose hope of a better life, become depressed or anxious, become paranoid and distrustful and spiral down into poor health, which also makes it more difficult for them to live a meaningful life. Even when they can afford rent and some food and bills, they generally can't afford anything else that adds meaning to their lives, like hobbies, socializing, even internet and cable sometimes. We don't tell wealthy people what to do with their money; we should trust people living in poverty in the same way."

The complexity of the current system, rather than meeting the specific needs of clients, means that some people do not get the help they need because they don't have the skills to navigate the bureaucracy. There are entire agencies devoted to helping clients interact with the income assistance system. Holly, for example, often accompanies clients to meetings with provincial income assistance caseworkers and devotes hours to working the telephones to ensure her clients receive the support to which they are entitled. If clients received a regular and predictable basic income, without complex and inconsistent eligibility rules, financial advisors would have the time to help clients who need to learn how to manage money. Clients who are not penalized for making mistakes, and whose income is not held hostage to control their behaviour, would be in a much stronger position to take control and build better lives.

**Reality Check: Financial literacy is a challenge for Canadians at all income levels. Providing information and support to all community members who want help is useful; forcing help on people who neither want it nor need it is patronizing.**

## MYTH #13

**We have no way to deliver a basic income. We have no list of all Canadians. The tax system is too slow and cumbersome and cannot adjust to changing circumstances, and too many people do not file taxes.**

One of the benefits of basic income, advocates argue, is that it is less bureaucratic than our current systems of support and could operate quite efficiently through the tax system. Critics who suggest otherwise usually imagine that the only way to deliver benefits through that system is the way we deliver the Canada Child Benefit or the Guaranteed Income Supplement. Both are traditional, refundable tax credits. In both cases, the benefit received this year depends on taxable income from last year. Even though people might receive benefits every month or every quarter, the amount they receive is determined by last year's tax return. It is possible to adjust these payments so that they reflect current rather than past income, but the ability to adjust is limited. This system could not work for the delivery of a basic income intended to replace provincial income assistance because the earnings of working-age adults might change dramatically from month to month. No one can wait until they next file taxes to receive a basic income.

COVID-19 drew our attention to the many people who were struggling before the pandemic, and made the limitations of our existing income support programs very clear. However, it also showed us that we have the capacity to deliver a basic income. The Canada Emergency Response Benefit demonstrated that it is possible to use Canada Revenue Agency accounts much more flexibly than was thought possible. People could reapply every month, using an expedited application form, and report their earned income that month. The payment could be delivered, or stopped, or adjusted accordingly. Income tax could be deducted at source, and adjusted monthly. It is, therefore, possible to adjust payments monthly using CRA accounts.

Critics also point out that many low-income people don't file tax returns. This, however, doesn't mean that CRA accounts can't be used to deliver benefits. The CERB allowed people who had never filed taxes to call a telephone number in order to apply. If benefits depend on current income rather than the taxable income reported last year, not having filed a return is not a barrier. However, many other benefits are delivered through the tax system and do require that someone file taxes in order to receive those benefits. Low-income people who don't file taxes miss out on these benefits. If a basic income made use of CRA accounts, applicants who apply by telephone could be encouraged to file tax returns so they don't miss out on other benefits.

Lindsay Tedds and her team at the University of Calgary have noted that 12 per cent of working-age Canadians do not file a tax return each year and therefore would not receive benefits through the tax system. Non-filing rates, according to their data, range from a low of 6.1 per cent in Quebec to a high of 15.9 per cent in Ontario.[21] Canadians with the lowest incomes are even less likely to file taxes and therefore miss out on government benefits. It was estimated that 40 per cent of eligible First Nations families did not receive the Canada Child Benefit in 2017. Only 3 per cent of Calgary's homeless received the GST credit and many income assistance recipients did not file taxes.[22]

These numbers, however, have led to the creation of public awareness campaigns and direct interventions to encourage people eligible for benefits delivered through the income tax system to file a tax return. A program in Manitoba for example, called "Get Your Benefits," partnered with primary health care providers to help people get the benefits to which they are entitled. The program is based on the insights of Gary Bloch who works at the Inner-City Clinic at St. Michael's Hospital in Toronto. Public health clinics, food banks and legal aid clinics are trusted and used by low-income people. Clients who came to a clinic or another partner agency were asked specifically about their financial situation and linked to volunteers who completed tax returns on their behalf and referred them to other resources as appropriate. This program, and others, have led to filing rates in Manitoba well above the national average, particularly among First Nations families.[23] Other low-income provinces, such as the Maritimes, have similar programs in place; even the CRA offers outreach services to encourage low-income people to file taxes. This may be a partial explanation for the somewhat unexpected finding that the richest provinces — Ontario, BC and Alberta — have the lowest tax filing rates.

There are ways to increase filing rates. An organization called Canadians for Tax Fairness notes that the Canada Revenue Agency already receives information from employers, banks and governments about most sources of income and has the capacity to automatically file taxes on behalf of low-income Canadians, ensuring they receive the benefits to which they are entitled. This is known as deemed filing and is consistent with government priorities.

If it were thought necessary to verify earned income before a basic income is delivered, it is worth recognizing the potential of a pilot conducted by Employment Insurance where employers were able to electronically update employment and earning data directly. This is similar to systems in use in many other countries. Clearly, getting a basic income to the people who need it is not a problem that cannot be solved.

**Reality Check: The technical capacity to deliver a responsive basic income exists.**

Chapter 9

# Can We Afford a Basic Income?

The pandemic year, 2020, began on an optimistic economic note. While several of the provinces struggled financially, the federal government was in excellent shape. The federal debt was low and easily manageable, both in absolute terms and relative to the performance of other high-income countries. The Parliamentary Budget Office (PBO) is an organization independent of the federal government that provides analysis on the state of the nation's finances, the government's estimates and trends in the Canadian economy. The PBO claimed as late as February 27, 2020 that the federal government could increase spending permanently by $41 billion each year without increasing taxes or making its debt unsustainable.[1] Within a matter of days, that optimism was called into question as non-essential businesses were closed across the country. The unavoidable federal response came at a price.

By April 30, the Public Budgetary Office had updated its forecasts. The planned $22 billion federal deficit for 2020–21 would balloon to as much as $252 billion, taking into account both the increased expenditure of the federal government on economic supports to workers and firms and the reduction in tax revenue associated with falling GDP. The federal debt would also increase, as a consequence of the higher deficit, to 48.4 per cent of GDP.[2] By July, the projected deficit had increased to $323 billion and the debt to $1.2 trillion — 49 per cent of GDP. It was equally clear that this update would be far from the last, since the trajectory of the recovery was essentially unknowable.

This news led some Canadians to adopt one of two extreme positions, neither of which stood up well to scrutiny. The "fiscal hawks," who prided themselves on "common sense," criticized the government for not having set aside money for emergencies like COVID-19, and claimed (contrary to the Parliamentary Budget Office report) that this temporary expenditure would burden our grandchildren unless we tightened our belts and reduced expenditures so that we could lower the debt. Others pointed out how easily the federal government could find the money for all these support programs when the middle class and businesses, large and small, would benefit. Clearly, they claimed, we could afford much more generous social programs if only we had the political will to do so.

Neither of these positions is persuasive. The Parliamentary Budget Office noted that the enormous 2020 deficit would not be permanent. As the economy recovered, federal expenditure on emergency supports would decline and tax revenue would recover. The deficit would fall to expected levels and the debt would stabilize. The Canadian economy, it noted, was capable of supporting much larger deficits for several years, as long as these were temporary. In fact, the federal government could borrow money to pay for these deficits at 0.5 per cent on ten-year bonds, and a little more than 1 per cent on thirty-year bonds. At 1 per cent, servicing an additional $343 billion of federal debt would cost only $3.4 billion a year — hardly onerous by any standard, and certainly not an amount that requires tax increases to sustain.

Nevertheless, COVID-19 created a public policy dilemma. Existing social programs like EI and provincial income assistance were clearly inadequate even in normal times and totally inadequate to meet unexpected events like a global pandemic or even a repeat of the 2008 financial shock. We needed a better social safety net. And yet, such enormous sums added to government expenditure and debt were troubling and the uncertainty that would necessarily govern the next few years was significant. Did the COVID-19 pandemic make getting our fiscal house in order the first priority for many years, relegating the development of a basic income to some far distant future time when economic upheaval wouldn't happen? Basic income in Canada had been postponed on precisely such grounds in the past. To answer this question, it helps to know how the federal government spends its money during normal, pre-pandemic, times.

## Federal Government Expenditures and Revenues In Normal Times

The 2019 federal government budget projected a deficit of $19.8 billion for the fiscal year 2019–20. Of course, this didn't take into account the additional expenditure caused by the pandemic which began just before the end of the fiscal year, but it does give us a picture of "normal" expenditures and revenue.

Figure 9.1 Federal Government Expenditures, 2019–20 (Billions of Dollars)

| EXPENDITURES | |
|---|---|
| Elderly benefits | 56.2 |
| Employment Insurance (EI) | 19.9 |
| Canada Child Benefit (CCB) | 24.3 |
| Canada Health Transfer to provinces (CHT) | 40.4 |
| CST | 14.6 |
| Equalization | 19.8 |
| Other transfers to government | 2.1 |
| Direct program expenditures | 152.1 |
| Debt service charges | 26.2 |

Source: Department of Finance.

Government expenditures are paid for through tax revenue, which is all ultimately paid by individual people, and by government borrowing. Since tax revenue pays for most of government expenditure, it helps to understand which taxes generate the revenue that the federal government relies on. About half of government revenue came from income tax on individuals, just over 14 per cent from corporation tax and almost 12 per cent from the GST.

Figure 9.2 Federal Government Tax Revenue, 2019–20 (Billions of Dollars)

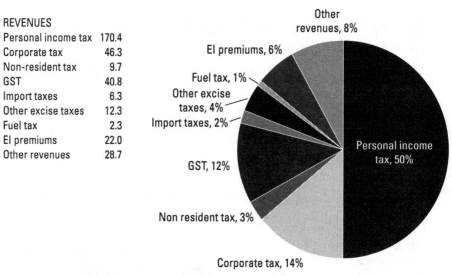

| REVENUES | |
|---|---|
| Personal income tax | 170.4 |
| Corporate tax | 46.3 |
| Non-resident tax | 9.7 |
| GST | 40.8 |
| Import taxes | 6.3 |
| Other excise taxes | 12.3 |
| Fuel tax | 2.3 |
| EI premiums | 22.0 |
| Other revenues | 28.7 |

Source: Department of Finance.

If expenditure is greater than tax revenue, the government will finance the resulting deficit by borrowing, either from Canadians directly, from the Bank of Canada or from foreigners. It borrows by issuing bonds on which it pays interest. The government deficit in 2019–20 was expected to be $19.8 billion at the time of the budget.[3] Any deficit is added to the stock of debt that was created by borrowing in the past. The debt, in 2019–20, incurred interest payments of $26.2 billion. Unlike households, governments do not have to pay off the debt. Debt becomes a problem only when the financing charges, the interest paid by the government to those who hold its bonds, become so large that its ability to pay for other things is affected. Interest rates have been so low for federal government debt that the current debt level is nowhere near that level. The federal government faces an interest rate as close to zero as one can imagine; some other countries are borrowing at negative rates of interest. Servicing this debt is far from burdensome. It is true that interest rates might rise at some future date — or they might not. If and when they do, it makes sense to worry then about the size of the debt and the amount of tax revenue required to pay interest on that debt. As long as the debt is not growing because of ongoing program expenditure, it is not a problem to be addressed. If governments are prepared to pay the interest on the debt, they can refinance it forever.

If a new program such as basic income were to be introduced, however, either the government must reduce its expenditure on something else, or increase its tax revenue, or rely on some combination of the two. The costs of an ongoing program cannot be paid for by government borrowing because that would lead to an ever-expanding federal government debt, and the service charges associated with that debt, even at low interest rates, would eventually be so large that we couldn't afford to pay for other social programs. The biggest difference between a temporary expenditure, such as the federal response to the pandemic, and a permanent and ongoing expenditure is that a temporary expenditure can be paid for by borrowing while permanent and ongoing expenditure should be paid for by tax revenue.

## How to Design a Basic Income

Every decision about how to design a basic income has important implications for cost, fairness and efficiency. There is no perfect design: each decision involves trade-offs. These decisions are based on value judgments rather than economics, so this is not a set of decisions to be left to experts. All Canadians have a stake in ensuring that our social policies reflect our collective values. Consequently, everyone needs to be engaged in a public conversation about fairness, the importance of work and self-sufficiency, how generous we want to be to people who have different values than we do, and how prepared we are to give the victims of bad luck or bad choices a second chance. These are some of the decisions that we need to talk about:

How high should the guarantee be?
The trade-off is obvious: the higher the guarantee, the more the program would cost. Moreover, the higher the guarantee, the more likely it would be that some people decide not to work at all. Since the purpose of a basic income is to address economic insecurity and poverty, it makes sense to set the guarantee close to the poverty line, allowing individuals to raise their standard of living higher by working and still receiving partial benefits.

How quickly should the benefit decline as income increases?
The more quickly the benefit declines, the less expensive a basic income would be for taxpayers. However, if benefits decline too quickly, people who work might decide that working an additional hour doesn't make sense for them. A part-time worker might choose not to look for full-time work, or people might work less overtime. If benefits decline quickly as income increases, fewer people would receive anything. The Canada Child Benefit declines at a very gradual rate as income increases; as a consequence, the program is expensive, but it benefits the majority of families. If many people benefit, the program might have more political support than a more targeted program.

Should basic income be based on individual income or on family income?
In Canada, we pay our income tax as individuals, so a family with one high-income earner will pay more in taxes than a family with an

identical total income divided between two earners. However, most of our benefits in Canada are based on family income. The Canada Child Benefit, for example, is based on the incomes of both parents, and income assistance in all provinces is based on total family income. The Guaranteed Income Supplement received by a married or common-law senior couple is lower than the amount that would be received by two unrelated people.

The justification for using family income is that it costs more for a single person to live on their own than it costs each of two people who can share some expenses. For example, a two-bedroom apartment does not usually cost twice as much as a one-bedroom apartment. Therefore, it might seem reasonable to choose a family as the benefit unit. But at a time when many couples do not officially marry, how desirable is it for the bureaucracy to determine the nature of the relationship between people who live together? If we simply take recipients at their word, we risk establishing a system that encourages people to misrepresent their circumstances. A benefit based on family income is one of the design features that current income assistance recipients resent bitterly, and it is a characteristic flaw in many Canadian social programs. The Canada Child Benefit, despite its many excellent features, is based on family income, and some single mothers have had their benefits reduced or clawed back when they were not able to demonstrate to the satisfaction of the Canada Revenue Agency that they were single parents.

Family relationships vary widely between population groups, by age, and even between similar groups in different provinces. Some marriages are formally sanctioned and relatively stable; other relationships are more fluid. Fewer couples choose to formally marry today as compared to a generation ago, and among those who do, first marriages generally occur at a later age than in the past. The decline in marriage rates does not mean that Canadians are no longer choosing committed, long-term relationships, but it does make it harder for authorities to determine the nature of the relationship between people who live together. If policies are based on a "family," then resources must be committed to policing personal relationships. This raises the cost of enforcing the policy and undermines one of the benefits of a basic income, which is that there should be no need for the government to intrude into personal decisions.

Defining income on the basis of whether it creates an incentive to marry or divorce may seem odd to anyone but an economist; most people seem to think such a personal decision would be made for other reasons. However, there is a historical reason to be sensitive to this issue. The negative income tax experiments that took place in the United States forty years ago foundered on precisely this issue. Early results seemed to suggest that recipient families in Seattle and Denver were more likely to divorce than were controls.[4] These results convinced some people that a basic income would discourage marriage, particularly among African American families. This led some early basic income advocates, such as Daniel Patrick Moynihan, to withdraw support because they believed that marriage was one of the best ways to reduce poverty among women and children.[5] A decade later, the data were re-analyzed, and the conclusion that recipients were more likely to divorce was called into question. However, by that time policy debate had already moved on to other issues, and basic income was not on the radar any longer.[6]

### Who receives the money?

When Family Allowances were first established in Canada, they were made payable to the mother because it was believed that the mother was more likely than the father to spend the money in ways that benefited the children. Some family benefits in Canada are now payable to the lower-income adult, which is an attempt to offset potential power differences within the family. Delivering support to the lower-paid adult gives that person, in theory, the financial capacity to leave a potentially violent marriage without worrying about whether they can afford to feed their children or keep them out of a shelter. In reality, of course, life is more challenging. Many people in oppressive relationships do not have control over their own money, and it really doesn't matter who the cheque is sent to or whose account receives the deposit. Family relationships are not so easily influenced.

The point, however, is that we can deliver the money to the lowest-paid adult however we define income; these are separate issues.

## What role does age play?

Depending on design, as much as one-third of the net costs of the basic income are required to support single adults between eighteen and twenty-four.[7] Not everyone in that age group is dependent on their parents, but including single adults living with their parents will raise the costs of a basic income significantly because this group includes many people working less than full-time at low-paying jobs. Sometimes, this is a choice made to facilitate education, and often the situation is temporary. How much should be spent to reduce the breadth and depth of poverty among a population that, in some but not all cases, has access to parental support? If payments are disallowed to single adults who live with their parents, many of these young people will simply move out. That does not mean that they will not remain financially dependent on their parents. If support is extended to all young people at age eighteen, is it certain that the money will not cause harm? There is always the temptation for older people to assume that young people do not have the foresight to make good decisions.

As an alternative, the qualifying age for a basic income could be set at twenty-five, and this limitation would be relatively simple and non-intrusive to enforce. However, increasing the qualifying age also causes difficulty because there is real poverty among eighteen- to twenty-four-year-olds. Young people, including especially those transitioning out of foster care, homeless youth and young parents, certainly experience poverty and economic insecurity. Moreover, this is the particular age group that most often encounters low-quality, low-paying work.

It is not clear whether a basic income or a more directed program that makes a benefit conditional on participation in approved work or study programs is the optimal response for this age group. It is simply not known how young people would respond to a basic income, or what the long-term consequences of their decisions might be. The benefits of a more intrusive, conditional program specifically for youth might exceed the costs. It is unfortunate that none of the basic income experiments anywhere in the world chose to investigate this issue.

How should basic income align with other social programs? Basic income is built on the idea that families know how to spend money better than do experts. There are, however, exceptions. Health care insurance is one such example. There is a lot of evidence that private health insurance leads to more inequitable, ineffective and expensive outcomes than public health insurance. Therefore, it makes sense to have public health insurance. Special benefits tied to income assistance are particularly badly designed. If someone who receives income assistance receives a benefit such as pharmaceutical drug coverage, why should a working individual with the same total income be denied such support? These kinds of benefits should be based on level of income rather than source of income.

The bigger question is which federal and provincial programs and tax credits ought to be replaced by a basic income. The Canada Pension Plan is a work-related public insurance plan that allows workers to save for retirement and insure against disability. It serves a useful purpose. Moreover, it has obligations to workers who have already contributed. Employment Insurance is more ambiguous. It provides support during temporary layoffs, and it is an insurance program entirely paid for by workers and employers. However, fewer than 40 per cent of displaced workers actually qualify for support when they need it, because they don't work enough hours to meet the eligibility requirement. Many of those who don't qualify are the least well-paid workers, a group that includes a disproportionate number of women, newcomers and racialized people. Some workers, mainly those in regular, full-time work, do much better with EI than they would under a modest basic income. However, others receive pitifully low payments. It makes sense to ask whether EI should be rolled into a basic income but, at the very least, the pandemic demonstrated that EI required extensive modification. It is hard to argue, for example, that EI regulations that differ by province are efficient, effective or fair. Other expenditures, such as the federal GST credit and the Canada Workers Benefit, might be rolled into a basic income with much less controversy.

This careful design work requires policy expertise and knowledge of the costs and effectiveness of current expenditures. People who currently benefit from existing programs and tax credits will, understandably, object to restructuring, but the decisions need to be based on clear principles. It may be possible to restructure programs so that no one is made worse off with a basic income than they would be under the current scheme, but it is not easy. More likely, there will be winners and losers as with any policy change, so the principles on which the redesign is based must be transparent.

What is less controversial is that programs designed to address other issues, such as addictions, disabilities and mental health challenges, cannot be replaced by a basic income. Individuals who benefit from such programs will still require support even if their material needs are better met. Basic income gives people money; it is not designed to address more profound social and health issues, although many of these issues are clearly made worse by poverty.

How should the money be paid?

Many single mothers complain that their Canada Child Benefit changes too slowly while their income assistance changes too much from month to month.

Some of the strongest support for basic income is associated with the belief that a lot of bureaucracy could be eliminated by paying a basic income through the tax system. Most people's tax forms are completed and their income tax reconciled once a year in April. If there is a refund, it arrives in one deposit soon after. If received, a GST credit or Canada Child Benefit might be paid monthly or quarterly, but it will normally be based on the previous year's taxable income, just as the Guaranteed Income Supplement for seniors is based on the previous year's taxable income. For low-income Canadians, and particularly for those who work and receive sporadic incomes, this poses a big problem. For working-age people, income and family composition can change a lot during the course of a year. People get married and divorced, change jobs, give birth or adopt and children move in or out. For basic income to be a primary means of support, it must be able to adjust to changing circumstances.

There is some capacity in the tax system to adjust payments for tax credits like the Canada Workers Benefit and the Canada Child Benefit, so that they are based on current and anticipated income rather than past income. Similarly, the Guaranteed Income Supplement can reflect expected income. These adjustments, however, are not automatic; they require specific requests and take time. But we shouldn't assume that the way the system does work is the way it must work.

People received CERB support very quickly through online CRA accounts used to administer income tax because policymakers decided that was a priority when the economy shut down during the COVID-19 pandemic. Students were required to report their income every month so benefits could, in principle, be adjusted to changing income. The federal government decided not to withhold tax on the CERB as it was paid, but they could have done so, which would minimize the adjustment required when income taxes are next filed. The federal government was already working on an e-payroll system that would allow automatic reporting by employers, as is done in many other countries. A clunky tax system has been tolerated for many years, assuming it was as good as it could be. The pandemic demonstrated just how much better social benefits can be delivered when the will exists. However, CRA accounts are not needed to deliver a basic income. A modified EI system or any other system could be used. What is important is to allow benefits to adjust quickly to changing circumstances, without the lengthy waits and mountains of paperwork that current systems require.

A basic income could be set up to introduce some much-needed financial stability into the lives of low-income people. A government payment that they know they will receive with certainty allows someone to plan their expenditures and to deal with unexpected needs. For a low-wage working person, in particular, a predictable basic income might be very useful. Wages can vary a lot from month to month, and it is possible that wage-earners will not know exactly how much they will earn until the cheque arrives. Hours of work may not be guaranteed. Wages might be paid into a bank account that is in overdraft and seized by the bank, or workers may receive less than they expected because their employer charges them for uniforms or other supplies. Wages might be withheld for a variety of reasons, some of them unexpected. Similarly, child support from an ex-partner may or may not arrive. By contrast, a fixed income paid by the government could be an important source of stability. However, if the government payment is also adjusted each month to account for volatile earnings, and especially if unexpected penalties are imposed on that income, any attempt to budget can be thrown into chaos.

As an alternative, basic income could be delivered through a modified system that reconciles accounts over a period of several months. Between adjustments, other income might fluctuate, but the recipient would receive a stable government payment. Someone who earns more than expected during this period will not be treated as having incurred a debt that must be repaid. Rather, basic income would be reduced going forward. Between adjustments, everyone would know with certainty how much they would receive.

There must also be a robust capacity to deal with unexpected emergencies. For that reason, some of the administrative capacity associated with income assistance must be maintained at the provincial level even after a basic income is introduced. This requirement, however, should be much less than that required by the current system, in which every payment is recalculated each month.

### Should there be an asset test?

The ability of people to participate in the economy depends on both their income and their wealth or assets. Some people have little wage income but hold significant wealth. This group might include seniors with small pensions and a lot of wealth tied up in housing. It might also include professionals, such as physicians, who incorporate and reinvest earnings in the corporation rather than taking them as income or dividends. The rules can be set to ensure that a basic income goes only to people who need it, eliminating professionals for example, but sometimes it is difficult to determine the appropriate response.

Fairness would seem to suggest that a basic income should be reduced for people with assets as it is for people with higher incomes. It is, however, not quite so simple. Financial assets held outside registered accounts typically generate incomes that will reduce the basic income benefit just as if they were wage incomes. Should the capital that people hold also reduce basic income? What about RRSPs, RESPs and TFSAs, which offer special tax treatment, as well as retained earnings in businesses, and real assets, such as vehicles and real estate? This is a very difficult political issue for any government. Assets held in registered accounts such as RRSPs and TFSAs have special tax treatment because a social decision has been made to encourage long-term savings. RESPs encourage saving for education. Should an individual who benefits from a basic income not also have the opportunity to save for retirement or for a child's education? Should someone who stops working for health reasons be forced to liquidate all their savings before they receive any help?

Until three years ago, I was a pharmaceutical sales rep. Most of my income was commissions and I did pretty good. My company didn't have a pension plan, but they matched contributions I made to my RRSP. I had retirement savings and my house was paid for. I had some other savings — not a lot, but I was comfortable. Then I lost my job when the company was bought up, then I got sick. So, I'm fifty-three and out of a job. No one is lining up to hire an old guy with cancer when they can get some twenty-five-year-old and pay them a lot less.

I'm pretty lucky. Lots of guys in chemo have got nothing. But I had money saved to retire when I'm sixty-five. It's not going to last very long if I start running it down at fifty-three. I can sell my house, but I've got to live somewhere. This job is all I've ever done but deliver pizza when I was a kid. Who's going to hire me? I'm either "over-qualified" or "just not competitive." No one says, "you're too old." — Karl

How should we accommodate real estate and other assets, such as vehicles? Most income assistance programs have raised asset limits to allow the ownership of (at least) modest vehicles, and few people are forced out of the family home when they require income assistance. How much is too much? Any jurisdiction that introduces a basic income will have to grapple with very different opinions. What seems obvious to some will seem far too generous to others.

Money is going to people who do not need it such as: my ex-friend who is sitting on $2 million in real estate and has been collecting "welfare" through her children for ten years because she doesn't "want a measly job for $40,000 a year." She receives family help, travels, dines at restaurants etc. Or, my nephew who makes $100,000 a year, took his family of five on two

overseas vacations in one year, receives a small payment for
his three children every month and asked to borrow $40 from
me. I don't agree that the programs in place now are helping
the people who really need it. If a guaranteed minimum
income is introduced, I hope assets, including principal
residence and vehicles, are taken into consideration.
— I. McInally

This is a challenging political issue, but it is important to allow people
to save and invest. Savings protect people from unexpected changes
in their circumstances. People with savings are less likely to rely on
credit cards or payday lenders and can borrow money on reasonable
terms from banks and credit unions when they need it. Savings create
economic security, which allows people to relocate for new job offers
or to take risks with self-employment. However, any government will
need to reconcile very different opinions about how much is too much.

## What Would a Basic Income Cost?
The Canada Emergency Response Benefit was not a basic income. It
was a temporary income support, the purpose of which was to allow
people to stay home during the worst period of a pandemic. The cost
of the CERB is more than a basic income would be during normal,
non-pandemic times because many of the people who relied upon
CERB would be working if their workplaces were not closed by government order. In fact, one of the benefits of a basic income is that it
would act as an automatic stabilizer, ensuring people have money to
spend when they need it without the government having to develop
a set of special programs to meet temporary needs. However, the
cost of a basic income during normal times is an important issue,
and that cost depends on exactly how it is designed. Consequently,
only the costs of specific proposals can be estimated. This book has
focused on a basic income where the benefit is reduced as other
income increases. There are several cost estimates for different ver-

sions of this proposal, all based on the careful use of a simulation model of the Canadian economy that is regularly used by the Parliamentary Budget Office to estimate the costs of policy proposals.

## The Cost of a National Program Modelled on the Ontario Experiment

A 2018 study by the Parliamentary Budget Office — the independent and non-partisan office that provides analyses of the state of the nation's finances — was the first to cut through some of the confusion about costs. At the height of debate about the short-lived Ontario Basic Income Guarantee experiment, Conservative Member of Parliament Pierre Poilievre asked a simple question: "If the Ontario scheme were to be rolled out across the country, how much would it cost?" Since Ontario had to make decisions about design elements to implement its pilot, the Parliamentary Budget Office had something concrete to work with.[8]

If every Canadian between eighteen and sixty-four were offered a basic income of $16,989 ($24,027 for couples), less 50 per cent of earned income, and if disabled people received an additional $6,000 per year, the gross cost to the federal budget would be a staggering $76 billion per year. (These odd levels of support were chosen because they were identical at the time to the amount of support someone would receive from Old Age Security and Guaranteed Income Supplement at the age of sixty-five.) However, the Parliamentary Budget Office noted, the federal government was currently spending $32.9 billion to support low-income Canadians in this age group. If the money the federal government was spending on refundable and non-refundable tax credits and special programs for low-income Canadians of working age was spent instead on a basic income, the federal government would only have to find $43.1 billion to pay for a national basic income.

This is still a great deal of money. However, the Ontario pilot was set up as a potential alternative to Ontario Works and the Ontario Disability Support Program — basic income assistance for working-age people with and without disabilities. In Ontario, these programs cost $8 billion each year, and if we assume there are similar costs in other provinces, that represents an additional $20 billion, not including the costs of administration.[9] If it were possible to reallocate this provincial expenditure to a national basic income, a challenging task we will consider in the next chapter, the net cost of a national basic income would fall to $23 billion. A net cost of $23 billion is starting to look decidedly less utopian. In fact, the Canada Child Benefit costs that much every year.[10] None of this takes into account any potential savings on the administration of provincial income assistance.

The upfront costs of delivering a basic income are important, because we need to ensure that we have tax revenue to pay for it. However, basic income should really be seen as an investment rather than a cost. While the fundamental purpose of introducing a basic income is to allow all Canadians to live modest but decent lives whatever economic challenges they face, there is a hard-edged economic rationale for addressing poverty: the consequences of poverty are expensive. In the Mincome experiment, hospitalizations fell by 8.5 per cent among basic income recipients relative to a group of similar people who acted as a control group; in 2019, Canada spent more than $70 billion on hospitals alone. Mincome also caused similar reductions in visits to family doctors. There are very few social problems that are not made worse by poverty. A basic income would be one way to slow the relentless increases in the costs of other social programs that enter people's lives after poverty has left its mark. Some advocates argue that savings on social programs would be greater than the costs of the program.[11]

## The Costs of Other Designs

Design issues are important because they are really about what is considered fair and just. As more and more people began to focus on a guaranteed livable income as the appropriate design of a basic income, the costs of different versions were estimated. Some offered larger or smaller guarantees, while others increased or reduced the amount by which the benefit declined as income increased. Some versions focused on adults between eighteen and sixty-four, reasoning that children and seniors already had access to forms of basic income through the Canada Child Benefit and Old Age Security/Guaranteed Income Supplement, while others included seniors. In each case, the cost of the basic income depended on the design features put in place.

For example, *Basic Income: Some Policy Options for Canada* by Chandra Pasma and Sheila Regehr uses the same methodology as the Parliamentary Budget Office to tackle the question of how these various design features affect the cost of offering a basic income.[12] They begin with several principles:

- Basic income is available to all Canadians, permanent residents and protected persons, and does not depend on employment status, availability for work, family composition or savings.

- Basic income is universally available when people need it. The only conditions are income and age.

- The maximum amount will ensure that everyone is above the poverty line, after all taxes and transfers are accounted for.

- When people work, they should always come out ahead. The benefit will not be reduced dollar for dollar.

- The benefit will decline gradually as income increases.

- Basic income will respond to fluctuating levels of income.

- Basic income and any tax changes will be such that benefits are greater for lower-income individuals and taxes are higher for higher-income individuals.

- Basic income and tax changes should respect gender equality.

- Basic income may replace some income security programs, but not at the expense of essential social services and supports such as affordable housing, health, dental and medical benefits for veterans, low-income Canadians or persons with disabilities.

- Basic income will not replace any social insurance programs, such as Employment Insurance or the Canada Pension Plan or Quebec Pension Plan.

- Basic income is national in scope, but may involve national and provincial programs.

They develop and calculate the cost for three different options that respect these principles:

- **Option 1**: an income-tested benefit for adults ages eighteen through sixty-four. Single adults receive $22,000 while couples receive $31,113. The benefit declines by forty cents for every dollar earned. Those aged sixty-five and above continue to receive Old Age Security and the Guaranteed Income Supplement, while children receive the Canada Child Benefit.

- **Option 2**: an income-tested benefit for adults over age eighteen. Single adults receive $22,000 while couples receive $31,113. The benefit declines by forty cents for every dollar earned. Children receive the CCB.

- **Option 3:** all adults over age eighteen receive $22,000 a year, regardless of income. Children receive the CCB.

Option 1 has the lowest gross cost of $134 billion annually. However, the authors find $136 billion to pay for it by eliminating the GST credit and the Canada Workers Benefit, increasing income taxes marginally for higher-income Canadians, eliminating a series of non-refundable tax credits and deductions and increasing corporate taxes from 15 to 20 per cent (small business taxes from 10.5 to 13.5 per cent). The basic income would replace provincial income assistance, so provinces would be expected to contribute a portion of the money they currently spend on income assistance.

Option 2 costs more because it includes seniors, but since basic income for seniors would replace Old Age Security and the Guaranteed Income Supplement, there is more money available to pay for it. The gross cost is $187 billion but the revenue to fund it is $189 billion.

Option 3 is the most expensive by far, so it requires considerably more income to pay for it. The gross cost is $637 billion a year, which would require more extensive tax increases. Everyone would pay significantly higher taxes from the first dollar earned. For most people, the $22,000 basic income they receive more than compensates for the additional taxes.

In every model, the poorest 50 per cent of Canadians benefit from a basic income. Poverty is virtually eliminated. The tax system is made much simpler and more transparent because the hidden benefits of deductions and non-refundable tax credits that benefit the highest-income Canadians are eliminated. There are limitations to this modelling exercise. It cannot take into account behavioural responses.

There are some interesting differences between the models. Option 2 includes seniors. Lower-income seniors benefit significantly, but higher-income seniors are worse off than they were before. This is because our current system is relatively generous towards high-income seniors; Old Age Security doesn't begin to decline until income reaches $79,054. Option 3 pays all adults the same benefit, regardless of whether they live alone or with others. This gives much greater independence to all adults and it eliminates the need for bureaucrats to determine whether someone is in a marital relationship with someone else. It affords much greater dignity, but dignity comes at a cost. Two adults who live together get less under Options 1 and 2 than do two adults living apart.

This set of calculations, along with the many others that have appeared, is great fun for policy nerds, but it does illustrate very clearly the trade-offs that are involved in designing a basic income. It is not any more complicated to design a basic income than it was to design the Canada Child Benefit, or Old Age Security and the Guaranteed Income Supplement before it, or any other benefit or tax. Any policy works to the advantage of some types of families and at the expense of others. Any policy requires a decision about how we will define income, which is really very complicated. Any policy requires us to determine whether or not savings or wealth should be taken into account. This document shows very clearly what the costs of our principles are. We can eliminate poverty in Canada. We cannot do so without raising tax revenue somehow. The more generous our basic income, the more it will cost. The more people who are included, the more it will cost.

Options 1 and 2 are generous basic income programs that are entirely feasible. They are not costless, but they are affordable if we choose to pay for them. We can generate the tax revenue required, however some people will certainly pay more in taxes if we choose to offer either program. As in the case of the Ontario model, there is no free lunch. There is a cost involved, but it is a cost worth paying.

It is worth thinking a bit about the relevance of Option 3. In most parts of the world, when people talk about a universal basic income (UBI) this is the model they mean. Everyone, rich or poor, receives money every month and taxes have to increase dramatically to pay for it. This model has not gained much traction in Canada among people who've thought about it for very long. As the modelling exercise shows, it is possible to generate the same net costs and pay for any kind of a basic income — in theory. However, in practice, Option 3 starts to look a good deal less feasible. Its gross cost is $637 billion a year, which is about twice what the federal government is currently spending on everything. Some of the money to fund it could be found by eliminating duplicated programs at the federal and provincial levels. But total tax revenue would also have to increase. I don't believe that Canadians are indifferent about the total size of the government, as measured by its tax revenue and total expenditure, and I certainly don't believe that high-income Canadians would be prepared to foot the tax bill. Critics of basic income often use the cost of Option 3 as a reason to dismiss much more modest and much more feasible basic income proposals, conveniently forgetting to mention that all serious basic income proposals in Canada reject this model and propose, instead, that basic income should be directed towards those in need.

This is an invitation to think hard about how Canadians support people who need help, and how tax revenue is collected from others to pay for it. Basic income redistributes income from the wealthy to the less wealthy; that is its purpose. Not everyone will gain financially. Everyone, however, will gain by living in a society that treats people with dignity, where all children have the ability to reach their potential and in which all Canadians can share the economic wealth of the country.

## How Behaviour Can Affect Costs

One of the limitations of trying to estimate the cost of any social program is that it is difficult to forecast the ways that human behaviour might change as a result of introducing the new program and the implications these changes will have for cost. For example, will a basic income encourage people to work fewer hours? Will it encourage some workers to stop working altogether? Or will it, as was the case in Finland and Utrecht, encourage people to move from low-paid, precarious jobs into regular, full-time work and to pay higher taxes as a consequence?

Economists like to talk about "incentivizing" behaviour and typically assume that we respond far more than we really do to monetary advantages and disadvantages.[13] This is what accounts for some of the extremely high estimates that some economists have attached to basic income.[14] Their concern with behavioural change is overstated. Most people working full-time are unlikely to quit their jobs when offered a basic income, and most don't have the flexibility to decide how many hours they would like to work each year. People work the hours they are asked to work. Other people are working part-time when they would work full-time if a job were open to them. When we look at other programs that change the incentives to work, the results are often ambiguous.[15] Despite the certainty with which many argue that a basic income will reduce work effort, there is very little empirical evidence to support such a claim, as we saw in Chapter 5.

How basic income is paid for is also relevant. A wealth tax could be imposed, for example. However, wealthy people will certainly try to move their assets to places where they can avoid paying the tax. As a consequence, any government that imposes a wealth tax often finds itself receiving far less revenue than it expected. There are a variety of ways to raise taxes, and each will have different effects on the economy. Critics focus on the potential impact of higher corporate taxes on business investment and of higher marginal tax rates on highly paid labour, arguing that not only will a basic income encourage the poor to work less, but it will also encourage firms to invest less in Canada. Professionals and other highly paid labour, they argue, will work less and relocate to lower tax jurisdictions, particularly the United States. (I have never understood why the same critics argue that giving money to poor people causes them to work less but giving money to rich people by cutting their taxes causes them to work more.) In any case, this fear too is dramatically overblown. There are many ways to increase taxes, most of which do not involve raising marginal income tax rates. The most obvious is to enforce existing tax law so that high-income earners actually pay the taxes they owe. Examining the various non-refundable tax credits that permeate the tax system and benefit mostly high-income earners is another. A third option is to increase consumption taxes such as the GST. While some worry that this would be particularly harmful to low-income people, these extra taxes would be more than offset by the basic income they would receive. The GST is a reasonably efficient way to ensure that high-income people actually pay at least some tax.

The estimates of the Parliamentary Budget Office effectively undermine the claim of unaffordability. While $23 billion annually sounds like a tremendous amount of money, it is a very small proportion of total federal expenditure. Even if we choose to increase taxes to pay for the program, the benefits will surely be worth the additional costs. In the words of journalist Andrew Coyne: "Three points on the GST to end poverty? Guaranteed income sounds like a good deal."[16]

## The Cost of a Basic Income During Pandemic Times

All of these studies have shown us that Canada can afford a basic income during ordinary times. It won't be costless and tax revenue would have to increase to pay for it, but the estimated cost of a modest basic income is not out of line with many other programs we already happily pay for, including pensions for seniors and the Canada Child Benefit. Basic income is not just a cost but rather an investment in families. It will lead to beneficial outcomes measured not only in quality of life, but also in hard fiscal terms. If people with a basic income don't have to rely on the health care system quite so much to deal with the consequences of hard lives, then the relentless growth of health care budgets across the country will slow. If fewer children end up in the foster care system because their families live with less stress and have more resources to provide for them, then the growth of child welfare budgets will moderate. If fewer people are criminalized for poverty-related crimes, then justice budgets will be constrained. These savings in other social programs cannot be used to pay the upfront costs of a basic income, but they do show us the long run financial benefits of investing in families before they need much more profound interventions to deal with the consequences of economic insecurity.

A basic income program has one other beneficial feature: it automatically expands during hard economic times to provide necessary support to families when the economy contracts, and it automatically shrinks when the economy recovers. When public health measures shut down many workplaces in response to COVID-19, the absence of a basic income program caused governments to scramble. In a few short weeks, they had to invent and implement a series of emergency measures like the CERB to limit the economic devastation and, because it was all done so quickly, there were glitches in the program design. If a basic income had been in place, the response would have been seamless. Families that lost income would apply to the basic income program that was already in place. That program would have automatically responded to their income loss. No one would have to decide when to end the program, because it would be permanent. As the economy recovered, people would go back to work and fewer would apply for support. The amount of money sent to Canadian families would automatically shrink. That is, a basic income acts as an automatic stabilizer for the economy, pumping more money out to families automatically when the economy contracts, and less when it recovers. Automatic stabilizers limit the destruction caused by economic recessions, and don't rely on governments to make good decisions quickly.

The cost of a basic income therefore depends on how well the economy is doing. If the economy is in good shape, employment rates are high and fewer people apply for basic income. Therefore, the cost of the program is small. During recessions, unemployment rises and wages fall. More people turn to basic income for extra help, and the costs of the program increase. The fluctuating costs of a basic income program are not a design flaw, but rather a beneficial feature. The basic income program absorbs the risks of economic change so that it doesn't fall on the backs of individual workers and families who can least afford it.

The cost of basic income would have been much greater during the pandemic year than it would be in normal times. This is precisely what the Parliamentary Budget Office discovered when it re-estimated the cost of the same program it investigated in 2018 for the year 2020. The Parliamentary Budget Office reported that the estimated gross cost of the program for the final six months of the fiscal year 2020 would be $47.5 billion, which was more than twice the cost of the estimate for 2018. The higher cost was due to the higher rates of unemployment and lower family incomes expected during these months as a result of COVID-19.[17] They also estimated the costs associated with different program designs. Any program put in place to address the unemployment caused by the response to COVID-19 would be very costly, and it is worth keeping in mind that the estimated cost of a basic income would be less than the cost of the CERB, and basic income would have the additional benefit of not penalizing workers who want to return to work.

If a basic income were to be implemented and made permanent, it would automatically respond to contractions like those caused by COVID-19, like the economic shock of 2008 and like the many earlier recessions that caused financial hardship for ordinary people just trying to pay the rent and feed their kids. It would automatically contract as the economy recovered and people went back to work. A basic income has two important features: it does not rely on governments to make good decisions in a timely manner, which is always hard and especially so during economic upheavals, and it shoulders the burden of economic events beyond the control of ordinary people. Recessions are not caused by supermarket cashiers, warehouse workers, restaurant servers, artists, teachers, physiotherapists or bartenders. It seems harsh to expect them to bear all the consequences.

## Developing a Canadian Basic Income
The design challenges associated with basic income are significant, but they are also an opportunity for all Canadians to reflect on

the kind of society that we want to build. Discussions about basic income, already in the air after the 2008 recession, acquired a new urgency during the pandemic. Changes that were already underway, such as the transition from storefronts to online retail and the growing reliance on knowledge workers hired for a single task without long-term commitment from an employer, accelerated. Other issues, such as the need to balance paid work with care work, took on a new urgency. Basic income was already being talked about by denizens of Silicon Valley and in the offices of the World Bank, the International Labour Organization and the Organisation for Economic Co-operation and Development well before the pandemic. Experimental results were trickling in from the Netherlands, Finland and Barcelona, and experiments continued in the United States and elsewhere. Spain was the first to declare that it would introduce a permanent basic income in response to the pandemic. Unconditional cash transfers have had remarkable results in low-income countries around the world. But every one of these instances takes the idea of basic income and makes it concrete by making very specific decisions about these design issues.

What decisions would best reflect Canadian values — our generosity, kindness and willingness to give people second chances and, at the same time, our resistance to those who would take advantage? What kind of a basic income is right for Canada?

# Chapter 10
# Getting from Here to There

The COVID-19 pandemic created a need, but also a unique opportunity for the federal government to address the limitations of existing income support policies. The Canada Emergency Response Benefit was first introduced as a very temporary four-month support program, but it was clear within a month of its introduction that financial supports would be required much longer as schools and summer camps waited to re-open, leaving parents with child care responsibilities, some cafés and restaurants closed permanently while others pivoted to take-out only and many retail shops filed for bankruptcy protection. Some people were called back to work quickly, notably in construction as provinces poured support into infrastructure, but others either had no jobs to return to or were unable to return to the jobs that existed because elementary schools remained closed. Simply extending the CERB was not sufficient, both because too many people did not qualify and because people who returned to work lost the entire benefit as soon as their monthly earnings exceeded $1,000. At the same time, the limitations of EI were so extensive that massive renovations would be required to provide support for Canadians still out of work. Consequently, when the federal government announced that people receiving support from the CERB would be transitioned to Employment Insurance, they also announced the creation of yet another transitional benefit to support the many who would not qualify.

As the first wave of the pandemic waned, new jobs began to appear and some employers reported difficulty attracting labour. It would take time for some employers to recognize that employees would return only when they could expect a safe working environment, care for their children and wages high enough to meet minimum needs. However, the pandemic also drew our attention to the low wages, poor working conditions and economic insecurity routinely endured by many low-wage workers even before COVID-19. The need for change was apparent. What was less obvious, but no less important, was the opportunity for policy change.

## Respecting Provincial Jurisdiction

One of the significant impediments to improving income support in Canada is the division of responsibilities between the federal government and the provinces. Income assistance is a provincial responsibility and provinces jealously guard their territories. However, income assistance is also costly for the provinces. During the pandemic, provincial tax revenues declined, exacerbating what was already a significant and growing problem for almost all of them. Newfoundland and Labrador had difficulty selling provincial bonds to finance its debt even before the closure. Manitoba had already called on the federal government to borrow on behalf of the provinces. Alberta, even before COVID-19 created economic chaos, was beginning to acknowledge that it could no longer count on recovery in the oil and gas sector to shield it from the consequences of its low-tax environment. While the fiscal situation of the federal government was strong, many provinces were struggling. Provinces have less capacity to raise taxes of all kinds, and they pay higher interest rates than the federal government on money they borrow. At the same time, provinces are responsible for health care, provincial income assistance and education. The federal government transfers money to the provinces to help pay for these responsibilities, but the costs of these programs are growing much more quickly than the money received from the federal government. The cost of providing health care, in particular, was already growing significantly faster than revenue because the population was aging. The pandemic laid bare the shortcomings of personal care homes — a provincial responsibility — in all provinces. Provincial finances were in poor shape even before the pandemic, and the reduced tax revenue and increased health care costs associated with COVID-19 did nothing to improve them.

If the federal government were to take on the financial burden associated with adult benefits, provinces would benefit financially. A basic income could, if it were offered at a reasonable level, replace provincial income assistance, which is everywhere a stigmatized, inadequate program of last resort. Provinces have jurisdiction over adult benefits, but the 2020 pandemic offered an opportunity to imagine how we might move forward.

During the first weeks of the pandemic, normally antagonistic provincial and federal relations thawed somewhat as various levels of government worked together to address the novel threat associated with the infection. It would have been nice, but unexpected, for the spirit of co-operation to carry over into the post-pandemic world. One way to address the fiscal straights of the provinces would have been for the federal government to offer working-age Canadians a basic income with political support from the provinces and First Nations governments. It was (barely) conceivable that all levels of government might have entered into negotiations in good faith. This level of co-operation hasn't often been seen and rarely lasts very long. This might have been the best outcome, but it was also the least likely.[1]

However, the federal government could provide leadership and offer a national basic income while respecting the jurisdictional sensitivities of the provinces and even advancing self-governance goals of First Nations. As governments contemplated how to end the emergency supports and began to think about the system that should replace them, the disparity between the financial health of the federal and provincial governments became ever clearer. The provinces, collectively, needed additional funding from the federal government if they were to meet their jurisdictional responsibilities after the pandemic. An ideal solution, from the perspective of the provinces, would be a simple transfer of funding from the federal government that they could spend however they liked. From the federal perspective, this was less desirable. The federal government would prefer to have some control over how the money might be spent.

If the federal government were to provide leadership by offering to provide all adults an income-tested guaranteed livable income at a level near the poverty line, it would alleviate some of the financial pressure on the provinces. While it would not be the most desirable outcome for any of the provinces, some would be sorely tempted. Any province that objected on constitutional grounds could be offered the standard deal usually negotiated with Quebec: a province prepared to offer its residents a benefit at least as good as the federal basic income would have the right to administer its own program in its own way with federal government financial support. And, while it would hardly be the desired outcome, any province that chose to do so could retain the right to opt out of the basic income altogether — and forego financial support from the federal government. Funding for a federal basic income would come from general tax revenue, so residents in provinces that opted out would, in essence, help to pay for a program from which their provincial legislatures had decided they should not benefit.

Each province could respond as it liked to a federal basic income. The federal basic income would provide a floor; nothing would prevent any province from offering additional benefits to people who had been receiving provincial income assistance. Most provinces would treat the basic income received by their residents as income for purposes of calculating provincial income assistance and disability support, and claw back provincial income assistance as a consequence. Others might choose to offer a top-up to meet local costs. All Canadians would have a guaranteed income significantly higher than any province now offers. The provinces would find themselves with fewer obligations to low-income residents who receive a federal basic income, which would give them the opportunity to reallocate provincial expenditure to programs designed to meet particular provincial and local needs. Provincial income assistance could be reduced to a much smaller program focused on direct services for people with disabilities, special cases, local needs and emergencies, with the bulk of provincial funding going to support public services. The federal government would have simultaneously addressed persistent poverty, ensured all Canadians' economic security and addressed the fiscal woes of the provinces. One way to protect the value of basic income and ensure that all Canadians would continue to receive an equitable share of economic growth is to peg increases in the basic income to the growth rate of the Canadian economy.[2]

This proposal would allow the federal government to do what the federal government does best — collect taxes and transfer money. Provincial and local governments, who are arguably closer to the people and more aware of local circumstances and needs, could focus on delivering specific services designed to meet unique needs. No province would be prevented from offering its residents a better program than the federal alternative, and every province would have the option to design and administer its own program, as long as it was at least as good as the federal program.

## Addressing Reconciliation and Enhancing Self-Governance

It has taken Canada a very long time to acknowledge the aspirations of Indigenous communities to govern and provide for themselves. An unwillingness to devolve control has had devastating consequences. Indigenous people who live off reserve would benefit from a national basic income just as would other residents of Canada. However Indigenous communities, such as reserves and independent Inuit communities, have a nation-to-nation relationship with the federal government that demands additional consideration. While the process of negotiation must be developed by the Indigenous and the federal government, there is a platform in place that could be used to co-create a basic income (or alternative) for delivery in Indigenous communities.

The role of the federal government should be to provide at least the same level of support for Indigenous people living on reserve as for other Canadians, and then to get out of the way and let Indigenous governments decide for themselves what they need. The federal government should be a willing, but non-controlling, partner. The creation of a national basic income is an opportunity to build on past successes and challenges, such as ongoing efforts to transfer greater control of health care to First Nations, and initiatives in education, child welfare and social assistance. The path to devolving control has been painfully slow with many barriers and setbacks, but Canadians have reached a point in our collective history when we can acknowledge that better outcomes result from collaboration and co-creation. The co-development of a basic income for Indigenous communities — reserves and independent Inuit communities — is an opportunity to test our commitment to reconciliation.

If Indigenous communities were to decide that a basic income is an appropriate policy, then the federal government should assist with administration and capacity building as requested. If they decide that a basic income is not appropriate, it isn't for other levels of governments to impose it on them. They should retain the right to opt out, but with a guarantee that, at minimum, per capita funding equivalent to the national basic income would be provided for whatever system is ultimately implemented. Assistance and funding to build administrative capacity is also essential, as is a recognition that this program in no way substitutes for investment in essential infrastructure and other necessary services.

Income assistance on reserve has been provided by the federal government often in partnership with, or under contract to, the provinces. The level of assistance received by someone on reserve is determined by the relevant provincial or territorial program, so someone living on reserve in Ontario, for example, would receive the same amount of money as someone receiving provincial income assistance and living elsewhere in Ontario. People living on reserve often live in subsidized housing, so the actual amount of money received in some cases is just the "basic needs" portion of provincial income assistance — usually slightly less than half the total. This program was evaluated, and the results along with a series of recommendations, were published in 2018.[3]

Indigenous Services Canada, which is the managerial body responsible for administering the program, responded to the evaluation by implementing a five-year staged response, with funding commitment in the federal budgets, to co-develop and implement operational and policy improvements to the program, with annual reviews to monitor progress. The staged approach recognized the complexity of the program and the connections between income assistance and other programs offered at federal, provincial and local levels. It was intended to allow time to engage First Nations and other stakeholders in a meaningful co-development process, and to accommodate changes in other complementary initiatives. This process created a mechanism by which First Nations can engage in the development of a culturally and geographically appropriate basic income which might, in the end, look very different from the basic income developed elsewhere in Canada.

The negotiation process does not mean that First Nations cannot benefit before this lengthy consultation runs its course. Income assistance on reserve is no more adequate than income assistance off reserve. If the federal government were to commit to a national basic income, it could immediately transfer to the income assistance program on reserve per-capita funding equivalent to the basic income offered off reserve. In the meantime, the federal government could commit to the platform established by the evaluation to co-create with First Nations and other stakeholders an appropriate income support policy to be administered by First Nations authorities with the administrative support and funding for capacity-building necessary to run the program.

## Overcoming Vested Interests

Any new policy will advantage some people and disadvantage others. Most of us fear losing what we already have more than we appreciate advantages that we hope to gain. Therefore, potential losers are always ready to complain while potential beneficiaries are cautious enough to wait and see whether the benefits they have been promised will actually materialize. In the case of basic income, the policy can be designed so that no one currently relying on existing income assistance programs will be worse off. That, however, does not mean that there is no one who suspects basic income will be worse for them than the current system.

The basic income experiments conducted during the 1970s demonstrate how easy it is for a good idea based on solid evidence to be shunted aside by interest groups. In the United States, the experiments were opposed by an informal and unstable, but nevertheless powerful, coalition made up of old-school Republicans who opposed any tax increases and all "entitlement" programs and "progressives" in the federal Department of Health, Education, and Welfare and the Department of Labor.

The opposition on the political right was expected. The opposition on the political left, however, was more of a surprise. Many of the people charged with overseeing the experiments were the same people who had built the existing welfare programs and were loyal to them. Some were incapable of imagining ways of delivering programs other than those that were currently in place, but more were simply committed to programs they believed to be essentially well designed but under-funded. Rather than embark on an untried basic income, they argued, it would be better to just increase the funding to existing programs.

That response, of course, downplays the flaws in the welfare programs that existed at the time. These flaws still characterize income assistance programs in Canada today. They were poorly designed programs not simply because they paid recipients too little, but because they were organized in ways that undermined individual autonomy. Caseworkers oversaw families, partly to help them make better life decisions and partly to ensure that the taxpayer was protected. This put caseworkers in an impossible position: how do you build trust with your clients when your loyalties are divided? The sheer mass of regulations means that recipients were almost always not in complete compliance; consequently, they were always subject to penalties that might or might not be imposed. People who have no experience with the income assistance system imagine that benefits are clear and well understood; in fact, many decisions are left to the discretion of frontline workers. All of this means that a recipient never knows how much they might receive, nor when it will arrive. Recipients are inundated with routine paperwork. Late compliance means another penalty or discretion denied. None of this supports autonomy or rational decision making. The solution is not just to "raise the rates" but to replace a fundamentally flawed template.

Opponents in the US Department of Labor, during the 1970s, brought a different perspective to the experiments. Their opposition was based on two points. They held a somewhat romantic attachment to the nobility and dignity of labour itself. They also believed that any improvement to social security was an implicit attack on the primacy of organized labour and, ultimately, the well-being of workers. The more fundamental opposition from those in the Department of Labor was a variant on an argument that has often been raised when labour advocates are confronted with proposed improvements to social security. The argument is that improvements to social security act as a subsidy to low wages, which allows employers to resist wage increases. Opponents in the Department of Labor believed that a basic income would undermine improvements in worker well-being that ought to be achieved through collective bargaining.

The third group of opponents in the 1970s was made up of people outside government involved in delivering very specific kinds of support to particular groups of people. Very often these were small-scale initiatives focused on the needs of a single neighbourhood or group of people, such as homeless people with mental health needs, or people with substance abuse issues living in a particular area of a city. These programs were often very effective for their recipients, but they required a lot of time and money to work well, and relied heavily on volunteer labour. They also addressed issues that were not shared by most low-income people. Advocates for such programs declared that their programs had proven successful, and the money being "wasted" on basic income should be reallocated to their programs because it was clear that basic income would not help their clients.

While well meaning, this opposition was based on the false belief that their clients were representative of those who would benefit from a basic income. While particular groups of low-income people might require specific supports well beyond basic income, most people who would benefit from a basic income — that is, most low-income people — did not require these supports. Some of the single-focus programs were simply not scalable. A program that requires dedicated workers delivering particular services to a well-defined group of recipients might be effective, but it cannot easily expand to address the needs of an entire population.

The same kind of opposition to basic income still persists in Canada today. If basic income in Canada is designed to replace provincial income assistance, it asks those who work within the current system to recognize its flaws. People who have worked hard to improve the system over time will have difficulty getting past the idea that all they need is more money to expand existing programs. Labour unions have played an important role in improving living standards over the past 150 years. Even though the private-sector unionization rate in Canada today is less than 15 per cent, it is hard for insiders to accept that the role of unions has fundamentally changed. Today, members are far more likely to be highly paid government and hospital workers than factory hands. New forms of employment, such as online platforms like TaskRabbit, Etsy or Mechanical Turk, resist labour organization. Well-meaning volunteers or underpaid workers in social services have devoted many hours and years of their lives to making life better for low-income people. Any changes, they believe, should come from those working on the front lines. Who are these outsiders who want to disrupt everything by introducing a basic income?

As basic income becomes better understood, some of this opposition is beginning to fade. There will still be a role for government employees who work within the existing system; imagine the benefits for both the worker and the client if a caseworker had the time to actually partner with clients to bring about positive change in their lives — that truly novel approach that worked so well in the Utrecht trust experiment. After all, the reason people take these jobs is because they want to help people. If less time is required to navigate a needlessly complex system, they might have that luxury. Labour unions still have a role to play today, but that role has changed. The programs that address the particular needs of specific neighbourhoods and groups of people are still very necessary. Everyone needs enough money to live a modest but comfortable life, and a basic income can deliver money far more efficiently than its alternatives. However, money alone will not solve all the ills of the world. There will always be a need for people to deliver specific programs for particular groups of people with special needs.

## Overcoming Taxpayer Resistance

It is challenging for some people to accept that basic income, important and beneficial as it is, will not pay for itself. Basic income is a program of income redistribution. Even if a basic income costs no more than $23 billion a year, some set of taxpayers will have to send more money to the government than they do now to pay for it. Imagining that we can somehow wrestle enough money out of the notorious "1 per cent" is fanciful; even though the extremely wealthy have obscene amounts of money, there are simply not enough of them to pay all the costs of a basic income. Wealth taxes have their own well-known limitations, not least of which is that most wealth is mobile internationally. We will not be able to find $23 billion a year by eliminating waste, eliminating tax fraud or being more efficient. Of course, the wealthiest people in Canada should pay all the taxes they are legally obligated to pay, but it is the people whose incomes fall in the highest 20 per cent of household incomes who will pay higher taxes to finance the program.

These people are not plutocrats; they are small business owners, professionals like doctors, accountants and lawyers, university professors, some media people and employees of foundations and think tanks. They are people who work hard to provide for themselves and their families, who pay their taxes and who struggle to balance their work obligations with the rest of their lives. These taxpayers are also very vocal and well connected. It is only reasonable that they should fight to protect their own interests, and that they should ask questions about why additional tax revenue is necessary. However, they are not the victims of globalization and technology that they sometimes imagine themselves to be. People with incomes in the top 20 per cent have benefited disproportionately from the economic changes in recent decades that have created new opportunities for work and investment. Yet they still worry about their future and that of their children; they work hard to find permanent, well-paying jobs, buy modest houses and pay for daycare. Paying for a basic income is not painless.

The people who will pay higher taxes to support a basic income are relatively high-income individuals, but they see themselves as middle class. Many will believe that they, alone, are responsible for their success, forgetting the investments that society made in the schools and universities that gave them the capacity to earn high incomes. Few will remember that the tax code has been written to allow them to protect some of their income and assets (in the forms of dividends and capital gains, for example) at the expense of others without investment income. High incomes for some are only possible because all taxpayers have invested in the infrastructure that makes the businesses they create feasible and lucrative, and in ensuring that the rule of law protects their property and communities. It is time to ask ourselves, as Canadians, whether we want our tax system to continue to favour the relatively well off — the professional and business classes — or whether we want to shift taxes just a bit to allow every person in Canada a better opportunity to reach their full capacity. There is, I believe, an appetite in this country to examine our entire tax system. Some of the pressure is coming from ordinary middle- and upper-middle-class people who wonder why their neighbours, who happen to be professionals like doctors or lawyers, can somehow arrange to have a salary paid into their corporation and transform their income into capital gains taxed at lower rates. Much less of the pressure is coming from low-income people who are trying to stay afloat because they recognize, quite rightly, that over the past two decades, tax reform has disproportionately benefited higher-income people.

Taxpayers are more likely to accept a tax if they believe it is applied fairly, and if the revenue from that tax is invested in something important. Accountability is a fair request. But accountability does not mean policing the expenditure or behaviour of individual families who receive a basic income. There are many examples of self-righteous scrutiny being passed off as "accountability." For example, in 2014, under Governor Paul LePage, the state of Maine decided to investigate families who received cash benefits through a federal program called Temporary Assistance for Needy Families (TANF). These benefits were loaded onto debit cards that left a digital record of when and where cash was withdrawn. The administration identified 3,650 transactions in which TANF recipients used ATMs in smoke shops, liquor stores and out-of-state locations. Then they released the data to the public, suggesting that TANF recipients were defrauding taxpayers by buying liquor, cigarettes and lottery tickets. Policymakers and the professional middle class then pushed the legislature to introduce a bill that would require TANF families to keep all cash receipts for twelve months for audit purposes and urged the governor to use the list to prosecute recipients for fraud. The "suspicious" transactions constituted only 0.3 per cent of the 1.1 million transactions during the period, and the record shows only where the money was withdrawn, and not what was purchased with the funds. Nevertheless, the purpose of the exercise was to stigmatize those who use social programs, and to reinforce the story that recipients are criminal, lazy, spendthrift addicts.[4]

When the Ford government in Ontario decided to cancel the Ontario basic income pilot, the minister of Social Services simultaneously announced that she had asked the auditor general to investigate "hundreds of millions of dollars" in fraud in social assistance payments. She offered no evidence to support the allegation and, two years later, the claim had quietly disappeared. When the CERB was introduced, we heard similar charges. The funniest was the notorious (and, needless to say, unsubstantiated) Twitter claim that someone knew someone who had registered his horses to receive financial support. (There was no explanation about how the horses had received birth certificates.) We worry a great deal about people in need taking advantage of programs set up to help those who need assistance, but few of us are as vocal about the well-documented tax fraud committed by relatively high-income individuals, for whom the benefits are much larger. The reality is that there is a small minority of people at every income level who will take advantage of any system we establish. All of our systems are set up to identify and prosecute "cheats," and the consequence is that these same systems disadvantage the vast majority of people who are honest and doing as well as they can. Their benefits are delayed, and they are inundated with demands that they prove they "deserve" the support they receive. This is not what I mean by accountability.

Accountability means that a government should commit to transparent reporting of the costs of a program and progress made towards clearly stated social goals. This might seem obvious, but it is not now an easy task to find the costs associated with income support. The Parliamentary Budget Office noted that the federal government spent $122 billion for tax expenditures (non-refundable tax credits and deductions) in 2017

— $122 billion that is not subject to program evaluations. There is no program of regular or ongoing examination to determine whether these tax expenditures meet their goals, or whether they give us good value for their cost. By contrast, federal program expenditures undergo regular evaluations. Provincial expenditures on income assistance are not knowable with certainty, even though many provinces have committed to "transparent government," because payments are aggregated with other expenditures, and the administrative costs are not clearly identified.

Since neither provincial nor federal governments report their expenditures in clear and useful ways, no one should be surprised that many taxpayers assume their tax payments disappear into great dark holes. Any taxpayer should be able to find out what programs cost, how the costs change over time, how many people benefit and whether beneficiaries are old or young, male or female, in families or living alone. We should know whether the programs meet the needs of families that receive support, and what proportion of families becomes more independent over time.

Taxes that support government programs can be levied in many ways, and it is reasonable to expect taxes to be efficient and well administered. Raising taxes to support basic income does not necessarily mean raising marginal income tax rates or even corporate taxes. There are many different kinds of taxes, but one place to begin is with the list of tax expenditures — $122 billion a year, remember, at the federal level alone — compiled by the Parliamentary Budget Office. Some of these expenditures are necessary and useful; others have lost whatever purpose they may once have had.

We do not need to wait for a review of the entire tax system to implement a basic income. There are several options available. However, any review of the tax system should have, as one goal, the identification of an income stream to support a fair and equitable basic income.

## There is No Perfect Time: Let's Begin Now

The initial impact of COVID-19 started to wane by the summer of 2020, but the economic consequences of the pandemic dragged on and it became clear that supports would have to stay in place longer than originally planned. As soon as infection and death rates began to subside, the voices of austerity grew louder. Some acknowledged that the temporary supports introduced during the shutdown — the CERB in particular — might have been necessary to induce workers to stay home during the worst of the pandemic, but as jobs started to come back, opposition to the CERB grew. Many argued that the increased debt associated with COVID-19 would only increase the challenge for an economy already burdened by an aging population. We needed workers back at work to stimulate growth. Others questioned direct payments to people at all.

It seemed prudent to ask whether to wait to talk about a basic income until the economy has recovered from the economic consequences of COVID-19. The temptation to wait before embarking on a bold, new social program until "the time is right" is deeply ingrained. The only problem is that the time is never right. There is always another new reason to delay, and another economic challenge on the horizon. There is always another new expenditure that must take precedence. After all, humans have lived with poverty and economic insecurity for millennia — what's another couple of years or decades? The poor can wait.

The case for basic income can be based on social justice or compassion. Alternatively, it can be demonstrated that accelerating economic change is increasing the number of people who would benefit from a basic income. Others might point to growing social inequality as a cautionary tale, and suggest that basic income is one way to quell social unrest. There is even a fiscal case: it already costs so much to deliver social programs to treat the consequences of poverty and economic insecurity. Basic income would invest a fraction of that expenditure upstream so that the worst effects of economic insecurity are eliminated before they happen. Basic income is an investment in families. But all these arguments inevitably face the claim that we cannot undertake even the modest expenditure associated with a basic income because this is not the right time.

Basic income is not about recovering from the immediate impact of COVID-19, and it's not about creating a utopia. It is a pragmatic policy that will make Canada more resilient by enabling everyone to meet our immediate needs when factors outside our control reduce our incomes. Once in place, a basic income acts as an automatic stabilizer; it will do its work without requiring co-operation from partisan politicians or rapid responses from weighty bureaucracies. As soon as our incomes fall, a basic income will allow us to pay the rent and put food on the table. When the economy recovers, it will allow us to take a chance on a job offer that might not pay enough to meet our needs. It will expand and contract in response to need without the mad scramble to create temporary support programs that will, inevitably, come too late, exclude too many people or embody design flaws that only become apparent later.

A basic income is not unaffordable in a wealthy country like Canada. It does not require massive tax increases, dramatic deficits or class warfare. We absorbed the Canada Child Benefit with no ill effects; in fact, the economic consequences have been overwhelmingly positive. The expected consequences of a basic income do not need to be compared with the expected consequences of every other way money could conceivably be spent; that is a recipe for the status quo. While there should be some idea of how to raise tax revenue to pay the expected costs of a basic income, it is not necessary to wait for the completion of a much-needed review of the entire tax system before a basic income can be introduced. The proposed basic income does not need to be perfect; the quest for perfection is another excuse to do nothing. The lurid claims that a basic income will be the end of capitalism or the beginning of an age of mass unemployment are more than a little overstated. We can, as we've done with every other program we've ever introduced, design the best basic income we can on the basis of what we know right now, and expect to adjust it after implementation. The time for change is now.

# Afterword

# The Pandemic as an Invitation to Change

Tacet is a musical term that indicates a voice or instrument does not sound. In orchestral scores it indicates a long period of time, typically an entire movement. *Violino Tacet*: the violin is silent. In many religious communities, there is an invitation to reflection — a time out from ordinary life for self-examination and reflection. St. Benedict called it *otium sanctum*, or holy leisure. A pause in the ordinary business of a frenzied life provides an opportunity to examine the way we live and interact with one another, to reconsider our priorities and clarify our intentions.

When a novel coronavirus made its way around the globe in the early months of 2020, public health regulations stepped in to ensure that life would not continue in the old ways. For decades, Canadians have known that dramatic and irreversible economic change was making our old ways of addressing persistent poverty and economic insecurity, which were never very good, even less effective. However, policymakers resisted the challenge to change those policies and instead made do, trying to reform ineffective, inadequate and stigmatizing policies by slapping on another patch and hoping that economic growth would, somehow, let us go on as we were without the necessary re-examination that could make all our lives more secure. Canadians lurched from recession to recession, from 1981 to 1991 to 2008 to 2020, each time sighing with relief when the stock market recovered and per capita GDP grew, as though either were the mark of a healthy society. And, in each case, we watched as our social safety net frayed even more, increasingly unable to address our needs in an interconnected world in which work had become ever more precarious.

The COVID-19 pandemic imposed the time out we thought we couldn't afford. It reminded all of us, in the most stark and vivid terms, that we are all connected to one another and that the health of one of us affects all of us. That is so for viruses, but it is also the case for economic well-being. The health of each one of us is enhanced when our relatives and neighbours have access to the tools and resources they need to live healthy lives. The well-being of each one of us depends on the well-being of others. Economic security is not a zero sum game; doing well economically does not mean that others must suffer.

Basic income is one component of a robust, responsive and comprehensive economic, health and social safety net, which includes universally accessible education, child care, mental and physical health strategies. It ensures that everyone has the capacity to live modestly, with dignity. We can ensure economic security for all of us.

# Acknowledgements

I am very grateful for the many, many people who helped me with this project. David Gray-Donald, my editor at Lorimer, decided I didn't have enough to do and set me the task of writing about future events in the past tense without sliding into the subjunctive. Go ahead; try it! Thanks to Richard Lobdell for putting up with my complaining. I'd like to thank Stephenson Strobel who acted as a research assistant for several years. The "two Davids" at Library and Archives Canada put up with my requests for access, and the many requests of journalists and documentary filmmakers who wanted to "film the boxes." Eric Richardson was a willing subject for many journalists, and an entrée into Dauphin society. CIHR (MOP-110984) and SSHRC (435-2015-1075) supported some of the research on which this book is based. I am also grateful to James Lorimer, Jim Turk and Ashley Bernicky at Lorimer.

# Further Reading

## Chapter 1

Many books have been published on the idea of basic income and approach the topic from a variety of perspectives. Of the following, some are very accessible while others provide a more complex, scholarly discussion of basic income.

Bregman, Rutger. *Utopia for Realists: The Case for a Universal Basic Income, Open Borders, and a 15-Hour Work Week.* Amsterdam: The Correspondent, 2016. This book, by a Dutch historian, is great fun to read. It is provocative, as its subtitle suggests, and very well written. Bregman focuses on a universal basic income (as opposed to a targeted benefit) and challenges us to imagine a future much different from the past.

Hasdell, Rebecca. *What we know about Universal Basic Income: a cross-synthesis of reviews.* Stanford Basic Income Lab, 2020. This is a very useful report on the evidence from various basic income and basic income like experiments. It reports on research using a variety of definitions of basic income. https://basicincome.stanford.edu/research/papers/what-we-know-about-universal-basic-income.

Hughes, Chris. *Fair Shot: Rethinking Inequality and How We Earn.* London: Bloomsbury, 2018. Chris Hughes (a Facebook co-founder) argues, in a well-written and entertaining book, that one-percenters like him should pay for a guaranteed income for everyone. He advocates a targeted benefit similar to the one adopted by Ontario for its pilot, which he provides support for in the book.

Lewchuk, Wayne, and Marlea Clarke. *Working Without Commitments: The Health Effects of Precarious Employment.* Montreal: McGill-Queen's University Press, 2011.

Lewchuk, Wayne, Michelynn LaFlèche, Diane Dyson, Luin Goldring, Alan Meisner, Stephanie Procyk, Dan Rosen, John Shields, Peter Viducis, and Sam Vrankulj. *It's More than Poverty: Employment Precarity and Employment Well-Being.* Poverty and Employment Precarity in Southern Ontario (PEPSO), 2013. Wayne Lewchuk is the Canadian expert on precarious employment. The book by Lewchuk and Clarke emphasizes the effects of precarity on health and well-being.

Standing, Guy. *Basic Income and How We Can Make It Happen.* London: Pelican Books, 2017.

Standing, Guy. *The Precariat: The New Dangerous Class.* London: Bloomsbury, 2011. Guy Standing is the international expert on the rise of the precariat — the insecurely employed underclass in today's economy — and a well-known advocate for basic income, which he, too, defines as a universal basic income given equally to everyone, rich or poor. The first book is intended as an entry-level account of the debate and is broadly accessible and the second focuses more closely on the economic effects of precarious labour.

Stern, Andy. *Raising the Floor: How a Universal Basic Income Can Renew Our Economy and Rebuild the American Dream.* New York: PublicAffairs, 2016. This book, by a well-known labour leader, focuses on changes in the labour market, especially in the United

States, and suggests that a universal basic income — a flat payment to everyone, rich or poor — is the appropriate way to renew the economy and rebuild the American dream.

Van Parijs, Philippe, and Yannick Vanderborght. *Basic Income: A Radical Proposal for a Free Society and a Sane Economy.* Cambridge, MA: Harvard University Press, 2017. This is a much more scholarly account of the debate that approaches the topic from the perspective of freedom. This book also treats universal basic income as the ideal.

World Bank, *Exploring Universal Basic Income: A Guide to Navigating Concepts, Evidence and Practices.* World Bank, 2020. This report focuses on Universal Basic Income – a uniform cash transfer extended to everyone which doesn't depend on their income. It is, however, a thorough report and very good reading. https://openknowledge. worldbank.org/handle/10986/32677

# Chapter 2

Baird, Sarah, Craig McIntosh, and Berk Özler. "Cash or Condition? Evidence from a Cash Transfer Experiment." *Quarterly Journal of Economics* 126, no. 4 (2011): 1709–53. A cash transfer program was established in Malawi, with some dramatic health results. This experiment compared a cash transfer that families received if they sent their adolescent daughters to school to a cash transfer that families received unconditionally. As might be expected, the conditional cash transfer was more successful at encouraging families to send their daughters to school, but an unintended outcome occurred in the unconditional arm that did not occur in the conditional arm: the incidence of HIV declined, and this was attributed to the fact that transactional sex work among girls in the poorest families declined when families received support.

Forget, Evelyn L., Alexander D. Peden, and Stephenson B. Strobel. "Cash Transfers, Basic Income and Community Building." *Social Inclusion* 1, no. 2 (2013): 84–91. http://www.cogitatiopress.com/ojs/index.php/socialinclusion/article/view/113.

Forget, Evelyn L. "New Questions, New data, Old interventions: The Health Effects of a Guaranteed Annual Income." *Journal of Preventive Medicine* 57, no. 6 (2013): 925–28. doi: 10.1016/j.ypmed.2013.05.029.

Forget, Evelyn L. "The Town with No Poverty: The Health Effects of a Canadian Guaranteed Annual Income Field Experiment." *Canadian Public Policy* 37, no. 3 (2011): 283–305. The Dauphin site of Mincome is responsible for broadening the debate over basic income in high-income countries to a consideration of health and well-being.

Owusu-Addo, Ebenezer, Andre M.N. Renzaho, and Ben J. Smith. "The Impact of Cash Transfers on Social Determinants of Health and Health Inequalities in Sub-Saharan Africa: A Systematic Review." *Health Policy and Planning* 5, no. 114 (2018). https://doi. org/10.1093/heapol/czy020. We should be careful about generalizing from the results of basic income (or cash transfer) programs in low- and middle-income countries, but the above is an excellent review of the health outcomes of a variety of such experiments in sub-Saharan Africa.

# Chapter 3

Martin, Danielle. *Better Now? Six Big Ideas to Improve Health Care for All Canadians*. Toronto: Penguin Canada, 2016. The relationship between poverty and poor health is pervasive. Almost any area of health is worsened by poverty. An interesting and accessible account is available in this book by Danielle Martin, who recounts her experiences in family medicine.

Raphael, David. *Social Determinants of Health: Canadian Perspectives*, 2nd ed. Toronto: Canadian Scholars' Press, 2009. A good discussion of the social determinants of health in a Canadian context is available here.  ﹅

Wilkinson, Richard G., and Kate Pickett. *The Spirit Level: Why Equality Is Better for Everyone*. London: Penguin, 2010. An accessible discussion of the role played by inequality on health outcomes is available in this very popular book.

The effects of chronic stress on long-term heath are also very well-documented in the medical literature:

Baum, Andrew, J.P. Garofalo, and Ann Marie Yali. "Socioeconomic Status and Chronic Stress: Does Stress Account for SES Effects on Health?" *Annals of the New York Academy of Sciences* 896 (1999): 131–44.

Cohen, Sheldon, Denise Janicki-Deverts, William J. Doyle, Gregory E. Miller, Ellen Frank, Bruce S. Rabin, and Ronald B. Turner. "Chronic Stress, Glucocorticoid Receptor Resistance, Inflammation, and Disease Risk." *Proceedings of the National Academy of Sciences* 109, no. 16 (2012): 5995–99.

Dickerson, Sally S., and Margaret E. Kemeny. "Acute Stressors and Cortisol Responses: A Theoretical Integration and Synthesis of Laboratory Research." *Psychological Bulletin* 130 (2004): 355–91.

Epel, Elissa S., Elizabeth H. Blackburn, Jue Lin, Firdaus S. Dhabhar, Nancy E. Adler, Jason D. Morrow, and Richard M. Cawthon. "Accelerated Telomere Shortening in Response to Life Stress." *Proceedings of the National Academy of Sciences of the United States of America* 101, no. 49 (2004): 17312–15.

Kopp, Mária S., and János Réthelyi. "Where Psychology Meets Physiology: Chronic Stress and Premature Mortality — The Central-Eastern European Health Paradox." *Brain Research Bulletin* 62, no. 5 (2004): 351–67.

Layte, Richard, and Christopher Whelan. "Who Feels Inferior? A Test of the Status Anxiety Hypothesis of Social Inequalities in Health." *GINI Discussion Paper* 78, 2013.

Loughnan, Steve, Peter Kuppens, Jüri Allik, Katalin Balazs, Soledad de Lemus, Kitty Dumont, Rafael Gargurevich, et al. "Economic Inequality Is Linked to Biased Self-Perception." *Psychological Science* 22 (2011): 1254–58.

Marin, Marie-France, Catherine Lord, Julie Andrews, Robert-Paul Juster, Shireen Sindi, Geneviève Arsenault-Lapierre, Alexandra J. Fiocco, and Sonia J. Lupien. "Chronic

Stress, Cognitive Functioning and Mental Health." *Neurobiology of Learning and Memory* 96, no. 4 (2011): 583–95.

Mitchell, Colter, John Hobcraft, Sarah S. McLanahan, Susan Rutherford Siegel, Arthur Berg, Jeanne Brooks-Gunn, Irwin Garfinkel, and Daniel Notterman. "Social Disadvantage, Genetic Sensitivity, and Children's Telomere Length." *Proceedings of the National Academy of Sciences* 111, no. 16 (2014): 5944–49.

Steptoe, Andrew, and Pamela J. Feldman. "Neighborhood Problems as Sources of Chronic Stress: Development of a Measure of Neighborhood Problems, and Associations with Socioeconomic Status and Health. *Annals of Behavioral Medicine* 23, no. 3 (2001): 177–85.

# Chapter 4
Brynjolfsson, Erik, and Andrew McAfee. *The Second Machine Age: Work Progress and Prosperity in a Time of Brilliant Technologies.* New York: WW Norton, 2014.

Ford, Martin. *Rise of the Robots: Technology and the Threat of a Jobless Future.* New York: Basic Books, 2016. Excellent discussions of a future without work can be found in both of the above titles.

David Graeber. *Bullshit Jobs: A Theory.* New York: Simon & Schuster, 2018. This is an entertaining read on the nature of jobs. Graeber effectively questions the identification of "work" with jobs that are accessed through the market for pay. He puts care work and artistic endeavour at the centre of human existence.

Lamb, Creig. 2016. *The Talented Mr. Robot: The Impact of Automation on Canada's Workforce.* Toronto: Brookfield Institute for Innovation + Entrepreneurship, 2016. http://brookfieldinstitute.ca/wp-content/uploads/2016/07/TheTalentedMrRobotReport. pdf. The challenges to the way we work brought about by technological change are pervasive in the popular literature. Lamb's text is an enjoyable read on this subject.

By contrast, if you are interested in the standard line that we are in the midst of a labour shortage, you'll find a plethora of articles in the business press. Newspaper articles and commentaries on Canada's imagined labour shortage are easy to find. The Canadian Federation of Independent Business sparked this article in *Huffington Post:*

Tencer, Daniel."Canada's Labour Shortage Intensifies, with Nearly 400,000 Vacant Jobs." *Huffington Post,* March 13, 2018. https://www.huffingtonpost.ca/2018/03/13/labour-shortage-canadajob-vacancies_a_23384818/.

Nearly simultaneously, a horde of articles declaring that "robots will take our jobs" appeared, for example:

Elliott, Larry. "Robots Will Take Our Jobs. We'd Better Plan Now Before It's Too Late." *Guardian,* February 1, 2018. https://www.theguardian.com/commentisfree/2018/feb/01/ robots-take-our-jobs-amazon-go-seattle.

# Chapter 5

Ariely, D. *Predictably Irrational. The Hidden Forces That Shape Our Decisions.* New York: HarperCollins, 2008. Dan Ariely can be found on TED Talks. This book is of particular relevance.

Folbre, Nancy. *The Invisible Heart: Economics and Family Values.* New York: New Press, 2001. Nancy Folbre has written a wonderful work on caring labour in the United States.

Loney, Shaun, with Will Braun. *An Army of Problem Solvers: Reconciliation and the Solutions Economy.* Altona, MB: Friesens, 2016.

Meghir, Costas, and David Phillips. "Labour Supply and Taxes." *Dimensions of Tax Design: The Mirrlees Review* (2010): 202–74. https://www.ifs.org.uk/mirrleesreview/dimensions/ch3.pdf. This is a good review of the standard economic analysis of labour incentives. It, like most economic analyses, defines work in a very narrow way and neglects the role of non-market work. Like most standard labour market analyses, it is very short-term in focus. It ignores the likelihood that some time out of the workforce may be essential to education and training that increases long-run productivity.

Skidelsky, Robert, and Edward Skidelsky. *How Much is Enough? Money and the Good Life.* London: Penguin, 2012. Others see basic income as a means of constraining our over-consuming lifestyles. Robert and Edward Skidelsky pick up the themes addressed by John Maynard Keynes (*Economic Opportunities for our Grandchildren*) and John Stuart Mill. All examine the philosophical underpinnings of economics and ask what kind of a society we want to create.

Srnicek, Nick, and Alex Williams. 2015. *Inventing the Future: Postcapitalism and a World Without Work.* New York: Verso, 2015. If you want to explore post-work imaginaries and the call for a new socialist imagination, try this one.

# Chapter 6

All Canadians should read the two volumes of the National Inquiry into Missing and Murdered Indigenous Women and Girls for the decolonizing lens it brings to gender justice:

*Reclaiming Power and Place: The Final Report of the National Inquiry into Missing and Murdered Indigenous Women and Girls,* Vols 1a and 1b. Ottawa: 2019. https://www.mmiwg-ffada.ca/final-report.

A special issue of *Basic Income Studies* published in December 2008 (Volume 3, Issue 3), entitled "Should Feminists Endorse Basic Income?" published varying perspectives.

Readers might also enjoy reading:

McKay, Ailsa. "Rethinking Work and Income Maintenance Policy: Promoting Gender Equality Through a Citizens' Basic Income." *Feminist Economics* 7, no. 1 (2001): 97–118.

McKay, Ailsa. "Why a Citizens' Basic Income? A Question of Gender Equality or Gender

Bias." *Work, Employment and Society* 21, no. 2 (2007): 337–48.

Regehr, Sheila. "Basic Income and Gender Equality: Reflections on the Potential for Good Policy in Canada." 2014. http://www.basicincome.org/bien/pdf/montreal2014/BIEN2014_Regehr.pdf.

Reynolds, Tracey. "Black Women, Gender Equality and Universal Basic Income." *Compass* (blog), January 27, 2017. https://www.compassonline.org.uk/black-women-gender-equality-anduniversal-basic-income.

# Chapter 7

Nordström Skans, Oskar. *Scarring Effects of the First Labor Market Experience.* IZA Discussion Paper No. 5565. Bonn, Germany: Institute for the Study of Labor, No. 5565, 2011. The literature on labour scarring is fairly technical and is mostly buried in economics journals, but this paper is particularly useful for understanding its effects.

# Chapter 8

Bregman, Rutger. *Utopia for Realists: The Case for a Universal Basic Income, Open Borders, and a 15-Hour Work Week.* Amsterdam: The Correspondent, 2016. This chapter has taken a very clear position that basic income is a simply a policy of redistribution, not different in kind from many other similar policies that we have already chosen to implement. This is a much more modest position than that taken by Rutger Bregman, who speculates in this book about a very different kind of world in which basic income plays a part.

# Chapter 9

Boadway, Robin W., Katherine Cuff, and Kourtney Koebel. *Designing a Basic Income Guarantee for Canada. Working Paper* No. 1371, Economics Department, Queen's University, Kingston, Ontario, 2016.

*Costing a National Guaranteed Basic Income Using the Ontario Basic Income Model.* Ottawa: Office of the Parliamentary Budget Officer, April 17, 2018.

*Federal Support for Low Income Families and Children.* Ottawa: Office of the Parliamentary Budget Officer, 2017.

Lammam, Charles, and Hugh MacIntyre. *The Practical Challenges of Creating a Guaranteed Annual Income.* Vancouver: Fraser Institute, 2015.

Macdonald, David. *A Policymaker's Guide to Basic Income.* Ottawa: Canadian Centre for Policy Alternatives, 2016. See Appendix for further discussion.

Pasma, Chandra and Sheila Regehr, *Basic Income: Some Policy Options for Canada.* Basic Income Canada Network, 2019. https://d3n8a8pro7vhmx.cloudfront.net/bicn/pages/3725/attachments/original/1579707497/Basic_Income-_Some_Policy_Options_for_Canada2.pdf?1579707497.

Stevens, Harvey, and Wayne Simpson. "Toward a National Universal Guaranteed Basic Income." *Canadian Public Policy* (2017): 120–39.

# Endnotes

## Chapter 1

1.  https://sencanada.ca/en/senators/pate-kim/interventions/536676/37.
    https://www.recoveryforall.ca/6pointplan.
    https://www.casw-acts.ca/en/promoting-equity-stronger-canada-future-canadian-social-policy.
    https://www.mmiwg-ffada.ca/final-report.
    https://www.anglican.ca/news/a-public-letter-on-guaranteed-basic-income/30026458.
    https://www.basicincomecanada.org/endorsements.
    https://www.obin.ca/a_public_letter_from_the_arts_community_for_a_basic_income_guarantee.
    *Report of the Special Senate Committee on Poverty* [Croll Commission] (Ottawa: Supply and Services, 1971).
    *Royal Commission on the Economic Union and Development Prospects Report* [McDonald Commission], 3 vols. (Ottawa: Supply and Services, 1985).
    *In From the Margins: A Call to Action on Poverty, Housing and Homelessness. Report of the Standing Senate Committee on Social Affairs, Science and Technology* (Ottawa: Supply and Services, 2009). https://sencanada.ca/content/sen/Committee/402/citi/rep/rep02dec09-e.pdf.
2.  Timo Verlaat, Marcel de Kruijk, Stephanie Rosenkranz, Loek Groot, and Mark Sanders, *Onderzoek Weten wat werkt: samen werken aan een betere bijstand, Eindrapport* (Utrecht: Utrecht University, 2020). An English-language summary is available here: https://www.uu.nl/en/publication/final-report-what-works-weten-wat-werkt.
    *The Final Report of the Finnish Basic Income Experiment* (in Finnish; English summary on p. 187ff.). http://urn.fi/URN:ISBN:978-952-00-9890-2
3.  The survey methodology and further discussion is available in their study report: Mohammad Ferdosi, Tom McDowell, Wayne Lewchuk, and Stephanie Ross, *Southern Ontario's Basic Income Experience* (Hamilton: Hamilton Community Foundation, Hamilton Roundtable for Poverty Reduction and Labour Studies at McMaster University, March 2020). https://labourstudies.mcmaster.ca/documents/southern-ontarios-basic-income-experience.pdf.
4.  Stephen Harrington, Jeff Moir, and J. Scott Allinson, *The Intelligence Revolution. Future-Proofing Canada's Workforce* (Deloitte, 2017). https://www2.deloitte.com/content/dam/Deloitte/ca/Documents/human-capital/ca-EN-HC-The-Intelligence-Revolution-FINAL-AODA.pdf.
5.  This limit varies by province and changes over time.
6.  Munir A. Sheikh, "Report Of The Commission For The Review Of Social Assistance In Ontario: Taking Stock Two Years Later," *SPP Research Papers* (Calgary: University of Calgary School of Policy Studies, 2015). https://www.policyschool.ca/publications/report-commission-review-social-assistance-ontario-taking-stock-two-years-later.
7.  Sung-Hee Jeon, Huju Liu, and Yuri Ostrovsky, "Measuring the Gig Economy in Canada Using Administrative Data," *Analytical Studies Branch Research Paper Series*, no. 437, Statistics Canada Catalogue no. 11F0019M (Ottawa: Statistics Canada, 2019).
8.  Wen-Hao Chen and Tahsin Mehdi, "Assessing Job Quality in Canada: A Multidimensional Approach," *Analytical Studies Branch Research Paper Series*, no. 412, Statistics Canada Catalogue no. 11F0019M (Ottawa: Statistics Canada, 2018).

9.  Statistics Canada, Table 14-10-0072-01,Job permanency (permanent and temporary) by industry, annual (x 1,000). doi: https://doi.org/10.25318/1410007201-eng.
10. René Morissette, "The Changing Job Landscape, 1981 to 2019," *Economic Insights No. 107*. Statistics Canada Catalogue no. 11-626-X (Ottawa: Statistics Canada, 2019).

# Chapter 2

1.  For a summary of Mincome in the context of the negative income tax experiments, see: Evelyn L. Forget, "The Town with No Poverty: The Health Effects of a Canadian Guaranteed Annual Income Field Experiment," *Canadian Public Policy* 37, no. 3 (2011): 283–305.
2.  See: *Poverty in Canada: Report of the Special Senate Committee on Poverty* [Croll Report] (Ottawa: Information Canada, 1971).
    *Welfare Recipients Speak for Themselves* [Federal-Provincial Study Group on Alienation] (Ottawa: Health and Welfare Canada, 1971).
    *Income Security for Canadians* (Ottawa: Health and Welfare Canada, 1970).
3.  David Calnitsky, "More Normal than Welfare: The Mincome Experiment, Stigma, and Community Experience," *Canadian Review of Sociology/Revue canadienne de sociologie*, 53, no. 1 (2016): 26–71.
4.  Derek Hum and Wayne Simpson, *Income Maintenance, Work Effort, and the Canadian Mincome Experiment*, study prepared for the Economic Council of Canada (Ottawa: Canada Communication Group, 1991).
5.  This is what happens for family doctors who are paid a fee for service. Many family doctors have other pay arrangements, including salaries from a clinic or a health authority, and these types of arrangements have increased over time. In the case of alternative payment arrangements, doctors are encouraged to "shadow bill" — that is, to complete the billing claim form even though it is not required for payment. That way, it still enters the database.
6.  Wayne Lewchuk and Marlea Clarke, *Working Without Commitments: The Health Effects of Precarious Employment* (Montreal: McGill-Queen's University Press, 2011).
7.  Based on my unsystematic reading of Mincome files.
8.  The survey methodology and further discussion is available in their study report: Mohammad Ferdosi, Tom McDowell, Wayne Lewchuk, and Stephanie Ross, *Southern Ontario's Basic Income Experience* (Hamilton: Hamilton Community Foundation, Hamilton Roundtable for Poverty Reduction and Labour Studies at McMaster University, March 2020). https://labourstudies.mcmaster.ca/documents/southern-ontarios-basic-income-experience.pdf.
9.  Olli Kangas, Signe Jauhiainen, Miska Simanainen, Minna Ylikännö (eds.), *The Basic Income Experiment 2017–2018 in Finland. Preliminary results* (Helsinki: Reports and Memorandums of the Ministry of Social Affairs and Health, 2019). http://julkaisut.valtioneuvosto.fi/bitstream/handle/10024/161361/Report_The%20Basic%20Income%20Experiment%2020172018%20in%20Finland.pdf.
10. *The Final Report of the Finnish Basic Income Experiment* (in Finnish; English summary on p. 187ff.). http://urn.fi/URN:ISBN:978-952-00-9890-2
11. Timo Verlaat, Marcel de Kruijk, Stephanie Rosenkranz, Loek Groot, and Mark Sanders, *Onderzoek Weten wat werkt: samen werken aan een betere bijstand, Eindrapport* (Utrecht: Utrecht University, 2020). An English-language summary is available here: https://www.uu.nl/en/publication/final-report-what-works-weten-wat-werkt.
12. Sarah Baird, Richard Garfein, Craig McIntosh, and Berk Ozler, "Effect of a Cash

Transfer Programme for Schooling on Prevalence of HIV and Herpes Simplex Type 2 in Malawi: A Cluster Randomised Trial," *Lancet* 379, no. 9823 (2012): 1320–29.

13. Sarath Davala, Renana Jhabvala, Guy Standing, and Soumya Kapoor Mehta, *Basic Income: A Transformative Policy for India* (London: Bloomsbury, 2015).

14. Andrea R. Ferro, Ana Lúcia Kassouf, and Deborah Levison, "The Impact of Conditional Cash Transfer Programs on Household Work Decisions in Brazil," in *Child Labor and the Transition between School and Work*, eds. Randall K.Q. Akee, Eric V. Edmonds, and Konstantinos Tatsiramos (Bingley, UK: Emerald Group Publishing Limited, 2010): 193–218.

15. Translated from Nathalia Carvalho Moreira, Marco Aurelio Marques Ferreira, Alfonso Augusto Teixera de Freitas Carvalho, and Ivan Beck Ckagnazaroff, "Empoderamento das mulheres beneficiárias do Programa Bolsa Família na percepção dos agentes dos Centros de Referência de Assistência Social," *Revista de Administração Pública* 46, no. 2 (2012): 403–23.

# Chapter 3

1. Essylt W. Jones, *Influenza 1918: Disease, Death and Struggle in Winnipeg* (Toronto: University of Toronto Press, 2007).

2. Randy Fransoo, Patricia Martens, The Need To Know Team, Heather Prior, Charles Burchill, Ina Koseva, and Leanne Rajotte, *Who is in our Hospitals . . . And Why?* (Winnipeg, MB: Manitoba Centre for Health Policy, September 2013).

3. R. Wilkins, *Mortality by Neighbourhood Income in Urban Canada from 1971 to 2001* (Ottawa: Statistics Canada, Health Analysis and Measurement Group, 2007).

4. Data from 2006–2011. Winnipeg Regional Health Authority Community Health Assessments.

5. Marni Brownell, Mariette Chartier, Rob Santos, Okechukwu Ekuma, Wendy Au, Joykrishna Sarkar, Leonard MacWilliam, Elaine Burland, Ina Koseva, and Wendy Guenette, *How Are Manitoba's Children Doing?* (Winnipeg, MB: Manitoba Centre for Health Policy, October 2012).

6. Patricia Martens, Marni Brownell, Wendy Au, Leonard MacWilliam, Heather Prior, Jennifer Schultz, Wendy Guenette, Lawrence Elliott, Shelley Buchan, Marcia Anderson, Patricia Caetano, Colleen Metge, Rob Santos and Karen Serwonka, *Health Inequities in Manitoba: Is the Socioeconomic Gap Widening or Narrowing Over Time?* (Winnipeg, MB: Manitoba Centre for Health Policy, September 2010).

7. WHO [World Health Organization], *The Economics of Social Determinants of Health and Health Inequalities: a resource book* (WHO Press, 2013): 6. https://www.who.int/social_determinants/publications/9789241548625/en.

8. Public Health Agency of Canada, *Social Determinants of Health and Health Inequalities*, last modified July 25, 2019. https://www.canada.ca/en/public-health/services/health-promotion/population-health/what-determines-health.html.

9. David Raphael, *Social Determinants of Health: Canadian Perspectives*, 2nd ed. (Toronto: Canadian Scholars' Press, 2009).

10. Göran Dahlgren and Margaret Whitehead, *Policies and Strategies to Promote Social Equity in Health* (Stockholm: Institute for Futures Studies, 1991).

11. Valerie Tarasuk, *Implications of a Basic Income Guarantee for Household Food Insecurity. Research Paper 24.* (Thunder Bay: Northern Policy Institute. June 2017). https://nccdh.ca/index.php?/resources/entry/implications-of-a-basic-income-guarantee-for-household-food-insecurity.

Lynn McIntyre, Daniel J. Dutton, Cynthia Kwok, and J.C. Herbert Emery. "Reduction of Food Insecurity among Low-Income Canadian Seniors as a Likely Impact of a Guaranteed Annual Income," *Canadian Public Policy* 42, no. 3 (2016): 274–86.

Lynn McIntyre, "Impact of a Guaranteed Annual Income Program on Canadian Seniors' Physical, Mental and Functional Health," *Canadian Journal of Public Health*, 107, no. 2 (2016): E176.

Joel Lexchin and Paul Grootendorst, "Effects of Prescription Drug User Fees on Drug and Health Services Use and on Health Status in Vulnerable Populations: A Systematic Review of the Evidence," *International Journal of Health Services*, 34, no. 1 (2004): 101–22.

12.  Sheldon Cohen, Denise Janicki-Deverts, William J. Doyle, Gregory E. Miller, Ellen Frank, Bruce S. Rabin, and Ronald B. Turner, "Chronic Stress, Glucocorticoid Receptor Resistance, Inflammation, and Disease Risk," *Proceedings of the National Academy of Sciences*, 109, no. 16 (2012): 5995–99.

Elissa S. Epel, Elizabeth H. Blackburn, Jue Lin, Firdaus S. Dhabhar, Nancy E. Adler, Jason D. Morrow, and Richard M. Cawthon, "Accelerated Telomere Shortening in Response to Life Stress," *Proceedings of the National Academy of Sciences of the United States of America*, 101, no. 49 (2004): 17312–15.

Marie-France Marin, Catherine Lord, Julie Andrews, Robert-Paul Juster, Shireen Sindi, Geneviève Arsenault-Lapierre, Alexandra J. Fiocco, and Sonia J. Lupien, "Chronic Stress, Cognitive Functioning and Mental Health," *Neurobiology of Learning and Memory*, 96, no. 4 (2011): 583–95.

A. Steptoe and P.J. Feldman, "Neighborhood Problems as Sources of Chronic Stress: Development of a Measure of Neighborhood Problems, and Associations with Socioeconomic Status and Health," *Annals of Behavioral Medicine* 23 no. 3 (August 2011): 177–85.

A. Baum, J. P. Garofalo, and A.M. Yali, "Socioeconomic Status and Chronic Stress: Does Stress Account for SES Effects on Health?" *Annals of the New York Academy of Sciences*, 896 (1999): 131–44.

13.  See: Richard G. Wilkinson and Kate Pickett, *The Spirit Level: Why Equality Is Better for Everyone* (London: Penguin, 2010). Some critics have argued that the observed results are not caused by inequality, but the authors and many others have provided compelling evidence. See: Kate E. Pickett and Richard G. Wilkinson, "Income Inequality and Health: A Causal Review," *Social Science & Medicine* 128 (2015): 316–26.

14.  See: Richard G. Wilkinson and Kate Pickett, "Income Inequality and Population Health: A Review and Explanation of the Evidence," *Social Science & Medicine* 62 (2006): 1768–84.

Richard G. Wilkinson, *Unhealthy Societies: the Afflictions of Inequality* (Routledge: London, 1996).

15.  Richard V. Reeves, *Dream Hoarders* (Washington: The Brookings Institution Press, 2017).

16.  The comparison is between member countries of the Organisation for Economic Cooperation and Development. The raw US score fell by 0.51 (on a 10-point scale).

17.  John F. Helliwell, Richard Layard, Jeffrey Sachs, and Jan-Emmanuel De Neve, eds. *World Happiness Report 2020* (New York: Sustainable Development Solutions Network, 2020). https://worldhappiness.report/ed/2020/#read.

18.  See: Robert de Vries, Samuel Gosling, and Jeff Potter, "Income Inequality and Personality: Are Less Equal States Less Agreeable?" *Social Science & Medicine* 72 (2011): 1978–85.

Marii Paskov and Caroline Dewilde, "Income Inequality and Solidarity in Europe,"

*Research in Social Stratification and Mobility* 30, no. 4 (2012): 415–32.

John F. Helliwell, Richard Layard, and Jeffrey Sachs, *World Happiness Report 2017* (New York: Sustainable Development Solutions Network, 2017).

19. The US Burden of Disease Collaborators, "The State of US Health, 1990–2016," *Journal of the American Medical Association* 319, no. 14 (2018): 1444–72.

20. This was the advertised wage for health care aids and personal care workers in Winnipeg in May 2020.

## Chapter 4

1. Catherine Clifford, "What Billionaires and Business Titans Say About Cash Handouts in 2017 (Hint: Lots!)," *CNBC Make It*, December 28, 2017, https://www.cnbc.com/2017/12/27/what-billionaires-say-about-universal-basic-income-in-2017.html.

2. Catherine Clifford, "Billionaire Richard Branson Weighs In on Fee Cash Handouts — There's a 'Real Danger' Tech Will Replace Jobs," *CNBC Make It*, August 16, 2017, https://www.cnbc.com/2017/08/16/billionaire-richard-branson-weighs-in-on-free-cash-handouts.html.

3. Chris Weller, "Mark Zuckerberg Calls for Exploring Basic Income in Harvard Commencement Speech," *Business Insider*, May 15, 2017, http://www.businessinsider.com/mark-zuckerberg-basic-income-harvard-speech-2017-5.

4. Nicole Goodking, "Stephen Hawking Advocated for Wealth Redistribution to Prevent Mass Poverty in His Final Reddit Posts," *Newsweek*, March 14, 2018, http://www.newsweek.com/stephen-hawking-wealth-redistribution-reddit-845497.

5. Sam Altman, "Basic Income," *Y-Combinator*, January 27, 2016, https://ycombinator.wpengine.com/basic-income.

6. Joel Lee, "Self Driving Cars Endanger Millions of American Jobs (And That's Okay)," *Mud*, June 19, 2015, http://www.makeuseof.com/tag/self-driving-cars-endanger-millions-american-jobs-thats-okay. See also: Gao et al. 2016.

7. P. Godsmark, *Automated Vehicles: the coming of the next disruptive technology*, (Conference Board of Canada, January 2015).

8. John Stuart Mill, *Principles of Political Economy with Some of their Applications to Social Philosophy*, book IV, chapter VI (London: 1848).

9. Ibid.

10. Adam Smith, *On the Wealth of Nations, vol. 2* (Oxford: Clarendon Press, 1869 [1776]), 365.

11. See: C. Frey and M. Osborne, *The Future Of Employment: How Susceptible are Jobs to Computerization* (Oxford Martin School. September 17, 2013). http://www.oxfordmartin.ox.ac.uk/downloads/academic/future-of-employment.pdf.

12. See: C. Lamb, *The Talented Mr. Robot: The Impact of Automation on Canada's Workforce* (Brookfield Institute for Innovation + Entrepreneurship, June 2016). https://brookfieldinstitute.ca/report/the-talented-mr-robot.

13. Canada and the Changing Nature of Work, *Policy Horizons* (Ottawa: Government of Canada, 2016). https://horizons.gc.ca/wp-content/uploads/2018/11/2016-0264-eng_0.pdf.

14. See: A. McElvoy, M. Valencia, R. Avent, "Ireland's Forbidden Fruit," *Economist*, August 30, 2016, http://www.economist.com/blogs/freeexchange/2016/08/money-talks-3.

## Chapter 5

1. A prairie word: "dainties" are small cookies and squares, often frozen by home bakers to be thawed and served for company or at church luncheons.

2. John Helliwell, Richard Layard, and Jeffrey Sachs, *World Happiness Report 2017* (New

York: Sustainable Development Solutions Network, 2017).

3.   "Affect" is a psychological term that describes how often people experience positive sensations, emotions and sentiments. Positive affect is associated with high energy, enthusiasm, activity and confidence; people with positive affect are often sociable, helpful and open-minded. Those with high negative affect are often distressed, sad, lethargic, anxious and depressed.

4.   "Life evaluation" is a psychological term that measures how meaningful and satisfactory individuals find their lives.

5.   Jonah N. Cohen, M. Taylor Dryman, Amanda Morrison, Kirsten Elizabeth Gilbert, Richard G. Heimberg and June Gruber, "Positive and Negative Affect as Links between Social Anxiety and Depression: Predicting Concurrent and Prospective Mood Symptoms in Unipolar and Bipolar Mood Disorders," *Behavior Therapy* 48, no. 6 (2017): 820–33. doi:10.1016/j.beth.2017.07.003.
     See also: Kristin Naragon and David Watson, "Positive Affectivity," in *The Encyclopedia of Positive Psychology*, ed. Shane J. Lopez (Hoboken, NJ: Wiley-Blackwell, 2009), 701–11.

6.   Maaike van der Noordt, Wilhelmina Ijzelenberg, Mariel Droomers, and Karin Proper, "Health Effects of Employment: A Systematic Review of Prospective Studies," *Occupational and Environmental Medicine* 71, no. 10 (2014): 730–36.

7.   Dan Ariely, "What Makes Us Feel Good About Our Work?" TEDTalk, October 2012, https://www.ted.com/talks/dan_ariely_what_makes_us_feel_good_about_our_work.

8.   Harold W. Watts and Albert Rees, eds., *The New Jersey Income-Maintenance Experiment*, vols. 2 & 3 (New York, Academic Press, 1977).

9.   Gary Burtless and Jerry Hausman, "The Effect of Taxation on Labor Supply: Evaluating the Gary Negative Income Tax Experiment," *Journal of Political Economy* 86, no. 6 (1978): 1103–30.

10.  Robert A. Levine, Harold Watts, Robinson Hollister, Walter Williams, Alice O'Connor, and Karl Widerquist, "A Retrospective on the Negative Income Tax Experiments: Looking Back at the Most Innovative Field Studies in Social Policy," in *The Ethics and Economics of the Basic Income Guarantee*, eds. Karl Widerquist, Michael Anthony Lewis and Steven Pressman (Aldershot: Ashgate, 2005), 95–106.

11.  Michael Hannan, Nancy Tuma, and Lyle Groeneveld, "Income and Independence Effects on Marital Dissolution: Results from the Seattle and Denver Income-Maintenance Experiments," *American Journal of Sociology* 84, no. 3 (1978): 611–33.

12.  Evelyn L. Forget, "The Town with No Poverty," *Canadian Public Policy* 37, no. 3 (2011): 283–305.

13.  In 1974, as the Mincome experiment ramped up, the Canadian labour force participation rate for men aged twenty-five to fifty-four was 94.5 per cent while that for women was 48.3 per cent. Between 1975 and 1978, the period of active experimentation, the rate for women increased monotonically from 50.7 to 56.2 per cent while that for men fluctuated between 94.3 per cent and 94.6 per cent. By 2014, the participation rate for men fell to 90.5 per cent while that for women rose to 81.9 per cent.

14.  Jitka Specianova, "Labor Supply Elasticity in the Unconditional Basic Income System: Data Sources and Methodological Issues," *European Scientific Journal* 14, no. 4 (2018).

15.  Kourtney Koebel and Tammy Schirle, "The Differential Impact of Universal Child Benefits on the Labour Supply of Married and Single Mothers," *Canadian Public Policy* 42, no. 1 (March 2016): 49–64.

16.  Juliet B. Schor, *The Overworked American* (New York: Basic Books, 1992).

# Chapter 6

1.  *Reclaiming Power and Place: The Final Report of the National Inquiry into Missing and Murdered Indigenous Women and Girls,* Vols 1a and 1b. (Ottawa: 2019). https://www.mmiwg-ffada.ca/final-report.
2.  See: Barbara R. Bergmann, "Basic Income Grants or the Welfare State: Which Better Promotes Gender Equality?" *Basic Income Studies* 3, no. 3 (2008): 1–7.
3.  See: Sheila Regehr, "Basic Income and Gender Equality: Reflections on the Potential for Good Policy in Canada" (2014). https://www.homelesshub.ca/resource/basic-income-and-gender-equality-reflections-potential-good-policy-canada.
4.  Ailsa McKay, "Why a Citizens' Basic Income? A Question of Gender Equality or Gender Bias," *Work, Employment and Society* 21, no. 2 (2007): 337–48.
    Carole Pateman, "Democratizing Citizenship: Some Advantages of a Basic Income," *Politics & Society* 32, no. 1 (2004): 89–105.
5.  See: Nancy Folbre, *The Invisible Heart: Economics and Family Values* (New Press, 2001).
6.  Statistics Canada, "Table 14-10-0327-02, Unemployment Rate, Participation Rate and Employment Rate by Sex, Annual." https://www150.statcan.gc.ca/t1/tbl1/en/tv.action?pid=1410032702.
7.  Statistics Canada, "Household Income in Canada: Key Results from the 2016 Census," *Daily,* September 13, 2017, http://www.statcan.gc.ca/daily-quotidien/170913/dq170913a-eng.htm.
8.  Statistics Canada, "Changes in Parents' Participation in Domestic Tasks and Care for Children from 1986 to 2015," *Daily,* June 1, 2017, http://www.statcan.gc.ca/daily-quotidien/170601/dq170601a-eng.htm.
9.  Calculated based on 2015 data in Statistics Canada, "Changing Profile of Stay at Home Parents," 2017, and 2014 data in Statistics Canada, "Lone-Parent Families," 2015.
10. Mary Ann Mason, Nicholas H. Wolfinger, and Marc Goulden, *Do Babies Matter? Gender and Family in the Ivory Tower* (University of Chicago Press, 2013).
11. See: Jeremy Greenwood, Nezih Guner, Georgi Kocharkov, and Cezar Santos, "Marry Your Like: Assortative Mating and Income Inequality," *American Economic Review* 104, no. 5 (2014): 348–53.
12. A special issue of *Basic Income Studies* published in December 2008, entitled "Should Feminists Endorse Basic Income?" publishes alternative perspectives. www.bepress.com/bis/vol3/iss3.
13. Statistics Canada, "Average and Median Total Income of Husband-Wife Families," CANSIM Table 202-0105.
14. "Persons Living Below the Poverty Line (Market Basket Measure), 2014–2018." https://www150.statcan.gc.ca/n1/daily-quotidien/200224/t002a-eng.htm.
15. See: Melissa Moyser, "Women and Paid Work," Statistics Canada 89-503X, March 9, 2017, http://www.statcan.gc.ca/pub/89-503-x/2015001/article/14694-eng.htm.
16. "Persons Living Below the Poverty Line (Market Basket Measure), 2014–2018," https://www150.statcan.gc.ca/n1/daily-quotidien/200224/t002a-eng.htm.
17. Qajaq Robinson was one of the commissioners charged with investigating the staggering issue of missing and murdered Indigenous women and girls. I am very grateful for her guidance in helping me to read the report and the narratives of the witnesses, and for helping me to understand what systemic violence really means, in concrete terms, to the people who experience it.
18. Josée Gabrielle Lavoie, Evelyn L. Forget, Tara Prakash, Matt Dahl, Patricia Martens, and John D. O'Neil, "Have Investments in On-Reserve Health Services and Initiatives Promoting Community Control Improved First Nations' Health in Manitoba?" *Social Science & Medicine* 71, no. 4 (2010):717–24.

# Chapter 7

1.  As measured by the after-tax Low Income Measure.
2.  2016 Census.
3.  Karl Widerquist and Michael W. Howard, eds., *Alaska's Permanent Fund Dividend: Examining its Suitability as a Model* (New York: Palgrave Macmillan, 2012). See also: Karl Widerquist and Michael W. Howard, eds., *Exporting the Alaska Model: Adapting the Permanent Fund Dividend for Reform around the World* (New York: Palgrave Macmillan, 2012).
4.  2016 Census.
5.  Susan M. Sawyer, Peter S. Azzopardi, Dakshitha Wickremarathne, and George C. Patton, "The Age of Adolescence," *Lancet Child and Adolescent Health 2* (2018): 223–28, doi: http://dx.doi.org/10.1016/S2352-4642(18)30022-1.
6.  Josh Brandon and Christina Maes Nino, *We Matter; We Count. The Final Report of the 2018 Winnipeg Street Census* (Winnipeg: Social Planning Council of Winnipeg, 2018). http://streetcensuswpg.ca/wp-content/uploads/2018/10/2018_FinalReport_Web.pdf.
7.  See, for example: G. Becker, *Human Capital: a theoretical and empirical analysis with special reference to education*, 3rd ed. (National Bureau of Economic Research, 1994).
    Andrew Clark, Yannis Georgellis, and Peter Sanfey, "Scarring: The Psychological Impact of Past Unemployment," *Economica* 68, no. 270 (2001): 221–41.
    Per-Anders Edin and Magnus Gustavsson, "Time Out of Work and Skill Depreciation," *Industrial and Labor Relations Review* 61, no. 2 (2008): 163–80.
    Ben Lockwood, "Information Externalities in the Labour Market and the Duration of Unemployment," *Review of Economic Studies* 58, no. 4 (1991): 733–53.
    Oskar Nördstrom Skans, *Scarring effects of the first labor market experience*, IZA Discussion Paper No. 5565 (Bonn, Germany: Institute for the Study of Labor, 2011).
    Christopher A. Pissarides, "Search Unemployment with On-the-Job Search," *Review of Economic Studies* 61, no. 3 (1994): 457–75.
8.  See, for example: *The Final Report of the Finnish Basic Income Experiment* (in Finnish; English summary on p. 187ff.). http://urn.fi/URN:ISBN:978-952-00-9890-2
    Timo Verlaat, Marcel de Kruijk, Stephanie Rosenkranz, Loek Groot, and Mark Sanders, *Onderzoek Weten wat werkt: samen werken aan een betere bijstand, Eindrapport* (Utrecht: Utrecht University, 2020). An English-language summary is available here: https://www.uu.nl/en/publication/final-report-what-works-weten-wat-werkt.
9.  Government of Canada, *Evaluation of the On-Reserve Income Assistance Program* (Ottawa: Evaluation, Performance Measurement and Review Branch, October 2018). https://www.sac-isc.gc.ca/eng/1557321693588/1557321741537.
10. See: John P. Martin, *Activation and Active Labour Market Policies in OECD Countries: Stylized Facts and Evidence on Their Effectiveness*, IZA Discussion Paper No. 84 (Bonn, Germany: Institute for the Study of Labor, 2014). http://ftp.iza.org/pp84.pdf.
11. 2016 Census.
12. 2012 Canadian Survey on Disabilities.
13. Katherine Wall, *Insights on Canadian Society: Low Income Among Persons with a Disability in Canada* (Ottawa: Statistics Canada, 2017).
14. Michael Mendelson, Ken Battle, Sherry Torjman, and Ernie Lightman, *A Basic Income Plan for Canadians with Severe Disabilities* (Ottawa: Caledon Institute, 2010). http://www.ccdonline.ca/en/socialpolicy/poverty-citizenship/income-security-reform/basic-income-plan-for-canadians-with-severe-disabilities.
15. Lucie Dumais, Alexandra Prohet, and Marie-Noëlle Ducharme in collaboration with

Léonie Archambault and Maude Ménard-Dunn, *Review of Extra Costs Associated with Disability* (Montreal: UQAM, 2015), http://www.ccdonline.ca/en/socialpolicy/poverty-citizenship/income-security-reform/extra-costs-linked-to-disability.

16. Kathy Tomlinson, "How Workers Comp Fanned the Flames of the Opioid Crisis," *Globe and Mail,* June 18, 2020, https://www.theglobeandmail.com/canada/article-how-workers-comp-fanned-the-flames-of-the-opioid-crisis.

17. These will be published in spring 2021 as:
Evelyn L. Forget and Hannah Owczar, *Broken Promises: Reclaiming Dignity in Canada's Working Cities* (Winnipeg: ARP Press, 2021).

# Chapter 8

1. See: Milton Friedman, *Capitalism and freedom: with the assistance of Rose D. Friedman* (Chicago: University of Chicago Press, 1962).

2. See: Charles Lammam and Hugh McIntyre, *The Practical Challenges of Creating a Guaranteed Annual Income* (Vancouver: Fraser Institute, 2015).

3. The comparable rates for persons with disabilities are $16,920 and $13,934, and for a single mother with a two-year-old $24,162 and $18,854. See: A. Tweddle, K. Battle, S. Torjman. Welfare in Canada 2013 (Caledon Institute. November, 2014), App. B1.

4. David Calnitsky, The Employer Response to the Guaranteed Annual Income, *Socio-Economic Review* (2018), doi: 10.1093/ser/mwy009.

5. I'm not sure the employers were correct about the causation. They knew Mincome was underway, so it was easy to blame the program for wage increases. However, the 1970s were a time of significant wage inflation across the country. I suspect higher wages had more to do with general trends than with Mincome.

6. For a discussion of the politics surrounding Family Allowances, see N. Christie. *Engendering the State: Family, Work, and Welfare in Canada* (Toronto: University of Toronto Press, 2000).

7. See: Hugh Grant, W.A. Mackintosh: The Life of a Canadian Economist (Montreal: McGillQueen's University Press, 2015), footnote 53.

8. Michael A.Clemens, Does Kicking Out Mexicans Create Jobs? *Politico Magazine,* February 15, 2017, https://www.politico.com/magazine/story/2017/02/mexico-immigrant-workers-jobs-americans-braceros-history-immigration-214784.

9. See: Sarah Cooper, Jesse Hajer, Shayna Plaut, Fast Facts: Now, more than ever, we need Rent Assist helping Manitobans. April 15 2020. Available: https://www.policyalternatives.ca/publications/commentary/fast-facts-now-more-ever-we-need-rent-assist-helping-manitobans.

10. Alex Himmelfarb and Roy Romanow, "We can end homelessness in Canada," *Globe and Mail,* January 16, 2017 [updated March 21, 2018] https://www.theglobeandmail.com/opinion/we-can-end-homelessness-in-canada/article33632029.

11. See: Alex Smith and Nasraddine Ammar, *Costing a National Guaranteed Basic Income Using the Ontario Basic Income Model,* (Parliamentary Budget Office Blog, April 17, 2018). https://www.pbo-dpb.gc.ca/web/default/files/Documents/Reports/2018/Basic%20Income/Basic_Income_Costing_EN.pdf.

12. There is an extensive history of the development of active labour market policies from the 1950s to the present in: Weishaupt, T. *From the Manpower Revolution to the Activation Paradigm: Explaining Institutional Continuity and Change in an Integrating Europe,* (Amsterdam: Amsterdam University Press, 2011).

13. See: OECD, Society at a Glance 2016: OECD Social Indicators, OECD Publishing,

Paris. http://dx.doi.org/10.1787/9789264261488-en.

14. See: John P. Martin, *Activation and Active Labour Market Policies in OECD Countries: Stylized Facts and Evidence on Their Effectiveness*, IZA Discussion Paper No. 84 (Bonn, Germany: Institute for the Study of Labor, 2014). http://ftp.iza.org/pp84.pdf.

15. See: J. Rothstein, Is the EITC as good as an NIT? Conditional cash transfers and tax incidence, *American Economic Journal: Economic Policy*, 2: 1(2010), pp.177–208.

16. See: Stephenson Strobel and E.L. Forget. Revitalizing poverty reduction and social inclusion. *Manitoba Law Journal*. 37 No. 2 (2015): 259–276.

17. See: Guest, Dennis, "Family Allowance". In *The Canadian Encyclopedia*. Historica Canada. Article published February 07, 2006; Last Edited December 18, 2013. https://thecanadianencyclopedia.ca/en/article/family-allowance.

18. See, for example: Robyn Maynard. *Policing Black Lives*. (Fernwood, 2017).
Lisa Monchalan. *The Colonial Problem: An Indigenous Perspective on Crime and Injustice in Canada*. (Toronto: University of Toronto Press, 2016).

19. Mohammad Ferdosi, Tom McDowell, Wayne Lewchuk, Stephanie Ross, *Southern Ontario's Basic Income Experience* (Hamilton: Hamilton Community Foundation, Hamilton Roundtable for Poverty Reduction and Labour Studies at McMaster University, March 2020). Available: https://labourstudies.mcmaster.ca/documents/southern-ontarios-basic-income-experience.pdf.

20. Sarath Davala, Renana Jhabvala, Guy Standing, and Soumya Kapoor Mehta, *Basic Income: A Transformative Policy for India* (London: Bloomsbury, 2015).

21. Anna Cameron, Lindsay M. Tedds, Jennifer Robson, Saul Schwarts, The Merits of Automatic Income Tax Assessments for Low-Income Canadians. Tax Policy Trends. (University of Calgary School of Public Policy, February 2020). Available: https://www.policyschool.ca/wp-content/uploads/2020/02/Tax-policy-Trends-Feb-2020.pdf.

22. John Stapleton, A Fortune Left on the Table. Why Should Low-Income Adults Have to Pass Up Government Benefits? (Open Policy Institute, 2018). Available: https://openpolicyontario.s3.amazonaws.com/uploads/2018/06/INFORMAL-A-Fortune-Left-R3.pdf.
Alicia Kalmanovitch, Nick Falvo, Britney Ardelli, Laurel Collier, Megan Hodgins, Megan Donnelly and Joel Sinclair, Point-In-Time Count Report (Calgary, Spring 2018). Available: http://calgaryhomeless.com/content/uploads/Calgary_PiT_Report_2018.pdf.
Prosper Canada, Increasing Indigenous Benefit Take-Up in Canada. (2018 Federal Budget Submission, 2018). Available: https://prospercanada.org/getattachment/f4add5df-0edb-4883-b804-60661f500c56/Increasing-Indigenous-benefit-take-up-in-Canada.aspx.

23. Get Your Benefits Manitoba. https://www.gov.mb.ca/health/primarycare/providers/getyourbenefits.html.

# Chapter 9

1. Parliamentary Budget Office. Fiscal Sustainability Report 2020. 27 February 2020. https://www.pbo-dpb.gc.ca/en/blog/news/RP-1920-029-S-fiscal-sustainability-report-2020-rapport-viabilite-financiere-2020.

2. Parliamentary Budget Office. Scenario Update Analysis: COVID-19 Pandemic and Oil Price Shocks. 30 April 2020. https://www.pbo-dpb.gc.ca/en/blog/news/RP-2021-005-S--scenario-analysis-update-COVID-19-pandemic-oil-price-shocks--mise-jour-analyse-scenario-chocs-dus-pandemie-COVID-19-chute-prix-petrole.
Parliamentary Budget Office. Economic and Fiscal Snapshot 2020, 8 July 2020. Available: https://www.canada.ca/en/department-finance/services/publications/economic-fiscal-snapshot.html.

3. This was updated to $26.6 billion in the December economic update: Department of Finance, Fiscal and Economic Update, 16 December 2019. Available: https://www.canada.ca/en/department-finance/news/2019/12/government-of-canada-releaseseconomic-and-fiscal-update.html.
4. See: Michael T. Hannan, Nancy Brandon Tuma and Lyle P. Groeneveld. Income and Independence Effects on Marital Dissolution: Results from the Seattle and Denver Income-Maintenance Experiments, *American Journal of Sociology* 84, no. 3 (1978): 611–33.
5. See: Daniel P. Moynihan, *The politics of a guaranteed income: The Nixon administration and the family assistance plan* (Vintage Books, 1973).
6. See: G.G. Cain and D.A. Wissoker, A Reanalyis of Marital Stability in the Seattle-Denver Income-Maintenance Experiment, *American Journal of Sociology* 95, no. 5 (March 1990): 1235–1269.
7. Thanks to Harvey Stevens for the estimate.
8. Parliamentary Budget Office. *Costing a National Guaranteed Basic Income Using the Ontario Basic Income Model.* 17 April 2018. https://www.pbo-dpb.gc.ca/web/default/files/Documents/Reports/2018/Basic%20Income/Basic_Income_Costing_EN.pdf.
9. It should be a simple matter to determine how much each province pays for income assistance, but that is not the case. These data are typically aggregated with other provincial programs in published data, and administrative costs are rarely identified with particular programs. In the past, the National Council on Welfare tracked provincial income assistance expenditure, but that body was disbanded in 2012. John Stapleton has picked up the mantle and estimates a total cost for Canada of nineteen billion dollars in 2017, not including administrative costs.
10. The Canadian Association of Social Workers estimated the combined costs of federal, provincial and municipal governments for income assistance at more than $185 billion (CASW, 2017).
11. Richard Pereira, The Cost of Universal Basic Income: Public Savings and Program Redundancy Exceed Cost, in *Financing Basic Income* (New York: Springer International, 2017), 9–45.
12. Chandra Pasma and Sheila Regehr, *Basic Income: Some Policy Options for Canada.* (Basic Income Canada Network, 2019). Available: https://d3n8a8pro7vhmx.cloudfront.net/bicn/pages/3725/attachments/original/1579707497/Basic_Income-_Some_Policy_Options_for_Canada2.pdf?1579707497.
13. See, for example: Dan Ariely, *Predictably Irrational. The Hidden Forces That Shape Our Decisions* (New York: HarperCollins, 2008).
14. See: Kevin Milligan, Dare to Dream but Do the Math, blog post, July 4, 2016, https://www.cdhowe.org/intelligence-memos/kevin-milligan-dare-dream-do-math. See also: Jonathan Rhys Kesselman, A Dubious Antipoverty Strategy: Guaranteeing Incomes for the Poor Is Politically Unfeasible and Financially Unsustainable, *Inroads* 34 (2014): 33–43, http://inroadsjournal.ca/a-dubious-antipoverty-strategy.
15. Koebel, Kourtney and Tammy Schirle. The Differential Impact of Universal Child Benefits on the Labour Supply of Married and Single Mothers, *Canadian Public Policy.* 42.1 (2016): 49-64. https://doi.org/10.3138/cpp.2015-049.
16. Andrew Coyne, Three Points on the GST to End Poverty? *National Post*, April 18, 2018, http://nationalpost.com/opinion/andrew-coyne-three-points-on-the-gst-to-end-poverty-guaranteed-income-sounds-like-a-good-deal
17. Parliamentary Budget Office, *Costing a National Guaranteed Basic Income During the*

*COVID pandemic*, 7 July 2020. Available: https://www.pbo-dpb.gc.ca/en/blog/news/RP-2021-014-M--costing-guaranteed-basic-income-during-covid-pandemic--estimation-couts-lies-un-revenu-base-garanti-pendant-pandemie-covid-19.

# Chapter 10

1.  See, for example: C. Lammam and H. McIntyre, The Practical Challenges of Creating a Guaranteed Annual Income in Canada (Vancouver: Fraser Institute, January 2015).
2.  Measured, for example, by real GDP per capita. A basic income that grows by the rate of increase of nominal GDP over time will protect payments from inflation and share the benefits of growth.
3.  Government of Canada, Evaluation of the On-Reserve Income Assistance Program. (Ottawa: Evaluation, Performance Measurement and Review Branch, October 2018). Available: https://www.sac-isc.gc.ca/eng/1557321693588/1557321741537
4.  Virginia Eubanks, The Digital Poorhouse, *Harper's Magazine*, January, 2018, 12.

# Index

Numbers in bold italics indicate illustrations.
A page number that appears in both plain text and bold italics indicates that a relevant illustration and additional related content appear on that page.